BEYOND ABORTION
A Chronicle of Fetal Experimentation

BEYOND ABORTION
A Chronicle of Fetal Experimentation

by Suzanne M. Rini

magnificat press
Avon-by-the-Sea, New Jersey

Beyond Abortion

Printed in the United States of America
ISBN 0-940543-13-3
Library of Congress catalog number: 88-060126
Magnificat Press
PO Box 365
Avon, NJ 07717

Beyond Abortion appeared in slightly different form as "A Look at Fetal Experimentation," a five-part supplement to the *Pittsburgh Catholic* newspaper, in 1986.

This book is dedicated, in its labors and in its completion, to my own children, Angela, Matthew and Carlos. Their lively presence has explained to me, in great part, my own humanity. To them I offer this book as an effort to secure a future less fraught with portentous and outrageous raids on human life than has been reported herein.

As well, to Michael.

As always, to my grandfather, Matthew Barone.

Acknowledgments

Gratitude is all mine for the help and vision of an array of people who helped this book to conclusion. My thanks to Mary Winter and Helen Cindrich of People Concerned for the Unborn Child in Pittsburgh for the beauty of their files and their knowledge on so many questions. The prior work of journalists Randy Engel, Paul Ramsey and William F. Brennan in this area will be immediately apparent as invaluable to all who read what follows. Father Peter Horton and Robert Melder of the *Pittsburgh Catholic* must be credited with believing in the notion that a series on this subject should be subsidized and published. I wish also to thank Michael Frazier for reading the first and subsequent drafts and suggesting changes that have made it more lucid and approachable.

Contents

We are determined to wrest by our scientific works some good out of guilt-laden harmfulness to unborn life.

—Paul Ramsey in *The Ethics of Fetal Research*

Preface

Doubt made this book.

In 1985, someone mentioned to me the "fact" of live, nontherapeutic fetal experimentation. My reaction was probably stronger than doubt, bordering more on disbelief. Yet the person in question was a credible source, saying too that a Chicago woman, Francene Markoweicz, had accumulated a file. I called her and she sent me that record, plucked and clipped from newspapers, newsletters and government documents. She of course deserves robust credit for her assiduous effort.

Yet Mrs. Markoweicz' collection seemed not to tell how or why such a phenomenon could spring up and thrive. Personally, that was my question. Professionally, my desire was to find out and as a journalist represent the public's right to know. Next, I called *The Pittsburgh Catholic,* where some of my work has appeared. Both its diocesan liaison, Fr. Peter Horton, and its editor, Robert Melder, agreed to commission and publish whatever it would be that I would find and write.

Nearly a year of investigation ensued, resulting in a research cache that had to be crated in order to be contained.

Finally, knowledge and analysis were wedded to fact. And finally, too, a sense of loss was added to shock. In this subject's details breathed evidence of a fissure in what we hold as civilization. Out of inquiry emerged the certainty that nontherapeutic fetal experimentation represented a dim horizon without end. Today, the fetus; who tomorrow? This book, then, is an attempt to answer that horrific question, one that has the power to unhinge or even destroy the bonds of the human family.

We come to the subject late. That is because the whole panoply of human fetal use stays in places where people have little to no access, and, supposedly, even less authority to tread. Also, this curious, disturbing subject is protected by a fact of human nature: it is unthinkable.

The whole practice of fetal use, especially in biomedical research, is rife and ingrained. What might have been called a fad initially is today so well advanced that it has announced its sealed success of using live fetal organs for transplants. The fad has burgeoned and exploded into a panacea.

It is ironic that the human fetus doomed to the abortion process, and so to death, is the sponsor of so many life-giving techniques. Indeed, that a fetus is condemned to abortion reigns as the arch reason given by medical researchers to condone and underwrite nontherapeutic experimentation on a living fetus about to die, one that has survived the abortion by accident (or by design), or one that is freshly dead. This cadre says it would, in fact, be *unethical* not to make use of these fetuses. A French researcher, Dr. Jean Bernard, has invented a maxim reflecting this position: "The means are necessarily unethical and ethically necessary."[1] Or, in its overused form, "The end justifies the means." Dr. Bernard's maxim is the very symbol of the current spirit of accommodation (and of real excitement) toward nontherapeutic research on the human fetus. The public, in its age-old search for cures, in its modern commitment to science, is being asked to regret or negate the means and to embrace the end and to call it humanitarian.

Fetal experimentation seems to be built, in its ethics, on shifting sand, and shifting sand is, in this case, the major convenience to assembling and perfecting ever more controversial and nontraditional biological and genetic tools away from public view. The researcher engaged in nontherapeutic experimentation on the living human fetus seems to feel secure in his means because he or she has seized the opportunity within a world that has decided, once again in history, to make graded pronouncements on human status and human value.

1

The New Barbarians

No sooner was the fetus denied its personhood in order to permit abortion (in the U.S. Supreme Court decision in *Roe v. Wade,* 1973) than the biomedical research profession entered the scene with plans to use the human fetus for much-coveted nontherapeutic human experimentation, generally forbidden under many of civilization's highest codes. Researchers' various specialties and inquiries called for using fetuses at various stages of development and in basically three life situations as they related to the abortion schedule:

The live in-utero fetus. The testing of drugs, of prenatal diagnostic techniques, of vaccines, of hypotheses about the effects of diet, stress, and maternal factors are some of the research objectives for this "class." These types of experiments have two phases: administering the drug, prenatal test, caloric deprivation, etc. to the still-living, in-utero fetus, and then examining the dead fetus, upon abortion, to assess the effects. In some cases, the fetus is actually killed by the experiment rather than by the abortion.

The viable fetus, ex-utero, still living after the abortion. This fetus would be analagous to a premature infant, except that the fetus would not be permitted to survive the experiment, whereas, most premature, wanted infants are helped to independence through medical technology. The viable fetus was included in several early, documented experiments but this class of fetus was disallowed for nontherapeutic experimentation with government funds once federal regulations were devised in 1976. However, these regulations do not govern experiments done with private monies.

The "previable" fetus, ex- or in-utero. This fetus is defined by the federal regulations as one about to be or already aborted (but aborted with some vital signs and therefore living). To meet this criterion, the fetus must be on the abortion schedule up to and including the second trimester, and weigh no more than 400 grams (about one pound). The thinking behind allowing this "class" of fetus for research is that it cannot survive on its own. However, some fetuses have survived with the help of ever-improving medical technology. Additionally, while federal regulations allow nontherapeutic research on these fetuses, most states now disallow it and further demand that any fetus surviving the abortion procedure, viable or not, must be helped to survival.

The dead fetus. Dead means clinically dead, that is, with no vital signs. This category of fetus would be said to be used to gain living tissues. While this is seen by many to be noncontroversial, others believe that it is unethical to use the living matter of these fetuses to benefit medical inquiry because they are not simply random victims, such as those of murder or accidents but are, rather, part of an entire class of human being denied intrinsic rights. The use of this class spurs the analogy of use of the body parts and tissues of concentration camp victims by the Nazis for anything from "medical progress" to soap and lampshades.

The outraged reader may ask if there are laws against this. There are, in fact, government regulations (not laws) and medical ethics codes that permit it. Strangely, there are also some state laws that forbid it; these seem, on the basis of evidence to be presented, to be equivocal and largely unenforced. For instance, in Massachusetts, live nontherapeutic experimentation and experimentation on dead fetuses is forbidden, unless by parental consent. Opponents of fetal research say that, according to such long-enduring standards as the Nuremberg Code and the Helsinki Accords, no human subject may be entered into nontherapeutic research *unless the subject him- or herself gives consent.* Thus, parental consent under such a rule is void, especially when the parent, in opting for abortion, has canceled guardianship over and care of the subject. But supporters of fetal research favor another facet of the Nuremberg Code that may be extremely persuasive in a society more and more used to medical progress. This Nuremberg article states that "The experiment should be such as to yield fruitful results for the good of society, [and be] unprocurable by other methods or means of study, and not random and unnecessary in nature." It is not hard for the reader to see that, in order to go forward, fetal experimentation has had to sacrifice the former article to the latter. In doing so, opponents of fetal experimentation believe that the human fetus, on the sole basis of its being unwanted and doomed to abortion, has been separated from all other human subjects of experimentation and subjected to procedures forbidden for all other humans, whether they are condemned to death or not.

A spectrum of fetal research is funded by a phalanx of the country's most sacred cows, who distribute copious monies to projects both here and abroad. Some of this research is currently confined to animal fetuses, but the agenda includes moving up to human ones once the data suggests that the animal models have been exhausted. Funders include the U.S. government's various agencies, mainly the National Institute of Child Health and Development (NICHD, formerly under HEW, which is now the Department of Health and Human Services). Other government funders are the Food and Drug Administration (FDA), the Environmental Protection Agency (EPA), U.S. Agency for International Development (AID) and—the most bizarre example—the military. Private funders have included the MacDonald's Kroc Medical Foundation, the Ford Foundation, The Muscular Dystrophy Association, the American Paralysis Association, the National Foundation/March of Dimes, and others.

Fetal experimentation has very many supporters. It also has an equal and opposing force who say that it should be universally forbidden in all of its forms. The latter view has been losing badly.

The particular, curious set of ethics favoring fetal use and experimentation is not common public knowledge today. Fetal experimentation and the debate surrounding it have been handled by the medical and academic elite. What has been missing is public disclosure and public participation.

The set of ethics supporting experimentation has been built around the supposed necessity of using the previable fetus who has survived the abortion process, or who has been arranged to be freshly dead for organ and tissue harvest. The medical researchers who support experimentation have tried to class these fetuses as "tissue." Their logic goes like this: the fetus cannot survive, therefore we can use it; and, since it cannot survive, it is merely a piece of tissue. It seems, however, that many researchers themselves admit that the living, previable fetus is not just a piece of tissue. Consider the remark of David G. Nathan in the *Villanova Law Review*[1]:

> The possibility that investigators might perform or tolerate ghastly intrauterine intrusions prior to abortion because they do not think of the fetus as a person, creates deep moral and ethical concerns. Indeed, a few of my colleagues occasionally lend some credence to that fear by referring to the fetus as just "a piece of tissue." Obviously the

> fetus is not just any piece of tissue. The fetus may not be a person in the *legal* sense, but *common* sense and dignity elevate it above the status of a gallbladder. The potential of a gallbladder is to become an older gallbladder, whereas the fetus has the potential to become a person.

He referred mainly to the fetus prior to abortion, but the word "tissue" has been used by researchers—who obviously know better than anyone—to refer to previable fetuses who have survived abortion, upon whom the researchers wish to experiment. Under current federal regulations, one may do anything except a procedure that directly stops the heartbeat.[2] But it is quite possible to remove vital organs, even the heart, without stopping the heartbeat directly. Researchers themselves have proven that.

For one example, we turn to the May 15, 1983, *American Journal of Obstetrics and Gynecology.* A letter from Drs. Bela Resch and Julius Papp was headlined "Effects of Caffeine on the Heart."[3] Resch and Papp, who had been doing the same horrendous experiments since 1973,[4] opened their letter with comments on a recent article in the *Journal*, "Caffeine and the Fetus: Is Trouble Brewing?" Their letter stated that "This [the known effects of caffeine] prompted us to study the responsiveness to caffeine in seven hearts isolated surgically from healthy human fetuses at legal termination of pregnancy." In an earlier report to the *Journal*,[5] they had put it even more graphically: "The hearts were dissected from the fetuses and were mounted in a thermostatically controlled bath containing modified Locke's solution gassed with 5 percent carbon dioxide in a 95 percent oxygen at a pH 7.4 . . . "

The U.S. regulations do not state that a previable fetus must be void of heartbeat before being dissected or experimented on. Researchers may kindly wait for a fetus to die, but they don't have to. By comparison, Australia's recently passed regulations (1984) explicitly state, as the American ones do not, that researchers must wait for a cessation of heartbeat before dissection. Besides being dissected for parts, under the U.S. regulations, a previable fetus may be observed, measured, have skin samples taken, all while the fetus is dying on the table.

The U.S. Supreme Court's *Roe v. Wade* decision on abortion (1973), although it never ruled on fetal experimentation at all, did say that the mother's rights cease to prevail once the fetus is expelled from the womb, and that with life outside the womb comes constitutional protection in full. Did the Court mean this to apply to fetuses that are previable as well as to those that are viable? Researchers have taken full advantage of the Court's error in not expanding its vision to take into account the phenomenon of fetal experimentation; it could have, because nontherapeutic experimentation on abortion victims began wholeheartedly in the late 1960's when states began to remove legal restrictions on abortion. The researchers have also tended to ignore the dichotomous, controversial fact that many states have a categorical ban on all nontherapeutic fetal experimentation and also frequently demand that every survivor of abortion be given medical assistance.

John P. Wilson, in the *Villanova Law Review* article cited earlier,[6] took up the question of whether or not the Supreme Court meant to protect the nonviable fetus ex utero as well as the viable one when either survives the abortion process:

> No doubt because the [Supreme Court] opinion focused on the right of a mother to obtain an abortion, almost no notice was taken of the status of a fetus following induced or spontaneous birth. The majority opinion noted that "the law has been reluctant to endorse any theory that life . . . begins before live birth." The term "live birth" was not defined, and the Court did not indicate whether the concept was in any way tied to viability.

Thus there is a great loophole in the Supreme Court decision, and researchers have rushed into it. Confusion reigns. For instance, California has a law that applies to fetal experimentation; it says that any fetus that survives the abortion procedure, regardless of viability or nonviability, must be given all of the helps given any premature infant. Yet in Massachusetts, in 1975, when Dr. Kenneth Edelin killed a live infant (not yet expelled from the womb) that had survived an abortion, he was first convicted by a jury and then, on appeal, exonerated by a superior court, which held that since the fetus was not viable, there was no law that forbade what he did.

Not only has the legal status of the previable fetus been left lying in the loophole, but no cases have, to this writer's knowledge, been heard concerning the researcher's *design* to produce a live fetus via abortion—a subject we shall take up in detail.

In all the ethical arguments over fetal experimentation, nowhere is there a statement quite like one from Dr. Paul Gill, Chairman of the Department of

Pathology at the University of Pittsburgh and working pathologist at Magee-Women's Hospital. Dr. Gill was frank and fierce, with volatile words for those who would protest nontherapeutic fetal research. If the opposition wins out, said Dr. Gill, "It would be a victory for the new barbarians."[7] To prove that research involving the fetus is necessary and not at all exploitation, as opponents say, of a caught and dehumanized class, he added, "The major source of medical advance has always come from research on tissues. The developing fetus is the developing situation. It's a developing human."[8]

This was exactly the thinking of researchers who in 1975 starved pregnant women who were going to abort their babies. The researchers did this to study the effects of malnutrition on fetuses. The results of their research were published in an article titled "The Dutch Famine." At that date there was a ban on all federally funded fetal experimentation, to give time for a special commission to debate the necessity and ethics of experimentation and to propose guidelines to the Secretary of Health, Education and Welfare, who would decide whether to adopt them. Obviously the researchers who perpetrated the cruelties of the Dutch Famine were not influenced by the consciousness raising that the commission was supposed to be inspiring at that moment. The term "consciousness raising" was used by a spokesman for the March of Dimes, R.P. Leavitt, to express his impression that the commission hearings were having that very effect on researchers.

The March of Dimes did not fund the Dutch Famine, but it too was contributing funds that were used to support live fetal experimentation during the ban on federal funding. Nor was the Dutch Famine experiment the only one like it. Women undergoing elective second-trimester abortion were starved for eighty-seven hours before abortion to check the effects of caloric deprivation on pregnancy.[9]

Both of these experiments come from the 1970's. Could they be done today under the current guidelines that govern public grants and are supposed to be the ideals for private grants reviewed and approved by hospital and institutional review boards?

Article 46.207 of the current federal regulations on fetal research[10] states, "No pregnant woman may be involved as a subject in an activity unless: (1) The purpose of the activity is to meet the health needs of the mother and the fetus will be placed at risk only to the minimum extent necessary to meet such needs, or (2) the risk to the fetus is minimal." If being reviewed under this section, it obviously would not be allowed, because the health needs of the mother would, in fact, be jeopardized. However, under 46.208[11], a section governing activities directed toward fetuses in utero as subjects rather than toward pregnant women, we read that research is permitted if "the purpose of the activity is to meet the health needs of the particular fetus and the fetus will be placed at risk only to the minimum extent necessary or (2) the risk to the fetus imposed by the research is minimal and the purpose of the activity is the development of important biomedical knowledge which cannot be obtained by other means."

This wording has been read by critics of the regulations as an open-door policy for experimentation on fetuses to be aborted. First of all, they say, to speak of the health needs of a fetus to be aborted is moot, and second of all the risk of any experiment *would* be minimal compared to the ultimate risk of abortion. An article titled "Fetal Research" in the *University of Miami Law Review*[12] stated:

> The use of a minimal risk standard is problematic because there is no indication in the regulations what that means.

It added:

> . . . differences of interpretation regarding what is risk to the fetus expected to be carried to term and what is risk to the fetus to be aborted did arise [in the deliberations of the Commission on Human Subjects preceding passage of the regulations] . . . even if the nonviable fetus is categorized separately as a being with the potentiality of becoming a person, once abortion or impending abortion removes that factor of potentiality, greater latitude in research can be justified . . . since the dying fetus cannot be injured for life and cannot be saved, the question of risk becomes less relevant. . . .

Ed Grogan and Dr. James Vaupel, in a coauthored critique of the government guidelines, wrote in 1980[13]: "Under this definition, minimal risk of injury to the child destined not to survive is not a consideration, but only minimal *risk* that an injured child *will survive* is a consideration."

This statement points out the greatest irony: for a fetus being aborted, the real risk of the experiment would not be injury but survival. John C. Fletcher, ethicist at the National Institute of Child Health and Development, upheld these two writers' view that minimal risk was left undefined and, in Fletcher's opinion, "should be clarified."[14]

Returning to the nature of the experiments, there is one that is often presented as evidence of the necessity of nontherapeutic fetal experimentation. It involved injecting pregnant women who had opted for abortion with live rubella virus when the vaccine was being developed. These women were then asked to continue their pregnancies for three to four weeks to determine if the virus crossed the placenta and caused death in the fetus. The virus did, and supporters of fetal research say that this experiment prevented the death of countless wanted fetuses. In the current federal regulations, we see under "General Limitations"[15] that researchers may have no part in "any decisions as to the timing, method, and procedures used to terminate the pregnancy . . . " Thus, it would seem that the experiment with rubella vaccine couldn't be done today, at least not with a federal grant. But pharmaceutical houses producing new vaccines are not eager to incite lawsuits by causing epidemic death from their products, and their practices and monies are not monitored by the government; therefore, similar experiments can be legally done today.

Researchers often offend the General Limitations when their funding comes from the private sector, and even when it comes from the public one. For example, researchers have experimented with abortion agents that can produce a live fetus; nor have the regulations at all prevented them from having a part in "the timing, method, and procedures" of the abortion. Additionally, *all* of the regulations can be waived if the Secretary of Health and Human Services should receive a research proposal that would offend the regulations in some or all parts but would promise important biomedical information supposedly unavailable any other way. If the rubella experiment were proposed for funding now, would it present enough of a promise of important new biomedical information that it would be granted?

But the necessity of the rubella experiment has been roundly argued. At the meetings of the Commission on the Protection of Human Subjects (1974–76), which preceded passage of the regulations in 1976 (slightly amended in 1983), Battelle-Columbus Research Laboratories were asked to do a study called "An Assessment of the Role of Research Involving the Living Human Foetus in Advances in Medical Science and Technology." It presented the rubella trials on fetuses to be aborted as a vindication of fetal research. After the Battelle-Columbus report, Dr. Robert E. Cooke, one of the twelve commissioners, took issue with this claim, as well as with many of the other supportive claims made in the study. In his critique[16] of the Battelle-Columbus report, Dr. Cooke wrote:

> . . . the use of pregnant women—intentionally vaccinated prior to abortion is said to have been essential to discover the threat to future fetuses. However, despite this report accidental vaccine infection of the fetus was reported shortly thereafter . . .

This means that a woman in a control group was given the vaccine, not realizing she was pregnant. She had a spontaneous abortion (miscarriage) due to the vaccine's impact on the fetus, who died. Upon autopsy, it was found that the vaccine had indeed crossed the placenta.

But today the rubella trials are still used to support nontherapeutic experiments on the fetus. For instance, in a packet of public relations materials from the March of Dimes,[17] one sheet stated, "The March of Dimes supports research to develop the best scientific information on human development before and after birth, and on those factors which may either cause birth defects or help to ensure healthy growth of the fetus and improve the outcome of pregnancy." The literature then pointed to key fetal experiments, among them, "Fetal tissue culture experiments [which] provided the key to development . . . of a vaccine against rubella . . . " It did not mention that the vaccine trials were done on live fetuses to be aborted.

Today, many experiments conducted on the fetus—both living in utero but to be aborted, and freshly dead from abortion or surviving an abortion with some vital signs–are connected to the growing fear of birth defects. This is a legitimate public concern, especially since, as *The New York Times* reported in 1984, the number of birth defects in the U.S. has doubled since the 1950's,[18] mainly due to drugs, carcinogens and mutating agents produced by the man-made environment of industry, food additives, chemical animal feeds, pesticides, waste dumps, radioactive fallout, etc. For the current experiments, the fetus has had to be conscripted in great numbers, and the necessity of nontherapeutic fetal experimentation proclaimed again.

For instance, in 1982, the March of Dimes paid for research done by Dr. Stanley Robboy, a pathologist at Massachusetts General Hospital and Harvard Medical School. This scientist has been able to transplant live fetal tissue into mice, an achievement the *New York Times* described only as "novel." To be of any use, tissues must be live. Dr. Robboy at that time was predicting that whole fetal organs—liver, kidney, heart—could also feasibly be transplanted into mice for testing the myriad of drugs and substances created by pharmaceutical houses and industry.

Dr. Robboy's desire to protect wanted fetuses from various poisons has been echoed elsewhere. The Laboratory for Embryology at the University of Washington, Seattle, has used very many aborted fetuses for the study of what are called teratogens, or mutation-causing agents.

In 1984, the Lab's work was furthered when the National Institute of Health gave the Lab's curator and founder, Dr. Thomas Hill Shepard, a $100,975 grant. He described the Lab's methods and services[19] as a collection program for the efficient procurement and distribution of fresh human embryonic and fetal specimens—a twenty-four-hour collection service. In the previous nineteen years the facility had collected over 6,000 specimens, which were distributed to more than 200 separate investigators. Some aborted fetuses were examined for abnormalities and what might have caused them. Others were serial-sectioned to supply teachers in high schools and colleges with specimens. The Lab maintains a computerized system that enables its personnel to provide data on animal tests and human risks of teratogenic agents.

The Laboratory was, in fact, founded in the 1950's after the thalidomide crisis. But the thalidomide babies were born alive precisely because there was no such service. Despite their limb deformities, they have been able to live useful and probably as happy lives as anyone else. Today, the Laboratory is instrumental in providing information that can lead to abortion for fear of bearing a defective child, in some greater or lesser degree—to what degree cannot yet be predicted by any prenatal test.

Because society continues to suffer under a deluge of lethal and harmful substances, "fresh," aborted fetuses arranged for testing and examination of deformities could be seen by researchers to be irreplaceable specimens. Some scientists disagree. Dr. Ross F. Nigrelli, director of the Laboratory of Marine Biochemistry and Ecology at the New York Aquarium, had this to say: "In testing drugs we use sea urchin eggs because the fertilization cycle is well known and the results are available within forty-eight hours. . . .We could have told them about thalidomide very quickly, had we tested it on sea urchin eggs."[20]

Another doctor who feels there is no need to rely on human fetuses for scientific investigation is Mark Ferguson, an anatomist at Queen's University in Belfast, Ireland. Ferguson has surgically corrected cleft palate in alligator fetuses while in the egg and has predicted that his technique will soon be used in fetal surgery to correct cleft palate in humans.

There are other examples of not succumbing to the panacea presented by the human fetus. The most stellar example is Dr. Jerome Lejeune, Nobel Prize–winning geneticist. His story is novelistic.

Long interested in Down's Syndrome, Dr. Lejeune found himself at the end of World War II with virtually no equipment and even put a morsel of paper under his microscope to balance it on a crooked table. He was in search of the genetic code for Down's Syndrome. He studied persons with the anomaly very closely. In fact, so observantly did he study them that he realized that their palm lines matched exactly those of the macaque, a species of monkey. He went to the Paris Natural Museum to check his hunch. He was correct. Because geneticists already knew the genetic makeup of the chromosomes of the macaque, Dr. Lejeune was able to find that Down's Syndrome was caused by a misattached chromosome.

Today, Lejeune is an ardent opponent of what is now taken to be the "cure" for Down's Syndrome: aborting the baby while in the womb after diagnosing the defect by amniocentesis, a procedure developed mainly by the March of Dimes using live fetal experimentation. Lejeune, for his brilliance and his opposition to the "fetus fad" and to eugenic abortion, has made enemies among supporters of nontherapeutic fetal research. Dr. Delacruz, a project director at the National Institute of Health, referred to Lejeune as "known to pontificate."[21] Dr. Gill, a pathologist from the University of Pittsburgh and Magee–Women's Hospital and a defender of fetal research, minimized Lejeune's creativity in discovering the code for Down's by saying that Lejeune's animal investigation and matching of palm lines were only "serendipity."[22]

Despite the urging of doctors such as Nigrelli, Ferguson and Lejeune, and because of the high availability of aborted fetuses, some workers in research have, in fact, eschewed animal studies altogether, and this is significant, because animal studies are supposed to precede any grants for experiments on humans. Yet, during the 1974-75 Commission on Human Subjects hearings at the NIH, it was revealed that *no animal studies* had preceded the live fetal research that bred amniocentesis, ultrasound and fetoscopy. Nor did any animal studies precede the most cruel experiments, the perfusion ones. In these, live babies of seven months gestation were aborted and hooked up to artificial placentas and perfused with oxygenated solution to see if they could respirate from the oxygen given through the skin. Again, the necessity of this experiment was heavily endorsed in the name of developing techniques to save premature wanted babies. Blinded by that feeling of necessity, the animal studies were not done as dictated by research ethics, and, in fact, one American researcher, Dr. Richard Chamberlain of George Washington Hospital, who performed such a perfusion experiment, was awarded the Research Prize of the American College of Obstetrics and Gynecology.

Far from upholding contemporary rationales for fetal experimentation, there are some who say that it has a chilling precedent. Dr. William Brennan, in his excellently researched book *The Abortion Holocaust,*[23] combined an incendiary title with meticulous, documented comparison of today's nontherapeutic fetal experiments to those done by the German doctors both before and after the rise of Nazism under Adolph Hitler.

Brennan's book has one chart that compares the testimony presented at the Nuremburg Doctors' Trial (1946-1947) to the U.S. Government guidelines for fetal research that exist today:

Concentration Camp Experiments	***Guidelines for Fetal Research***
Time of Performance	
Nontherapeutic experiments were conducted on camp inmates before, during and after extermination.	Nontherapeutic research directed toward the fetus in anticipation of, during or after abortion may be conducted or supported.
Purpose of Research	
"Entirely new data will be secured for science. The problems in question can only be solved on human beings." (Justification for the high altitude experiments performed at Dachau, Dr. Sigmund Rascher, 1942)	The development of important biomedical knowledge that cannot be obtained by alternative means is a justification for nontherapeutic research directed toward the fetus.

Previous Animal Studies	
"After numerous experiments on animals," the sea water experiments were performed on Dachau inmates.	Investigations on pertinent animal models should precede fetal research.

Consent for Experiments	
Consent for the sulfanilamide experiments came from the "legal authorities."	Consent for fetal research must be obtained from the mother.

Fetal experimentation, like all other kinds of nontherapeutic experimentation, may be one subject on which there is no middle ground, no ability "to agree to disagree." Today, fetal experimentation goes forward because of a complex of reasons, ranging from an argument for necessity, to nondisclosure to the public. It has resulted in an unseen but real civil war. Those who are against it are labeled, in a pro-abortion climate, "new barbarians" or fanatically backward. Pitched against this charge is a countercharge that makes comparisons between nontherapeutic fetal research and the atrocities enacted by actual barbarians of the twentieth century, over whose deathcamps is inscribed "Never Again."

Do we say, "Let the dead bury the dead," and go forward with nontherapeutic fetal experimentation, or do we stand fast on the ideal of both the sacrosanctity of life and the Hippocratic tradition, the essence of the latter being to "do no harm"? This choice has been the focus of the ongoing ethical debate. It is an interesting, if closed and curious, debate, begun in the 1970's. But let's pull back the elitist, private curtain for all to learn its ropes and its characters.

Very often sought out for his perspective has been ethicist Joseph Fletcher, a self-admitted casuist, i.e., situation ethicist. Fletcher's support for fetal experimentation has been absolute and based on his familiar underlying theme, his belief that there are no universal principles but only the inherent morality of each situation as it evolves. A quote from his *Moral Responsibility*[24] explains his "love" ethic:

> . . . Christian ethics is not a scheme of codified conduct. It is a purposive effort to relate love to a world of relativities through a casuistry obedient to love. . . . The first question of ethics is not "How do we behave?" but "What do we want?" . . .
>
> [Jesus] left no doubt whatsoever that *the ultimate norm of Christian decisions is love: nothing else.*

Fletcher applied this norm of "only love" to fetal research and came up on its side. At the 1974-75 hearings of the Commission for the Protection of Human Subjects, he said that a fetus is only "precious" when its potential for life is wanted, that the fetus is expendable if its existence threatens the quality of life of our other children.[25] "To treat live fetuses as 'untouchable' is absurd; variables such as their functional condition and health prospects, costs of treatment both financially and emotionally . . . whether they are destined for termination—these factors should enter into the decisional mix."[26] As to never experimenting on an infant capable of survival, he said, "The good intention of one government official, who said, 'If you have a viable fetus you are precisely in the same position you would be with a minor child,' is more and more taking on the appearance of the grotesque."[27] Fletcher also denied that any nontherapeutic experimentation on a live fetus to be or already aborted should be avoided. "Common sense, in any case, does not allow that a fetus which is inviable or to be terminated can be 'harmed' or 'injured' or 'insulted,' since acts of battery and mayhem presuppose a living, independent individual biologically. . . . An injustice predicates a person."[28]

Fletcher's vehemence against those who would protect especially the living, previable (20 gestational weeks or less) fetus is matched only by the outspoken support of Sisela Bok, Ph.D., for research on fetuses aborted or to be aborted even up to the third trimester. She also shared her thoughts at the hearings of the Commission on Human Subjects:

> This group of cells cannot feel the anguish or pain connected with death, nor can it fear death. Its experiencing of life has not yet begun; it is not yet conscious of the interruption of life nor of the loss of anything it has come to value in life. Nor is it tied by bonds of affection to others. If the abortion is desired by both parents, no grief will be caused such as that which accompanies the death of a child. Almost no human care and emotion and resources have been invested

> in it. Nor is such an early abortion and consequent research brutalizing for the person voluntarily performing it, or a threat to society. Because there is no semblance of human form, no conscious life or capability to live independently, no knowledge of death, no sense of pain, words such as "harm" or "deprive" cannot be meaningfully used in the context of early abortion and fetal research.[29]

In sum, Ms. Bok maintained that the fetus up to the third trimester cannot even be considered a *subject* of research, because it is an *object.*

Both Bok and Fletcher held that the human fetus' life has meaning only in the sense that it can benefit the living. Doctors, then, according to this school of ethics, are entitled to make value judgments about which lives have value and which do not. Fredric Wertham, M.D., in *A Sign for Cain,*[30] his brilliant book on violence in American society, quoted Dr. Christoph Hufeland (1762-1836), who stated that the medical profession runs a very self-destructive risk when proffering "love" to some and necessary sacrifice to others: "If the physician presumes to take into consideration in his work whether a life has value or not, the consequences are boundless, and the physician becomes the most dangerous man in the state."

Directly opposite the opinions of Fletcher and Bok are those of Hans Jonas, a philosopher who has written extensively on human experimentation. However, for the most part, he has received little notice among the ethicists usually called upon to pronounce on human fetal experimentation. That deletion seems significant by its absence.

In 1969, when the issue of fetal use began to surface in scholarly publications, *Daedalus,* the journal of the American Academy of Arts and Sciences, dedicated an entire issue to human experimentation. Jonas wrote[31]:

> . . . the doctor's imaginary speech would run, for instance, like this: "There is nothing more I can do for you. But you can do something for me. Speaking no longer as your physician but on behalf of medical science, we could learn a great deal about future cases of this kind if you would permit me to perform certain experiments on you. It is understood that you would not benefit from any knowledge we might gain; but future patients would.

Jonas maintained that such an attitude crosses the line of the permissible, even if the medical rubrics of consent, risk and the objective of the experiment are met. Jonas insisted that a "residue of identification" must be left to the patient, assuring the patient "that it is his own affliction, his own kind of suffering which he helps to alleviate in others, and so in a sense it is his own cause. It is totally indefensible to rob the unfortunate of this intimacy with the purpose and make his misfortune a convenience . . . "

Jonas seemed well aware that his strict point of view would cause many to accuse him of impeding "progress." And he spoke to just that point:

> Let me say . . . that if some of the practical implications of my reasonings are felt to work out toward a slower rate of progress, this should not cause too great dismay. Let us not forget that progress is an optional goal, not an unconditional commitment, and that its tempo in particular, compulsive as it may become, has nothing sacred about it. Let us also remember that a slower progress in the conquest of disease would not threaten society, grievous as it is to those who have to deplore that their particular disease be not yet conquered, but that society would indeed be threatened by the erosion of those moral values whose loss, possibly by too ruthless a pursuit of scientific progress, would make its most dazzling triumphs not worth having. Let us finally remember that it cannot be the aim of progress to abolish the lot of mortality. Of some ill or other, each of us will die. Our mortal condition is upon us with harshness but also wisdom—because without it there would not be the eternally renewed promise of the freshness, immediacy and eagerness of youth; nor, without it, would there be for any of us the incentive to number our days and make them count. With all our striving to wrest from our mortality what we can, we should bear its burden with patience and dignity.

Dr. Jonas scaled the heights. Others bring us back to a society quite locked into denying its mortality and willing to sacrifice whatever is at hand to waylay it. Mrs. Bernice McLernihan, Chairman of the Board of Magee–Women's Hospital, had this to say about the validity of fetal experimentation as an entry to well-being for others: "When I'm seventy or so, I want those techniques to be available for me."[32] Mrs. McLernihan is probably representative of a great number of people in society today, wedded to pragmatism rather than to any heightened sense of the sacred.

There have always been those naughty enough to try to stick a wedge into the power of the medical profession's eagerness to say what will or won't be done with humans. George Bernard Shaw put it to us with piercing and characteristic wit in *The Doctor's Dilemma.* He set up therein that dark side of man, that human propensity to take universals into one's own hands. Wrote Shaw in the play's preface: "No man is allowed to put his mother into the stove because he desires to know how long an adult woman will survive at a temperature of 500 degrees farenheit, no matter how important or interesting that particular addition to the store of human knowledge may be."[33] It is interesting to remember that Shaw's play was not made out of whole cloth. It was, rather, based on his conversation with a doctor friend of his who told him quite bluntly how he would choose to save certain patients over others, using a scale of their usefulness and potential up against what he called a "scarcity" of medical resources.

Unfortunately, what Shaw drew in play form in the late nineteenth and early twentieth century, the second half of the century has seen. When written, Shaw's play had not yet been taken at its word.

Earlier in the eighteenth century, Johnathan Swift wrote *A Modest Proposal for Preventing the Children of Poor People from Being a Burden to their Parents and for Making them Beneficial to the Public.* Today, we are also beset with "modest proposals" such as one recorded at the Hastings-on-Hudson Ethics Institute in New York, where all strains of opinion mix rather eerily together. As Swift proposed raising children for food, so today there are some avid to grow fetuses for their organs.

This modest proposal is written up as "Case 477,"[34] meaning that it is a real case, already written into history.

> Case 477: Mr. R, a twenty-eight-year-old engineer, has been on dialysis for 3 years, and is growing desperate because of the restrictions it places on his life. . . .
>
> Mr. R has already investigated the possibility of obtaining a transplant. However, he had been adopted as an infant and does not know his natural family. In addition, tests show that he has a rare tissue type that makes it highly unlikely that a suitable cadaver kidney can be found.
>
> . . . his wife suggests a solution to the transplant surgeon. She will . . . become pregnant, and after five or six months, have an

> abortion. The kidneys from the fetus could then be transplanted in her husband.
>
> The surgeon knows that technically such a transplant could be performed, and that the graft would probably not be rejected. He also knows that Mr. R has threatened to commit suicide if he has to remain on dialysis for an indefinite period.
>
> Should he agree to transplant the kidney of a deliberately conceived and aborted fetus?

Mary Anne Warren, a philosopher at San Francisco State University, asked to comment on the ethics of the case above, went one better by making her own modest proposal: "Can the Fetus Be an Organ Farm?"[35]

Ms. Warren set up her final endorsement this way: she asked what is the moral status of the five- or six-month-gestational fetus,

> . . . whether or not it should be considered a human being with a full-fledged right to life. . . . Unless . . . one supposes that mere biological parenthood confers the right to kill one's offspring, at any age, one must conclude that if a fetus of this age is a human being with full moral rights then the woman's proposal is tantamount to murder. On the other hand, if a fetus does not have a significant right to life, then the plan raises no serious moral problem, and provided that the operation has a good chance of saving her husband's life without seriously endangering hers, it certainly should be performed.

The next point in Warren's essay regards the moral status criteria of "problematic entities." Her list of these includes "fetuses . . . nonhuman animals, alien life forms, intelligent machines . . . " She told us that "it will not do to make genetic humanity (mere genetic affiliation with the human species) either a necessary or a sufficient condition for the possession of full moral rights. . . . My candidate for a species-neutral criterion for the possession of full moral rights is what I call *personhood.* A person . . . has the (actual, not merely potential) capacity for consciousness, complex and sophisticated perception, rationality, self-awareness, and self-motivated behavior. . . . Fetuses, one might say, as yet have no will; they do not desire life, or anything else . . . "

Ms. Warren then counseled us that not all might approve her criterion, because "fetuses, especially those as old as five or six months, elicit our sympathy, and tempt us to endow them with moral rights, not only because they are potential people, but because they look disconcertingly like people; their physical features are recognizably human." She assured us that "this sympathy is misplaced, unless there is a good deal more conscious activity in the fetal 'mind' than we have any reason to suspect." Ms. Warren closed with a neat maxim: "In such cases, a proper respect for the right to life requires that it not be respected where it does not exist."

Readers may be temporarily relieved to know that the surgeon in question turned down the prospect Mr. and Mrs. R. outlined to him. However, when this piece was written by Ms. Warren in 1978, the concept of fetus as an organ farm was already being practiced.

In 1972, *Time* had already reported that Dr. Arthur Ammann of the University of California's San Francisco Medical Center had transplanted a fetal thymus into a five-year-old-girl.[36] The fetus has special properties that make its organs optimum for transplant. The same thing was found in Australia in the early 1980's in the case of transplantation of fetal pancreas islets into diabetes victims. This research will soon become clinical rather than experimental. In 1972, Dr. Samuel Kountz, a kidney specialist from the University of California medical center, said he would like to try an even bolder operation—the transplant of a fetal kidney.

Obviously, the only ethical stumbling block for the surgeon in Case 477 was that the couple premeditated the conception of the child for organ harvest. Doctors such as Dr. Ammann do not have to confront that particular nugget of ethical bother. "We don't go around soliciting abortions. These are abortions that are already being done for other reasons."[37] (A Pittsburgh transplant specialist, Thomas Starzl, said he would find fetal transplants "objectionable.")

There are some opponents of fetal experimentation and use who feel that it is a symptom of doom-wishing, that fooling around with human biomedical and genetic material matches the mission man went on when he split the atom and created ultimate weapons. The clearest, most consistent voice hitting this point is theologian Paul Ramsey. He has indicated that those who do the cavorting with the risky and the unknown and cavort, moreover, at the expense of human subjects, are playing God[38]:

> All this adds up to man's limitless dominion over man. Who will be the Creator and who the creatures, who the masters who the

slaves, who the miracle workers and who the things, at the end of these converging lines.

Ramsey placed the aborted or to-be-aborted fetus on the list of the dying. In *The Ethics of Fetal Research,*[39] he wrote:

> In cases of induced abortion the fetal human being resembles not only the dying, it also closely resembles the condemned . . .

Ramsey added to this in an interview with Maggie Scarf in the *New York Times Magazine* in 1975,[40] when there blew up the first public furor over fetal experimentation. He said:

> Capital punishment presented us with a similar "golden opportunity" to do high-risk medical experimentation. After all, the condemned prisoner, like the living previable fetus, was going to die anyhow. . . . So why is it that we didn't research someone in that position to death? Such experimentation could, you know, have been seen as "ennobling" the death of the human subject by using him to make great contributions to mankind.

Ramsey's point was upheld by others. John Wilson, in the *Villanova Law Review* article quoted earlier, wrote that simply because the fetus is condemned to death in the abortion procedure does not verify the right to experiment on it.

Ramsey also traced much of the problem of fetal experimentation to our difficulty with sexuality and to our "modern" propensity to "reify" (make a thing of) sex. In *Fabricated Man,* he seemed to pray in print:

> Perhaps God will let loose another St. Augustine upon this planet, and the wounds men have inflicted upon themselves in the modern period by "thing-i-fying" the *carnal* life may begin to be healed.[41]

The point Ramsey made about "ennobling" the fetus as an excuse to do nontherapeutic research has not been neglected by others. This was exactly the point propounded in the pages of the *Atlantic* in 1975.[42] Willard Gaylin, M.D., and Marc Lappé, Ph.D., both of the Hastings-on-Hudson Ethics Institute, wrote, "At some point it becomes unethical *not* to do fetal experimentation. We believe that point has been reached when the research has as its objective the saving of the lives (or the reduction of defects) of other, wanted fetuses." Elsewhere in the article, they wrote, "Perhaps its death [the aborted fetus] can be ennobled because it served those more fortunate."

Gaylin and Lappé also argued that any intrusion on the fetus to be aborted could not logically be agonized over, considering its ultimate fate:

> Absolute and complete defense of the dignity and autonomous rights of the fetus seems bizarre when contrasted with the current government approval and public acceptance of abortion. In abortion, we condone procedures which subject the fetus to dismemberment, salt-induced osmotic shock, or surgical extirpation [cutting off of extremities or limbs]. No experimentation so far imagined would do the same.

So, there is a considerable effort on the research side to part company with the framers, supporters and practitioners of abortion. The researcher is far more humane, said Gaylin and Lappé.

Yet Gaylin and Lappé, who know research very well, did not tell the truth when writing for laymen in the pages of the *Atlantic.* First of all, as to their assurance that "no experimentation so far imagined" would be as mutilating as abortion: In fact, the very *extirpation* they spoke of in relation to the abortion procedure had already occurred in the much-publicized experimentation that involved the decapitation of fetuses in 1974 in Helsinki, Finland, an experiment in which American doctors participated. As reported earlier, Dr. Bela Resch has intermittently reported to his American colleagues on his pet experiment that involves surgical removal of beating fetal hearts for perfusion experiments.

Nor is Gaylin and Lappé's claim that the researcher is no kin to the abortionist able to hold up against past and present evidence. For a current example of the researcher's involvement in the abortion trade, we turn to Dr. Steven D'Ambrosio. In 1982, he received a $311,411 grant from the EPA. In his grant proposal, Dr. D'Ambrosio mentioned that he had a "unique source" of fetal organs. For his experiment "Fate of DNA Damage in Human Fetal Cells," Dr. D'Ambrosio said he would use human fetal "dermis, brain and kidney."[43] That seems to express a considerable stake in the abortion process. Yet a bright ethicist can take that disallowed closeness and other nettles out of nontherapeutic fetal experimentation, even D'Ambrosio's kind, which mutilates live fetal organs. Sometimes the ethical rationale, provided by a specialist, can detract attention from the realities of the experiment. The following is one example of this.

In 1980, a controversy hit the Notre Dame University's Department of Chemistry. Dr. Subhash C. Basu there discovered a link between the absence of enzymes and various brain diseases, a discovery that might help ameliorate such diseases in the future. His research was conducted on a cell culture from the cerebrum of a twenty-week-old diseased fetus. The fetus was obtained by a Prostaglandin E abortion; this could indicate that the fetus was born with some vital signs and vivisected, as prostaglandins are the favorite abortion inducers of researchers looking for live and intact organs for experiments.

The experiment was news, but so were the controversy and ethical gymnastics that accompanied it. When the experiment was initially proposed three years earlier, the Notre Dame Committee for the Protection of Human Subjects approved Dr. Basu's plan, and the Board of Trustees upheld the decision. A theologian there avowed that an experiment on the body of an aborted baby (he did not specify living or dead) is not intrinsically immoral. He offered an analogy likening this type of experiment to an experiment on a murder victim. Thus, claimed the theologian, the experiment was not deprived of "moral validity" provided that the body had been obtained with the consent of the proper custodian.

The theologian's argument neatly omitted the method of abortion, notorious for yielding live fetuses. It ignored the question of whether the researcher "ordered" a diseased-brain fetus from an area obstetrician, which would mean that he broke the general ethical rule of having no connection to the abortion process. After all, for a diseased brain to be used for research, it has to be fresh; an obstetrician or collaborating pathologist must dispatch such a fetus or that organ to the researcher very quickly or fix it in freezing nitrogen because he knows he has a "client." Finally, the theologian's argument ignored the fact that the researchers as a group have at their disposal not random, unpredicted murder victims but an array of disenfranchised living human subjects that have been condemned to die.

Rather than compare the aborted baby to a murder victim, which is rather inane upon examination, Dr. Bernard Nathanson, one of today's most active foes of abortion, conjures a stronger image: the aborted child is equal to a slave. His remarks accompanying his film *The Silent Scream* are pertinent to this report because Dr. Nathanson's complete retreat from abortion was impelled by his experience with fetal experimentation, a fact little known or logged by the media.

Said Nathanson, after first describing his prior career as a pro-abortion figure, who himself had presided over 70,000 abortions and trained countless others to perform them as well[44]:

> At the end of 1972, I . . . took up a research position as chief and director of fetology at St. Luke's Hospital, a part of Columbia University's medical school.
>
> Fetology was a new science: it was made possible by the development of new technologies such as ultrasound, fetal heart monitoring, amniocentesis and immunochemistry, all of which had a confluence in being the new science of fetology. [All of these depended for their development on experimentation performed on live fetuses to be aborted.] Fetology is the most dynamic, most explosive science in medicine today. Ten years ago, if one searched the medical world literature, one would find about 100 reports a year. If one searches the world literature today, one would find about 5000. . . .
>
> I spent four years in that science, cheek by jowl, working with the human unborn and it was during those years that the scientific data and my perception about the unborn began to change.

Nathanson did not become a total advocate of the fetus overnight. He stayed in fetology, that is, human fetal experimentation, until 1979, with increasing doubts that the fetus was the nonperson he had claimed it to be, and gradually forging a new position:

> I perceive the issue of abortion and the human unborn as the last major oppressed, decimated and disenfranchised minority in this country and I liken the current situation to what was occurring in this country in the 1830's and 1840's with respect to black persons in the U.S. who were oppressed, decimated and disenfranchised.

He told of a letter Ronald Reagan wrote deploring the pain that the fetus undergoes, a position shared by both ultra-rightwing journalists such as George Will and left-liberal ones such as Nat Hentoff. The letter was repudiated by the press for the most part. Additionally, the American College of Obstetricians and

Gynecologists responded to Reagan's letter, saying its points were unfounded. Twenty-six members of the American College of Obstetricians and Gynecologists then responded in protest to the College's assertions, Nathanson among them.

Is Nathanson right? Does fetal experimentation, by presenting the researcher and the public with a live human subject of nontherapeutic research, challenge the nonperson and "tissue" school of thought on the fetus? Does the fetus' aliveness, which is coveted by researchers, and ability to sponsor life for others, ironically but actually prove the fetus' own life?

Nathanson is no ethicist schooled as much in verbal obfuscation as in thought. Nathanson is a walking conversion experience, and, as we shall see, there may be more doctors who, knee-deep in live fetal experimentation, are coming upon the humanity of the fetus they once could kill or cure as they wished, or upon whom they could suffer any torture or any novel plan. Nathanson may not realize it, but he is tied to at least one academic ethicist in his own activist position of opposing abortion based on his experience with fetal experimentation. Paul Ramsey wrote in 1975:

> Far from abortion settling the question of fetal research, it could be that sober reflection on the use of the human fetus in research could unsettle the abortion issue.[45]

2

A Catalogue of Fetal Use

Including a selection of 1984–85 National Institute of Health grants for fetal experimentation.

In *Roe v. Wade,* the 1973 Supreme Court decision establishing abortion on demand, the ruling stated that, in deference to the mother, responsibility for disposal of the aborted fetus may fall to the institution where the abortion is performed. This usually means incineration, or, in some states, incineration or interment. That does not mean that a mother cannot bury her own aborted child. Magee–Women's Hospital in Pittsburgh reported that it does give mothers that option but that "very few" take it.

Germaine Greer, in her book *Sex and Destiny*, recorded that some "primitive" societies have other rubrics for burial of aborted babies. She cited the fact that in preagricultural societies, because of fixed food supplies, women often abort babies that cannot be supported by the group. In Brazil, Yanomamö women desiring abortion have their female friends jump on their abdomen until the fetus is separated from the uterine wall, often at the expense of the mother's health, even her life. But these Yanomamö women, and others, bury their aborted babies. Some bury them under their dwellings, name them, and subsequently give that name to another, liveborn child.

Thus we see that in the "modern" world, the trend is much away from the practices of the more personal, "primitive" one. What has resulted is a mighty availability of fetal bodies for myriad and often even ritualistic uses. The fetal body seems to be coveted—and feared. For instance, Dick Hatch of WPIT Radio of Pittsburgh reported that labs at Women's Health Services had signs placed in them asking doctors not to carry dead fetuses without wrapping them, since it disturbs the patients.

Only by realizing the spectrum of uses for fetal bodies can readers see that there seems to be a veritable fetal fetish—among doctors, artists, soldiers, pathologists, book publishers and more. The thesis of *Sex and Destiny* is that the West is turning its back on its own fertility, rejecting its progeny in any number of ways. Perhaps this phenomenon, which Greer said stems from an inability to understand and manage sexuality itself, would be one way of viewing the following catalogue of fetal uses, supplied here to give the reader a capsule view of what has been happening to the bodies of fetuses. This sampling is also an effort to show that biomedical experimentation cannot be separated in essence from any of the following; fetal use is a strange terrain without a map, but is nevertheless the surreal landscape that has become life.

1. By 1976, the staff of the District of Columbia General Hospital was regularly doing abortions, and some enterprising staffers there had an idea—the *Washington Post* revealed that year that Columbia General made over $88,000 from commercial sales of the fetuses it had aborted, fetuses they had *already* been paid to abort. An opportunity for profit presented itself, and they accepted it. What was done with the money was as crass as the sales themselves. The profits were used for such mundane expenses as "sending physicians to conventions and buying soft drinks and cookies for visiting professors." After that incident exploded in the *Post*, the trade seemingly went underground, at Columbia and everywhere else, including places where it hadn't been reported. A former abortion nurse in a Southern hospital said that fetuses there were routinely packed in ice after the abortions. "We wondered what happened to them then," she said. "But we never asked and were never told."

2. In 1977, the *Village Voice* carried another verification of fetal traffic.[2] This time it involved the Army research center at Fort Detrick in Maryland, whose premises are shared with the National Cancer Institute's labs. The *Voice* had learned, via a Japanese politician's report to the Tokyo Diet (parliament), that human fetal internal organs, such as livers and kidneys, were being shipped from South Korea to Fort Detrick via Japanese airlines. Detrick is the infamous installation for alleged chemical and biological warfare production, a charge continually denied by the Army, which says it only manufactures vaccines there for use in defense against germ and chemical warfare agents.

According to the Japanese report, the tissues and organs were being used to manufacture Korean hemorrhagic fever, a deadly virus that struck down U.S. troops during the Korean conflict. Quipped the *Voice:* "The peninsula of Korea is enjoying the dubious privilege of not only supplying the fever itself but also the foetal material for its potential mastery by human science." The *Voice* also verified that, before the Supreme Court decision, researchers looked to Sweden as a source of live human cells. But after the U.S. abortion decision, "American women began to provide a steadily growing supply of the needed product. . . . Horrible [is] the possibility that . . . doctors were encouraging abortions on women well beyond the third month of pregnancy—by such time the parts of the embryo are notably developed and thus infinitely more valuable for medical researchers."

The *Voice* report also took up the subject of Flow Laboratories, an international biological lab supplier of all types (including fetal) of biological materials. Then-director Joseph Hall told the *Voice* that Flow was one of the U.S. companies that had indeed received fetal parts from Seoul. "It's not the kind of thing one sees at the corner drugstore or supermarket," said Hall, adding that it is vital all the same. He also said that about six or seven U.S. companies purchase fetal material from pathologists for $20 to $25 a batch (today that figure is allegedly $35 a batch but no one seems willing to disclose how many, and of what, are in a batch).

Checking on this 1977 report, this writer called Fort Detrick. Public affairs spokesman Chuck Daicy at first seemed skeptical that the *Voice* report could be true. But I had already checked with Flow Labs, which verified that they had prepared cell lines from the fetal organs via a contract with the Army. After some "digging," Daicy called me back and said yes, Human Cell Line MRC-5, sold by Flow, and derived from human fetal lung tissue, is today being used to develop a vaccine (not a virus) to fight not Korean hemorrhagic fever, but Argentinian hemorrhagic fever. The Army, then, was doing something with human fetal cell lines, but maintained it was no longer receiving fetuses. This is because they were able to have Flow Labs seed as much cell stock from the original shipment of fetuses from Korea as they would need for some time.

As to Flow, it has been a target of French pro-life activists, who have appeared on news programs in front of Flow's Paris headquarters. This is because Flow's catalogue has advertised "Whole Human Embryo" and various whole fetal organs. But, explained Douglas Porretz, P.R. person at Flow, they are not at all selling whole organs or whole embryos. They are selling the cell lines derived from the original, called "primary," fetuses. Occasionally, Flow said, it will use a primary fetus for a new stock. Flow also had, said Porretz, a contract from the NIH to grow and store seed stocks.

Janet Ditmore, a researcher at Flow, lamented that Flow cannot obtain any fresh aborted babies. Ms. Ditmore said that the fetal kidney is the optimum medium for studying cancer. This reporter told her that many other researchers *are* obtaining fetal organs or whole fetuses and I gave her many examples. She was nonplussed. I mentioned this anomaly of Flow being unable to obtain fetuses to Richard Doerflinger of the Bishops' Pro-Life Committee in Washington, who knows much about the history of fetal experimentation. I asked him what he made of Ditmore's claim, but without telling him my own hypothesis. He came up with exactly my own line of thought: that after the Washington General Hospital scandal, when that hospital profited from fetal sales, the trade, as many claim, really did go underground. Other researchers (see NIH grants for 1984-85) told me that they either operate on a closed circuit, that is, making arrangements with obstetricians and pathologists in their areas to get and prepare fetal organs for them upon abortion, or, if this is difficult, they trek to foreign countries where obtaining fetuses is much easier. This is the result of publicity, in itself healthy, but bad publicity results in it becoming more difficult for reporters to find ready examples of fetal use.

3. *The American Type Culture Collection,* in its Second Edition, 1979, described "Characteristics of a Human Diploid Cell Designated MRC-5." This is the cell line used by Flow in the military experiments. The primary stock was cultured from a fourteen-week-old male fetus in the U.S. who was removed from a twenty-seven-year old woman, allegedly for psychiatric reasons.

4. In the 1980's, a new rabies vaccine, distributed by the Merieux Institute in Virginia, was developed, also using the MRC-5 cell line. It was found to work in 100% of the people vaccinated before they were exposed to the disease. It also worked in 99.9% of those treated after they had been bitten by rabid animals.

5. *The Chicago Sun-Times* of July 26, 1977, reported that an Ohio medical research company was testing brains, hearts and other organs of one hundred fetuses as part of a $350,000 pesticide research contract for the Environmental Protection Agency. The *Sun Times* wrote, "The research is being conducted by Dr. Raymond Thabet, head of Automated Medical Services, a Mansfield (Ohio) firm that was the only bidder for the contract. Thabet, who is also the Richland county coroner, refused to discuss his methods for collecting the fetuses or to answer any other questions about the contract." The organs were collected from fetuses at various stages of development, then frozen in dry ice and later reduced to gas, either chemically or through burning, for the purpose of analyzing their pesticide content. One EPA official said "there was some dispute" over whether the fetuses to be used in the experiment were considered living. This report pointed out the central role played by pathologists whether they work in a hospital or in a private lab. The pathologists receive the fetal body, dead or alive. They do the preparation ordered by the researchers. Mr. Thabet, however, was an exception, who, like the literary characters in Southern towns who are at once sheriff, jailer and judge, played the role of both pathologist and researcher.

6. The most horrendous event yet discovered involving the role of a pathologist occurred in 1982 in Wilmington, California, Los Angeles County. The Martin Container Company was repossessing for nonpayment on a twenty-foot container on the property of pathologist Mel Weisberg. Medical writer Rex Dalton wrote in the Torrance, California, *Daily Breeze*[3]: ". . . hundreds of fetuses, some more than five months developed with expressions on their faces, have been discovered in a large shipping container in Wilmington."

Martin, the owner of the container rented to Weisberg, who at the time was not in evidence, had asked a crew to clean it out. Wrote Dalton, "They came back and said they couldn't do it. They got sick." All of the fetuses, stacked eight feet high in jars filled with formaldehyde and in cartons, some as old as twenty-eight weeks gestation, were tagged with points of origin. They came from doctors and clinics throughout Southern California, the San Joaquin Valley, St. Louis, MO, and the Jefferson County Health Department in Missouri.

Los Angeles District Attorney Robert Philipbosian arranged with Valhalla Cemetery to inter the 16,500 aborted fetuses. The D.A. was moved to do this out of respect for the fetuses, whom he maintained were human beings even if denied legal personhood under the law. He made the arrangement with Valhalla on his own and was well within California law, which allows for incineration or interment of aborted fetuses. In the meantime, the drama was enlarged.

The Catholic League for Religious Freedom and Civil Rights, Southern California Chapter, went to Valhalla's administrator and arranged, without consulting the D.A., for a religious ceremony to be performed over the mass grave and a plaque placed on the grave. At this point, the ACLU intervened and filed a brief on behalf of the Feminist Women's Health Center, Inc. The brief maintained that the D.A. had violated church-state separation. But Philipbosian said he had not done that at all and that the Catholic League had contracted on their own for the religious service. That was in 1982.

As of 1985, the fetuses were still sitting in the original container in a county workyard, awaiting a hearing of the case before the California Supreme court. Philipbosian is finished with his term as D.A. and the new man in that office had kept to his position. Mr. Albergate, a spokesman for the D.A.'s office, said "The ACLU seems to want to insist that the fetuses are only tissue. That seems to be the philosophical point beneath their surface charge of violation of church and state separation."

The six-year case in California points up the adamance of the "tissue school," repeating the common appeal to the public made by pro-abortion and pro-experimentation cadres. The D.A. especially wanted interment for the fetuses of advanced gestational age, who would have been victims of illegal abortions. Even this was prevented under the terms of the brief filed by the ACLU.

7. In 1973 and 1976 the *Journal of Endocrinology and Metabolism* reported that fifty-four babies of ten to twenty-five weeks gestation were delivered alive by hysterotomy and that immediately after delivery each was cut open and that sex organs and adrenal glands were removed for experimentation. Others had their hearts punctured while still alive. Criminal charges were filed by the Provincial Attorney General in Manitoba against the doctors who delivered these infants and those who experimented upon them.

8. *The New York Times* reported on July 2, 1972, that scientists at the National Institute of Health had captured but not yet identified a flu called "the Norwalk agent." NIH researchers collected specimens from patients affected by scattered outbreaks of the flu in various parts of the country beginning in the late 1960's. They then tried to grow the virus in human fetal tissues. Dr. Dolin at the NIH told reporter L.K. Altman that the technique "relies on cells taken from the intestines of human fetuses obtained from therapeutic abortions in private hospitals." Said Dolin, "The key to success was nothing very sophisticated." He said that his team learned early that fetal specimens must be prepared in the operating room immediately after an abortion and not several hours later.[4]

9. In Denver, dentists in research experimented on the lower mandible (jaw) of 300 aborted fetuses. Dr. Charles Tobin, a researcher, told Frank Morriss of *The Wanderer* in a report dated March 2, 1972, that he had several sources for obtaining the fetuses, the main one being Denver's General Rose, a private hospital that in 1971 led the state with 993 abortions. Dr. M. Ovitz, pathologist at General Rose, confirmed that. He said that fetuses are supplied to such researchers under the general release of "tissue." A patient permission form signed by mothers was required. "In this case," said Dr. Ovitz, "the tissue would be the fetus." Mothers only *released* the "tissue" but were not told of the experimentation to follow. Dr. Tobin, in turn, said that when he finished with the fetuses, he cremated them.[5]

10. Dr. D. Lee Miller of Children's Hospital in Pittsburgh worked in the 1970's on allergic antibodies responsible for hay fever and other allergic diseases. To determine directly if fetuses can synthesize the antibody, tissues were obtained from human fetuses of 8.5 to 21 weeks gestation at the time of their abortion. The tissues were cultured. It was found that the human fetus is capable of producing the antibody as early as eleven weeks. This means that even newborn infants could manifest allergic diseases triggered by the environment.

11. In March 1979, Denis Gospodarowicz, Professor of Biochemistry in Medicine at the University of California Moffitt Hospital in San Francisco, applied to the National Institute of Health for a grant to fund his study of transplantation of corneal endothelia and the clinical implications.

Besides asking the NIH to pay for weekly "trips to the slaughterhouse for aortic arch and eyes," he also requested $1500 "for a trip to Lima, Peru," where a Dr. Francisco Contreras would help him "obtain fetal ocular tissues obtained at therapeutic abortions."[6]

12. Another grant application was made to the NIH in 1979 by Anthony Pearson at the University of Oregon Medical School, where he was director of research studies. His area of investigation was "The development of the eye and its adnexa (human)."[7]

Under "Goals," he flashed a bit of humor and a complaint: "The usual neurological methods are not always predictable. The staining of a series of human embryo sections on many slides is tedious. As a result of this, human developmental neurology has become a neglected field. I need a technician with the skill of a Ramon y Cajal. One would think that with an increase in the number of abortions performed in recent years, the supply of human embryos for research studies would have increased. The reverse of this has been the case. I have received only a few embryos during the past year. I must explore more productive avenues for obtaining embryos. In the past I have gotten a few embryos from Japan. . . ."

Under the section of his grant subtitled "Study on Eyelid Development," Pearson wrote that Part I of that study would be "based on observations on a large number of specimens and photographs of several hundred embryos many of which were obtained in Japan."

13. A report in *Child and Family* in 1970 stated that Dr. Jerald Gaull, at the time Chief of Pediatrics at the New York State Institute for Basic Research in

Mental Retardation at the Willowbrook home in Staten Island, was making periodic trips to Finland "to experiment on aborted but still-living fetuses." He severed the nerve connections between brain and body, then surgically removed the brain, lungs, liver and kidneys for study and dissection. In defending this type of research, Gaull was quoted as saying, "What needs to be said is that we need to get information that will help the unborn who are going to be born, not aborted. Rather than it being immoral, what we are trying to do, it is immoral—it is a terrible perversion of ethics—to throw these fetuses in the incinerator as is usually done, rather than to get some useful information." He described his career: "I'm interested in the fetus' biochemical development. We must know much more about development for intelligent genetic counselling. My coworkers and I have even studied the whole, intact fetus, injecting radioisotopes and following certain chemical reactions. In Europe we have studied the transfer of amino acids—body building blocks—from mother to fetus while the umbilical cord was still intact. We also maintain our own bank of fetal tissue. Banks like this should be established everywhere so these tissues can be distributed to investigators instead of being thrown away."

14. Experimentation with prenatal and neonatal human beings was the subject of an article in the *Marriage and Family Newsletter,* January 1972. Author John Harrington wrote, "While organ storage will probably be the main source of supply for "spare-part" operations in the next fifty years or so, beyond that we can expect to see a far more radical alternative: the growing of organs from embryonic tissue, in whatever quantities required. The maintaining of cells and tissue in culture is now a well-developed technique, the first steps in which were taken more than a half-century ago by an American, Ross Harrison, who maintained nerve cells alive in isolation. Since the war, notably at the Strangeways Laboratory in England, a start was made on maintaining organs. First, small thigh bones, taken from an embryo, were grown to many times their initial size. More recently, in Paris, Etienne Wolf has grown embryonic tissue destined to become not only bone but skin and testis; he has even been able to change the sex of gonadal tissue by the application of hormones. He is now working on the growing of eyes.[9]

15. Experiments on the brains of unborn infants at the University of Rochester Medical Center were reported in *Science,* Aug. 27, 1971. Researchers removed brain sections from babies of ten to nineteen weeks gestation, and kept the brain sections alive for five months, subjecting them to exhaustive tests.[10]

16. Human fetal antigens, used as cancer markers in lab tests, were acquired by Joshua Fierer of Columbia University by homogenizing babies directly from the abortion suction machine, according to the *Journal of the American Medical Assn.*, March 26, 1973.

17. The use of live human fetuses in experiments for the cosmetic industry were reported in the *Cork* (Ireland) *Examiner* Aug. 25, 1983[12]: "Laboratories in Europe, which serve the cosmetic industry in the preparation of beauty products, are experimenting on live human fetuses. This horrific claim is made in an as yet unpublished report to a Committee of the European Parliament. . . . In his report [to the European Parliament, Italian Christian Democrat Member of Parliament Alberto Ghergo] says that in (unnamed) European embroyological laboratories experiments are being carried out on foetuses between 12 and 21 weeks. These are removed whole and alive by means of hysterotomy (Caesarean Section). . . . The embroyos are dissected in order to remove certain organs (pancreas, thymus, brain, etc.) which are frozen by liquid nitrogen vapours. Other embroyos are frozen on extraction from the mothers' womb to be set aside for various uses.

"According to his report, the use of foetuses has given rise to a dense network of economic interests 'ranging from traffic in them, with financial incentives to encourage mothers to become donors, to laboratory manipulation.'" Mr. Ghergo's remarks were made before the Legal Affairs Committee of the Parliament. He spoke of the "regular and consistent pronouncements" of civilization—"the Hippocratic Oath, the Geneva Declaration (1948) the International Code of Medical Ethics (1949) and the Helsinki Charter (1964)." He also pointed out that "in 1978 the Council of Europe adopted a resolution recommending the Member States to lay down special rules for the protection of embryos." Ghergo also quoted Pope John Paul I's statement made in 1978 before the International Congress on Organ Transplants: "Man must not be transformed into an experimental subject."

Ghergo then went on to say that today it is not blind dogma that inhibits changes in scientific procedure as was true in the days of Galileo, "but the knowledge, acquired with progress, that science must be based above all on the universal values of respect for human life.

"Must the weak become the pawns of the strong?" he asked. "Have the higher interests of science become absolute, unconditional values?" A contingent thought might also be: has medical science assumed today a position over human affairs with the dogmatism that it says it despises in history and that was held by religion? Is it possible that society might be on the verge of being stripped of its humanity by science the way that Galileo, et al., were stripped of their right of inquiry by the Church? Certainly science today is very free to inquire, but it seems to want that freedom to go unchecked even in the most ethically controversial areas, so controversial that they could change man's perception of his humanity—and perhaps, in some dim future, the very criteria for it.

Ghergo asked the Parliament to consider fetal trafficking. He did not bow to politesse, but grouped medical researcher in with common profiteer: "The use made nowadays of live and dead human fetuses has assumed such proportions that this phenomenon must be examined bearing in mind the confidential and even clandestine nature of such practices. . . .

"It appears that there is a trade in foetuses and embryonic tissue between [European Economic] Community countries and between the latter and third countries. Appropriate Community provisions are desirable in this field, above all to prevent the legislation governing it in the various Member States from actually being evaded."

Ghergo distinguished between living, vivisected fetuses and tissues gained from dead fetuses. He felt that tissue from dead fetuses "may be compared with the transplant of tissues removed from cadavers." Although he said, "No special problems arise here," he recommended that national provisions be harmonized at the Community level. Ghergo did not mention the fact that some fetuses are aborted alive, allowed to expire without medical intervention and then harvested for tissue and organs.

18. On June 29, 1980, *The Chicago Tribune* ran a story headlined "Beauty may be only placenta-deep." After citing the natural fad in health and beauty aids, reporter Marianne Taylor wrote, "Perhaps the most earthy of the earthy ingredients found in cosmetics is protein . . . The source of the ingredient, however, also serves to turn stomachs. . . . An elite group of lotions and shampoos, about 5 percent of all protein products, contains the most expensive protein—processed from human afterbirths."

She went on to describe the acquisition of the placentas by processing firms that serve the cosmetic industry. Not only the placenta, but the sac surrounding the fetus inside the womb "are collected regularly from hospitals across the nation." One U.S. processor supplies most manufacturers: RITA Organics in Crystal Lake, IL.

RITA Organics fielded all of Ms. Taylor's questions with complete aplomb. They described the processing procedure: "placentas are thawed, sliced and forced through filters." Unwanted materials are then extracted. What is left is a snowy powder. Three to four days of processing yield only 400 grams; the cosmetic manufacturers pay $3,500 to $5,000 a pound.

RITA's profitability was not specifically mentioned. But hospitals were selling placentas at 50¢ to 75¢ each. Mr. Steve Goode, President of RITA, had this to say: "If someone doesn't buy it, then the hospital will have to pay scavengers to haul it away." Or, he added, they would have to burn it and use up valued energy. Obviously, these masterfully drawn utilitarian notes were supposed to sedate the bystanders.

"Birth of a Lotion" by Sandy Rovner in the *Washington Post,* May 15, 1982, explored the same subject, with more comments from Goode. He mentioned that he had processed the placentas of two of his grandchildren. He also stated, "There is more to the placenta than anyone would believe. It contains everything a human body needs." However, the Food and Drug Administration believes that to be just so much advertisement. A spokesperson there countered Mr. Goode: "There is no biologically active material left in those extracts . . . If it had anything active in it, it would have to be registered as a drug rather than a cosmetic. I guess the purpose is somehow to make the product distinct from someone else's." As usual, the consumer is the victim of his own zeal and is sold a placebo, except that in this case there is a moral dimension to the placenta trade.

Goode said that about fifty companies in the U.S. use the processed placenta but wouldn't divulge the names.

Richard Kaitz, executive vice president of Palm Beach Beauty Products Co., manufacturer of hair products and face creams called "Placenta Plus," does buy some of Goode's placentas and the rest from another processor in New York. He said he pays $3,400 a pound and uses "about 50 to 60 cents worth in a 16-ounce bottle of shampoo." This represents about ten percent of the product's retail cost. Cosmetic firms are not required to list their "secret ingredients" with the FDA under the current regulations. The FDA does say that it has had some complaints about the use of human placenta in products and some requests to remove them. The FDA counters by saying that it has nothing to do with legalized abortion and regulates only the grade and safety of ingredients.

While the idea of placenta as an ingredient excites many, it sickens others. There is also the question of consumer rights. In the case of placentas taken from abortions, those opposed to abortion would not want to buy products associated with it. Other consumers may not want to put human ingredients on their face or hair and may further disapprove of profiting from abortion, if not of abortion itself.

19. The cosmetic industry's use of placentas does not really prepare one for the following. Judy Narigian of the Boston Women's Health Collective related in the *Post* article cited above that she was once approached by an Italian doctor who was advocating the rights of women to control their own placentas. He suggested setting up placenta banks and believed that the placenta might carry some immunological benefits. Ms. Narigian did not mention if this was to be a commercial proposition. Another person, Dr. Allan Weingold, chairman of the obstetrics and gynecology department at George Washington University Medical Center, said that about seventy-five percent of that hospital's placentas are collected by agents of several pharmaceutical houses. The membranes have also been used for primary burn coverage. But some patients, he said, take their placentas home with them to cook and eat them, "following the natural trend." Dr. Weingold was untroubled because other animals, he noted, eat their placentas too.

20. In 1976, several news media discovered the existence of Turtox-Cambosco, a firm based in Chicago and at the time a subsidiary of Macmillan publishing company. The company's catalogue listed "embedments of human embryos" for $97.80 and stated, "These embryos range from 3 to 4 months in age. They have been bisected along the median, cleared and mounted naturally. Specify age or ages desired."[13] Turtox-Cambosco was a major supplier of biologicals, supplying schools and colleges, but also individuals.

One man had a quarrel with the firm. Gilbert Durand of the Durand Investment Company in Glendale, CA, was, in 1976, a Macmillan stockholder. He came across a Turtox advertisement touting the company as a subsidiary of Macmillan. Durand called Macmillan headquarters in New York and asked for the facts. James McIlhenny, then executive vice president at Macmillan, told Durand that the company only accepted donated human fetal material from natural miscarriages and not from induced abortions. The latter were not acceptable not for moral considerations but because of "the damage incurred in the abortion process." Macmillan is said to have since relinquished its ownership of the company.

There may not only be a cult of the fetus but also a raging lack of creativity in society at large. Durand pointed out that there is no educational advantage in using a real fetus as opposed to a facsimile. "Has not our technology and artistry reached the point when a plastic, three-dimensional facsimile embryo would serve the educational process better and cheaper?"

Readers will wonder what the laws are about such trade. Unfortunately, the laws in every state are dissimilar. Some effort is being made by pro-life organizations to cull the separate laws and analyze them. At this point it can only be said that some laws allow for trade that has been called "trafficking" and others explicitly forbid any trade in human organs of any kind.

21. *The Arizona Republic,* on March 2, 1981, carried a report by Randy Collier[14]: "State officials are investigating reports that doctors affiliated with the Valley Abortion Center performed experiments on fetuses although such tests are prohibited by state law . . .

"Pregnant women volunteered for E.R. Squibb & Sons Laboratories' experiments involving hypertension medication . . . Drs. Robert Tamis, Robert Wechsler and Mark Gross purportedly provided free abortions to 14 women, most of whom had been referred by the Maricopa County Hospital, in return for the women's cooperation in the testing of a Squibb-manufactured drug called Nadolol.

"The women, all of whom were in their second trimester of pregnancy, reportedly were informed exactly what the tests entailed. A spokesman for Doctors Hospital said Tuesday that Tamis, head of the hospital's obstetrics-gynecology department, acknowledged the experiments.

"The spokesman, Randy Heller, quoted Tamis as saying Squibb approached him nine months ago asking if he would seek volunteers for the experiment."

Robert Schwadron, public affairs director at Squibb's headquarters in Princeton, N.J., said, "The experiments met all federal drug-administration requirements." They were, however, in violation of Arizona law. According to the *Republic* report, Schwadron "said that women used for the experiment were given the drug for five days. Each day, the women were examined, blood was drawn and amniotic fluid was taken from the womb. . . . On the fifth day, the abortion procedure was begun at the center, where the women were injected with prostaglandin solution. They then were taken to Doctors Hospital, where the fetuses were delivered."

After quoting Schwadron, the report mentioned that two former nurses at the clinic said Squibb paid the center $10,000.

22. In 1975, Dr. Maurice J. Mahoney testified before the National Commission for the Protection of Human Subjects. Dr. Mahoney made a scan of recent medical literature to make his report on "The Nature and Extent of

Research Involving Living Human Fetuses."[15] Research using the clearly dead fetus was excluded from this report. Dr. Mahoney found published records of numerous experiments on living fetuses.

Drugs were given to mothers for the purpose of studying placental passage and fetal distribution patterns. Fetal tissues were analyzed shortly after the death of the fetus. Dr. Mahoney's report did not indicate whether the fetus died from any of the drugs. Dr. Mahoney pointed out that dead fetuses are also used in completing studies that began while the fetus was still alive in utero.

In a study of cutaneous respiration, fifteen fetuses who were judged to be alive by a pulsating cord or visible heartbeat were immersed in a salt solution with oxygen at high pressure. If a pulsating cord or visible heartbeat was not present, the fetus' thorax was opened and the heart was observed directly. If the heart was found to be still beating, the fetus was returned to the immersion chamber. The study was aimed at developing a temporary fetal incubator.

In a similar experiment, seven previable fetuses, also obtained from legally induced abortions, were submerged in a sugar solution. They were perfused with blood through umbilical vessels and kept in a plexiglass oxygenator. The fetuses carried out movements of the head, body and limbs during the perfusion. If perfusion was stopped, gasping efforts by the fetus would increase and the fetus would characteristically die in about twenty minutes.

In eight-week-gestational infants, growth hormone and insulin assays were obtained from the umbilical vein while the placenta was still in utero. The study increased knowledge of endocrine function during fetal life.

Other fetuses, most older than twenty-eight weeks and so presumed viable, had blood drained from their heads. This study's purpose was to gain information about intrauterine malnutrition.

23. In 1983, members of the British Parliament heard protest from the Society for the Protection of Unborn Children concerning a claim that live aborted fetuses were subjected to electric shock for experimental purposes. The claim was attributed to Dr. Robert Edwards, test-tube baby pioneer, as reported in the British newspaper *The Guardian,* September 29, 1982.[16] Edwards claimed that scientists have subjected sixteen-week-old aborted fetuses to electric shock in order to measure their development. Dr. Edwards said that asking patients' permission to perform experiments on their live aborted babies was not necessary. "It is hardly the right of the mother," said Edwards, "who has condemned her fetus to be aborted to then give consent for it to be experimented upon."

24. From a Leaflet advertising Californie Esthetique products[17] in Cannes,

France: "Beauty by Freezing: A revolutionary treatment of cellular regeneration uses freezing. Since the work of Dr. Alexis Carrel, we know that young cells applied to old tissues are able to regenerate them. These cells are the more effective if they are living.

"Exclusively taken from fetuses, these cells, no longer independent, do not carry antibodies and so reduce to a minimum any risk of allergic reaction.

"Red bottle contains placenta, spleen, liver and thymus of the fetus.

"White bottle contains material drawn from intestinal membrane."

25. The *Village Voice* is known for its New York arts beat. On January 27, 1979, it reported on Spider Webb, "the premiere skin engraver."[18] Spider engraved a fetus which he bought for $300 from a person who threw in a bottle full of human fingers. Foto, a Manhattan gallery exhibited the fetus, accompanied by a film of Spider doing the actual engraving. Said Spider, "It was harder on Gatewood (the filmaker). "When he developed his film, the prints scared the shit out of him. He had to take two valium and go to bed." Webb hinted that he was ready to engrave the free fingers next.

Thus ends this partial catalogue. Readers may want to consider not only Germaine Greer's thesis that Western society is turning its back on its own fertility, but also the words of Saul Bellow as quoted in *U.S. News and World Report* in 1982[19]:

> Everything [in modern times] is done brutally and in haste and processed quickly. We are divested of the deeper human meaning that has traditionally been attached to human life . . .
>
> There is no sacred space around human beings any more. It's not necessary to approach them with the tentativeness and respect that civilization always accorded them. People are now out there in the open: They're fair game. . . .
>
> Our humanity is at risk. It's too powerful a thing to just lie down and give up the ghost. But we have to face the fact that it is in danger. It is at risk because the feeling that life is sacred has died away in this century.

Selected 1984-85 National Institute of Health Fetal Research Grants

The 1984-85 grants for fetal research from the National Institute of Health do lack the bizarre and cruel character of the now infamous experiments of the late 60's and early 70's. But the current projects are far from controversial—they demonstrate how the NIH regulations have, in some or large part, been ignored, skirted, or relatively interpreted by the NIH itself. Because the NIH Ethics Advisory Board was long ago disbanded, any debate over whether some of the projects should have been funded at all, from an ethical standpoint, is not even a possibility.

One of the most problematic projects is the $1.2 million grant given to five medical research centers to study the ability of chorionic villi sampling to yield as precise a prenatal diagnosis between eight and eleven weeks as amniocentesis can at fourteen to sixteen weeks. The NIH, because it is trying hard to avoid the controversiality of funding nontherapeutic experimentation on previable, living fetuses, has given the money only for the data collection. Thus, it can say quite truthfully that it is not funding the cvs itself. Yet it is collecting data by means of a procedure that John C. Fletcher, ethicist at the NIH, said is unable to meet the definition of therapeutic for the fetuses undergoing the test. Also, the worldwide loss from the test is believed to be two percent, which Fletcher considered high. Therefore, it can be safely said that the cvs procedure, now being done in the trials on women at risk for carrying genetic and inborn anomalies, can lead to the death of infants undergoing the test; so the test exceeds the minimal-risk definition in the NIH regulations, which requires that no fetus be entered into research the risks of which would exceed any situation the fetus would normally experience.

The cvs trials are not taking place on fetuses to be aborted. Rather they are being done on yet another newly defined class of research subjects: "fetuses at risk" for genetic, chromosomal or cellular defects. The researchers' logic about experimenting nontherapeutically on a fetus to be aborted was that no injury due to the experiment is pertinent because the fetus is going to die anyway. With cvs, the logic seems to be that imposing the nontherapeutic cvs on an alive, at-risk, in-utero fetus, and thereby possibly suggesting a eugenic abortion or prompting miscarriage, is worth the risk of injury to the fetus because it can prevent a "defective" from being born.

Dr. George Rhoades, director of the NIH data collection project, reported that some women in the study, upon receiving a cvs report that their infant is carrying a defect, have opted for abortion. Both Fletcher and Rhoades, when asked if the cvs test is therapeutic for the infant involved, although admitting it is not, also tried to beg toward the idea of the development of future therapies, such as gene-mending, etc., to help such infants. If therapy were definitely on the horizon, it would certainly have to be introduced as a support for cvs. But to do cvs in the therapeutic lacuna which now exists, and which is admitted by both sources at the NIH, leaves it with only a eugenic quotient to ponder. Dr. Rhoades admitted that "at this point, therapy is not the main thing." Dr. Fletcher conceded that were there an Ethical Advisory Board sitting at the NIH, even the data collection project might not have been funded because the research subjects involved are previable, living fetuses, a class that normally demands a waiver of all regulations if the research is nontherapeutic but can yield "important biomedical knowledge unavailable by any other means." At present, all that cvs can contribute to the latter is an earlier method of prenatal diagnosis that can enable parents to abort a handicapped fetus, as Fletcher said, without the same feeling of guilt as when doing so via amniocentesis in the third trimester of pregnancy. The mask of voluntarism also haunts the project, for researchers at the four centers are approaching women "at risk" with the "option" of partaking of the cvs "opportunity." Ultimately, the women "volunteer" and also pay for the test.

Also bundled deep within the cvs trials is another controversy. If the test is nontherapeutic, then there is the question as to whether it is afly of the law in states where the trials are taking place. For instance, one of the research centers is at the University of Pennsylvania, another at the University of California. Both of these states forbid any nontherapeutic procedure on any live fetus, whether viable or nonviable, to be aborted or not, in utero or ex. This reporter asked Dr. Fletcher if, in general, the NIH regulations, which do allow nontherapeutic procedures on live fetuses, are in serious conflict with many state laws. Fletcher conceded, "You certainly have something there." Readers may assess that many quandaries and controversies still remain in the realm of fetal experimentation, yet there are few governmental mechanisms—such as an Ethical Advisory Board—by means of which they can undergo scrutiny and resolution. There are even fewer means—that is, none—by which the public can get in on any discussion.

NIH-funded research projects[20]

S.S. Robertson of Case Western Reserve University, Cleveland: "Neurobehavioral Organization of Fetus and Neonate" ($51,498). Robertson, who has a Ph.D. in developmental psychology, characterizes his research as "not invasive," aimed at tracking fetal activity in the second half of gestation, and then comparing his findings with work he's done on eleven other primates. Dr. Robertson attached a pressure transducer to the mother's abdomen every other week during the second half of pregnancy and then during labor. Robertson saw his method of checking up on the fetus as an alternative to ultrasound, which is invasive and, according to reports in *Science* magazine, is more damaging in some cases to the fetus than formerly thought. Yet Robertson did not think that his procedure would ever become widely used, mainly because it is very labor-intensive. The thrust, he said, is therefore not clinical, but in the realm of new knowledge.

Gerald R. Cunha, University of California, San Francisco: "Normal and Abnormal Utero-Vaginal Development" ($229,382).

Dr. Cunha reported that he used "completely non-viable" aborted specimens' reproductive tracts. These came, he said, from first-trimester dilation-and-curretage abortions or from second-trimester dilation and evacuation; in both methods, the fetus is shredded. He then took hairless mice and transplanted some of the fetal reproductive tract into the mouse. Doses of DES and of other drugs, such as the fertility drug Clomid, were then injected into the mouse, because, as Cunha said, "Obviously you can't shoot up a lady with DES." The objective is to study "how DES elicited the malformations" for which it is now infamous.

Cunha's research again raises the basic question: whether science has a right to use tissue from dead fetuses who have been denied legal personhood under the law, thereby creating a cheap class of research subjects, free of ethical restraints. As the Warnock report of Ulster, Ireland, recently pointed out, much of society polled in that country found it unacceptable for human embryos to be gestated in the bodies of animals, namely sheep. Cunha's experiment, and others like it, while it did not use a live fetus, still raised the question of whether any trans-species transplantation violates longstanding protocols and rules on what can be done with human organs. Another concern is the fact that mutilation, rather than transplantation into a diseased victim for the sake of regeneration, took place in the experiment.

Cunha did make an important find: that Clomid, an anti-estrogen fertility drug, produces an effect on the female reproductive tract similar to that of DES. Cunha approached Merrill Drug Co., makers of Clomid, to see if they might be interested "for the sake of self-interest" in looking further into the question of Clomid's effects. Cunha was surprised to find that they weren't.

For the use of fetal tissues, Cunha asked only for the verbal consent of the mother. He said that his view all along in the debate about using fetuses from abortion has been, "Let's use this tissue." He added, "There are animal models for studying everything we do. It's likely we won't learn anything new [by working on animals]. [But] when you get a positive result in a human, you can be sure."

Dr. E. Kolodny, Tay-Sachs Prevention Program, Eunice K. Shriver Center for Mental Retardation, Inc., Waltham, MA ($27,962). Dr. Kolodny said that he was doing no research on fetal material. Yet the precis of his grant as provided by the NIH includes this statement: "The Genetics Unit will improve techniques for the prenatal detection of metabolic and chromosomel disorders and neural tube defects." Dr. Kolodny would not verify the means by which this is done. All previous prenatal diagnostic techniques' research required and used living fetuses.

Donald Pious, Developmental Biology Program, University of Washington, Seattle ($67,726). Dr. Pious' project did not involve fetuses but had an impact on them in two realms: the first is contemporary, prenatal diagnosis; the second, futuristic—the ability to cure genetic anomalies through gene therapy. His work was in gene mapping, taking blood from a range of adult humans, then culturing cells from the blood and treating them to break up DNA. Pious reported that his work did not involve gene therapy, which, he said, was being done experimentally by others in this country. Pious' project represented a two-edged sword presented by biomedical researchers to the fetus and to society. Gerald Stine asked in *Society and Human Genetics* whether fetuses should be allowed to undergo any prenatal diagnostic test that has no therapeutic possibility. That question could be extended to the work of Pious and others. Should they work only on that aspect of gene mapping that will result in therapy? Or, if a prenatal diagnostic component of the work is found and proven, should it only be applied in cases where known therapies exist? Of course, with the current abortion law able to inveigh against the rights of the normal fetus, how much less is the protection for handicapped fetuses in the face not only of abortion options but also prenatal diagnostic ones?

Dr. Ronan O'Rahilly, University of California at Davis: "Development of Nervous System" ($142,490). Dr. O'Rahilly answered his own phone at the Carnegie Collection of Embryos, and didn't mind saying why: "We're not very well supported." The Carnegie Collection, which O'Rahilly called "the bureau of standards for human embryology," was suffering, he said, from "young people not coming in" and from general lack of support. Asked if the Collection was gotten from abortuses, O'Rahilly emphatically replied, "No. And that's the beauty of it. No controversy at all."

He described how twenty to forty years ago, the Collection was begun by Dr. Rock. "When a woman came in for hysterectomy, we figured out when to do it based on her cycle on chance there might be an embryo." The extraction of the fetus, he said, was "very laborious." Other specimens of varying gestational ranges were all obtained from miscarriage or stillbirth. O'Rahilly also said that younger researchers are not, these days, inclined to work from morphological or anatomical studies for their investigations.

This is in contrast to another grant holder from the NIH for 1984-85, Dr. Thomas Hill Shephard, of the University of Washington in Seattle. Dr. Shephard's copious journal articles speak of his "24-hour collection of fresh abortuses." He has also reported supplying fetal tissues to a few hundred researchers. Shephard's operation is, in contrast to Dr. O'Rahilly's, very well funded, receiving $100,975 from the NIH in 1984-85. O'Rahilly said that his 1984-85 grant would have to last several years and would be only for maintenance rather than expansion. Shephard, on the other hand, has been getting generous grants year after year.

Dr. Karen Holbrook, University of Washington, Seattle: "Fetal Skin Biology" ($239,740). Dr. Holbrook has received, as she reported in two journal articles,[21] as many as "sixty human embryos . . . obtained by hysterectomy, hysterotomy or saline suction abortion . . . through the courtesy of Dr. Thomas Shephard, Director of the Central Laboratory for Human Embryology." These specimens have been used in much of Dr. Holbrook's work on fetal skin and hair. For use under her 1984-85 grant, she received fetal skin biopsies from two sources. The first was normal abortuses of the first, second and third trimesters. When asked about their state upon abortion, she said, "Hopefully they are not born alive. It's better to avoid that. The skin is taken after fetal demise." The other source was fetoscopies taken of live, in-utero fetuses at various colleges where Dr. Holbrook had connections. Dr. Holbrook was trying to track epidermal diseases so they could be diagnosed in the womb. Asked if these—one being the so-called "fishscale" disease—are fatal, Dr. Holbrook said "No, but they ruin your life." When asked if she was concerned about the eugenic abortions that result from her work, she said, "Some say we are giving parents the direction to abort, but we see it as giving people the chance to have a normal baby." This is the rhetoric made famous by the March of Dimes, and which all subsequent workers in techniques and research leading to eugenic abortion are fond of repeating.

Two other issues haunt the work of Dr. Holbrook. One is that her source of tissue has been, via Shephard, from hysterotomy, as stated in her articles. The infamous experiments of the 60's and 70's that used live, intact babies born of hysterotomy prove clearly that the technique is used to get live specimens for research. Yet Holbrook could say that her tissue was taken "after fetal demise." What was the state of the fetus before the dissection for tissue or the delivery of the whole embryo to the Center for Embryology? Although the NIH has a category for allowing research on living, nonviable fetuses, many states demand that any live-born fetus, whether from abortion or not, whether viable or not, be given medical intervention. If this was not being done in the states from which Shephard obtained fetuses, then are researchers, although within the limits of the federal regulations, complicit in allowing fetal death for the sake of increasing the availability of "tissue" for research projects?

Some light can be thrown on the subject from a March 1985 memo that was filtered to this reporter from the head of the local Pittsburgh chapter of People Concerned for the Unborn Child. She, Mary Winter, in turn, received it from a source at Magee–Women's Hospital in the same city. The memo read, "Under the new guidelines recommended by NIH, any termination of second trimester pregnancies that results in a live birth should be reported to the Pathology Department." PCUC asked state Representative Stephen Freind, sponsor of Pennsylvania statutes on fetal experimentation, to ask the head of the Department of Obstetrics and Gynecology at Magee and author of the memo, Terry Hyashi, to explain the memo and to state how and if it conforms to the state statute demanding medical intervention for all live-born fetuses, even those from abortion. Hyashi responded to Freind only by way of asking how he came by the memo. Magee–Women's Hospital President George Szygkowski told this reporter in February 1985 that "Magee-Women's does give out fetal tissues to researchers via autopsy and does not require the written consent of the mother for this." Thus, there remains the question as to the state of fetuses born alive via abortion procedures such as second-trimester prostaglandin and hysterotomy being cannibalized for research and not being allowed to define, as the Edelin jury proposed, their own ability to survive. Ethicist Fletcher, mentioned above, said, "The mother is not entitled to the death of her fetus" (in a liveborn abortion).

Researchers such as Dr. Holbrook, who receive tissues from hysterotomy, and from second-trimester abortions by methods notorious for producing live babies, too glibly state that their tissues come from "dead fetuses." There is an intermediate stage about which few will talk.

This same issue is represented by a comment made by Dr. Paul V. Haydock, University of Washington, Seattle, who holds a $17,736 NIH grant for 1984-85 for the study of "Epidermal MRNA Expression During Human Fetal Development. Asked from what "class of fetuses"—viable, previable but living, previable but dead, etc.—his tissues came, Haydock replied that he couldn't even say as the pathologists with whom he had his arrangements took care of this.

Dr. Bernard Gondos, University of Connecticut at Farmington: "Gonadal Differentiation in the Human Fetus" ($104,870). One of Dr. Gondos' difficulties was "the constriction in this country of the twenty-week limit on abortion." Most of his specimens, he said, were in the "previable dead" category. Even so, he found it "difficult to obtain the tissue as soon as possible. Fewer and fewer obstetricians want to be involved. First they are too busy, second, because of the Edelin case they are hesitant." Because Gondos was "just not getting enough specimens," he planned on taking a sabbatical to Denmark to solve his specimen deficiency. Gondos also said that he preferred abortions done by evacu-extraction, prostaglandin and, his first choice, hysterotomy. "With d&c they are too ruined; I'm forced to go to other countries," he said. Clips from research projects done in Denmark during the 60's and early 70's reveal less-restrictive rules on live abortions, which are also more common in just such countries as Denmark. For instance, Dr. David Gitlin of the University of Pittsburgh used Denmark as the locus for his work on alphafetoprotein. For his experiments, hysterotomy-born fetuses were dissected and "individual organs or tissues were cultured separately." In one case, "the very youngest embryo was too small to permit adequate dissection for separate organs . . . and therefore, the entire embryo was minced, mixing the tissues."

NIH regulations do not disallow using such liveborn fetuses for research, as long as the procedure does not stop the heartbeat of itself and does not prolong the life of the fetus. But it may be just as inhuman to watch a liveborn fetus die on the table and then proceed to harvest it for organs and tissues.

Dr. Bruce Carr, University of Texas Health Science Center at Dallas: "Human Fetal Liver: Cholesterol and Lipoprotein Metabolism" ($76,424). Dr. Carr said he got his first- and second-trimester fetuses from private abortion clinics. "We dispose of them through the department of cell biology." His work was "geared toward the theory that the fetus derives its cholesterol from its liver. Dr. Carr emphasized that "we don't buy these tissues." However, he thought that new challenges to abortion might induce a change and that even getting tissues from explicitly dead fetuses "may not be allowed." Dr. Carr was not personally for abortion but believed that work on specimens such as the ones he used is valuable.

Dr. Urvashi Surti, Magee–Women's Hospital, Pittsburgh: "Cellular and Molecular Genetics Studies" ($59,193). Her work entailed using the bodies (mostly disintegrated) of partial and complete moles, that is, a conceptus without an embryo, to try to determine what the genetic code for this condition might be. Molar pregnancies often lead to a form of treatable cancer in the mother called choriocarcinoma. Surti's work may be one of the rare cases where work on fetal tissues is not controversial because in this case there is no embryo and also because the health of the mother is clearly at stake.

3

The Federal Regulations on Nontherapeutic Fetal Experimentation

> In all talk of ethics involving experimentation on humans scientists tend to specify that . . . the benefits must outweigh the risks. That is a highly subjective measure. Scientists are all too prone to assume that the benefits will always outweigh the risks. In view of their theoretical commitment to peer review and informed consent, the risk-benefit measure can come out as a loophole. The ends justify the means. The same sort of argument is used by policemen who defend searches without a warrant by contending triumphantly that after all they came up with useful evidence.
>
> —Vance Packard
> *The People Shapers*[1]

It is remarkable that theologian Paul Ramsey became the investigative reporter of the National Commission on Human Subjects which lasted from 1974 to 1976. This commission bred the final government regulations on fetal research, which remain in force today.

Ramsey's "little book," as he calls it, *The Ethics of Fetal Research,* acts as the only living document recording the events leading up to the appointment of the commission. Ramsey compared the commission itself and the way it went about its business to two 1970's controversies that had, at their heart, the lack of public disclosure about matters of great interest to and impact on the public.

Ramsey's observations are a good introduction to the commission and the regulations its spawned:

> My quandary is, I believe, our quandary in democratic societies. How shall medical policy be formulated and enacted in matters that obviously involve serious moral and social questions, as well as scientific or technical questions? Should that be done by a process that terminates in the Secretary of Health, Education, and Welfare, with no appeal and with little public voice in the production of the regulations; with openness only through written comments submitted after the proposals have been drafted and . . . published twice before the promulgation deadline?
>
> Here we have a sort of Daniel Ellsberg, Pentagon Papers, problem. The case might also be compared with recent allegations that the Atomic Energy Commission has not been candid about its own experts' studies of the dangers in nuclear reactors and power plants.[2]

Today, Dr. Ramsey's questions about how policy is made, and whether it should include the public, are as ever-burning. The facts and chronology of events leading up to the commission's founding, as Ramsey himself reported on it, ask this question: Was not the public meant to remain dumb and unincluded? Another question follows: was the commission mounted to convince the public that it was truly interested in a debate on nontherapeutic fetal experimentation even while deciding the outcome beforehand? The questions still hold.

The promulgated image of the commission from inside the National Institute of Health is that the commission was mounted to look into fetal research (and behavioral research on other human subjects) because the medical research community was eager to discern the public conscience on the matter. That image seems to have been constructed as a political smokescreen to obscure the fact that the research community and the NIH as its main funding vehicle were caught holding a freewheeling position toward human fetuses on the abortion schedule as research subjects.

The commission came into being this way . . .

On April 12, 1973, about one hundred female students from the Stone Ridge Country Day School of the Sacred Heart joined students from the Landon Episcopalian Boys School to demonstrate at the NIH against the government's permissive attitude toward nontherapeutic fetal research. The students had read about it in the *Washington Post* two days earlier.[3]

The Post learned of the easygoing policy from an article in *The American Journal of Obstetrics and Gynecology* published earlier in 1973. This article published documents that, in turn, had been written as early as 1971, but which only in 1973 came under consideration at the NIH. Between those years, researchers were engaged actively in various kinds of live fetal research using abortion subjects. The *Ob/Gyn* reporter had not been invited to the NIH to attend the meeting to review these documents. The reporter, in fact, had simply slipped in with his tape recorder and documented the proceedings.

At that meeting, the Advisory Council of the NIH repeated what it had already proposed in March of 1972: that fetal research should go forward with proper ethical and scientific guidelines. It stated that researchers should not be involved in the abortion procedures themselves, and that the rights of the mother and of the fetus should be "fully considered." The travesty of this seemingly protective language was challenged by Ramsey in *The Ethics of Fetal Research:* "It was not explained how the human fetus can be said still to be a bearer of 'rights' or what rights remain, if the experiments are done when abortion is in view or has already been set on course."

At the same time that these sweeping generalities were erected, another set of recommendations from September 1971 were also offered from the Study Section on Embryology and Development of the NIH. This document was supposed to be the one to "protect" human fetuses by distinguishing two "classes" of them. The first is the fetal patient. Readers will notice that the word "patient" implies "person" and meant to the NIH a wanted fetus. The second "class" was the "abortus," described neutrally as an "isolated product of planned or spontaneous termination of pregnancy during the first 20 weeks of gestation." This fetal subject was given no protective or personal consideration or status. Regulations on this fetal subject, said the recommendations, should not at all differ from those governing research on tissues or organs.

The Post reporter picked up the lead from Ob/Gyn and went out into the street, that is, to the research establishment, to collect statements. The reporter got a fistful of them, all militantly defensive of the necessity of live fetal research on aborted fetuses.

One such staunch defender was Dr. Kurt Hirschhorn, an advisory board member of The March of Dimes and a researcher at New York's Mt. Sinai Hospital and Medical School. His specialty has been, and is now, tracking down abnormalities via prenatal diagnostic techniques. Hirschhorn is also an evangelist for the cost/benefit analysis of selective abortion of the defective. At the time, he said, "How do we know what drugs do to the fetus unless we find out?" Through nontherapeutic research he hoped to learn more about cell differentiation and inborn anomalies. "It is not possible to make this fetus into a child," he said, "therefore we can consider it as nothing more than a piece of tissue."[4]

Dr. David Gitlin, then of the University of Pittsburgh Children's Hospital, said, "We used to do research on the intact fetus. Now we take tissues—the brain has stopped functioning but the tissues are still alive. I very frequently go to friends in Scandinavia. Without them I couldn't work."[5] Gitlin's testimony is important because it asks whether the fact that a fetus is dead lessens the ethical weight of using aborted babies for experiments. Although the baby is not subjected to pain, the real question is whether society has the right to help itself to the living remains of humans that have been denied personhood. An analogy would be that most citizens find it outrageous and a breach of all civilized codes that the Nazis tried to transplant still viable limbs from just gassed inmates onto injured German soldiers.

Gitlin's work, especially his flights to Scandinavia, was part of the fashionable trek abroad by researchers in the early 1970's, when second-trimester abortions were more common in Europe than in the U.S. These were done by a procedure called hysterotomy, a miniature Caesarean section in which the fetus is born alive with all or some vital signs.

The Post also interviewed Dr. Robert Schwartz, chief of pediatrics at Cleveland Metropolitan General Hospital; he is now deceased. Dr. Schwartz would figure in a report that appeared a few months later in *Medical World News* on June 8, 1973. Schwartz was in the habit of going to Finland to the University of Helsinki, where he took part in experiments to study brain fuels. The rubrics of the experiments involved severing ("extirpating" it is called medically) the heads of twelve "pre-viable" fetuses obtained by hysterotomy. The heads were then perfused through the internal carotid arteries with recirculating bicarbonate mediums equilibrized with a gaseous oxygen–carbon dioxide mixture.

Schwartz worked on this with another researcher, Dr. Peter J. Adam, an associate professor of pediatrics at Case Western Reserve University in Cleveland. Their monies were a commingling of private and public funds. Adam, in defending the necessity of such research in order to gain knowledge of benefit to fetuses that will survive, articulated his reasoning on why the problems of consent of the mother are null and void for fetal experimentation on aborted babies, stating that legal considerations and the principles of informed consent are irrelevant: "Whose right are we going to protect when we've already decided the fetus won't live?"[6] It is this attitude, built profoundly and clearly on the same rationalization as abortion on demand, that is responsible for researchers' going forward with nontherapeutic fetal experimentation. They have few legal inhibitions in their way. With the aborted fetus legally a nonperson, with state laws forbidding experimentation completely unenforced, with foreign countries readily accessed, and with the permissive NIH regulations and even more permissive private funders, the researcher knows that much can be said against the ethics of his or her choice but that the climate, especially the law and mores, are on his side.

What *The Washington Post* was doing, without realizing it at that moment, was documenting the birth of the "tissue" school of thought concerning the aborted human fetus. As well, they were seeing the first verbalization by the research community that they had adopted a high-minded feeling of mission for the living as they moved in to collect the living spoils created by abortion.

At the time, it was not only researchers from outside the NIH bureaucracy who were already deep into the "tissue" mentality. Dr. D.T. Chalkley of the NIH Institutional Relations Branch said succinctly, "If you have a clearly nonviable fetus you are in a position to . . . possibly . . . treat it as nonviable tissue."[7]

Dr. Andrew Hellegers, physician and professor of obstetrics and then-director of the Kennedy Institute for the Study of Human Reproduction and Bioethics (he is now deceased), rebutted this reasoning. Although he favored fetal research, he opposed live experiments. "If it is going to die, you might as well use it. It appears that we want to make the chance for survival the reason for the experiment." That, he pointed out, was the approach of the Nazi doctors.

Thus we find that in 1973 we had the "tissue school" well entrenched. There was also Hellegers' prototypical statement comparing that school of thought to deathcamp logic. Both of these schools of thought are frequently expressed today and ought to give the public the realization that we have been immersed, since 1973, in evidence that we may have a biocracy within a democracy, one with its own definitions of human life and the rightful province of biomedical research.

What we also see at this early date in the story is that researchers were protective and adamant about continuing the research. The intermingling of grants from various sources, described in the *Post* story, allowed one project to be described in several ways both to cull monies and to allay ethical problems. One grant could be strictly for bringing back blood samples or travel to a project that actually entailed a very objectionable experiment. The same situation exists today. A researcher may state in a proposal that he or she will be working on tissue or organs from an aborted fetus, but will not say whether the fetus was aborted alive and then allowed to expire unaided before dissection. In fact, today many researchers with whom this reporter spoke maintain that they do not know anything about the state of the fetuses before tissue is taken. This is left to a pathologist who in turn is in contact with an obstetrician.

Also, then as now, there was no definitive way to know all that was being done in nontherapeutic fetal research. There was and is no compulsory registry of experiments. Obtaining copies of grant proposals from the NIH and other government agencies requires use of the Freedom of Information Act with its delays and high charges. Private foundations have no mandate to disclose grant proposals in any form. In 1973, some researchers told *The Post* that they did not even work on grants, but used their own monies. And the international sharing of scientific information and resources, basically a good thing, also compounds the problem of ready access to details.

The moment *The Post* disclosed its unsettling news, that news began to be cosmetized. Dr. Robert Berliner, then deputy director for science at the NIH, said, "The NIH does not now support research on live aborted human fetuses and does not contemplate approving the support of such research."[8] This indicated either a lapse of memory or a desire to throw facts into doubt, for *The Post* had already reported that Drs. Schwartz and Gitlin were in part, on NIH grants when they did their fetal research abroad. The disclaimer by Berliner was weakened by the assertion that, as one scientist put it, "Dozens of people have done it as part of their projects though they might not use their NIH funding for this part."

Seven months after Berliner declared that the NIH was not supporting live fetal research, the NIH issued a document titled "Protection of Human Subjects: Policies and Procedures." It published notice of these recommendations in the *Federal Register* as a way of publicly asking Secretary of Health, Education and Welfare Casper Weinberger to turn them into policy, an act within his power.

But these guidelines were never pressed into regulation because Weinberger delayed endorsement. In *The Ethics of Fetal Research,* Ramsey analyzed the politics involved. "The delay of the secretary's promulgation for so many months might at the time have supported the suspicion that, on the matter of fetal research, the document was being weakened."[9]

In July of 1974, Congress intervened, passing a National Research Act, "Protection of Human Subjects of Biomedical and Behavioral Research." Under the act, a commission with a term of only two years was appointed to make recommendations for regulations on human experimentation in general, with a subsection for fetal experimentation. After this commission presented its recommendations, the Secretary of HEW was to respond to them publicly. If he chose to reject the recommendations, he had to publish his reasons for doing so.

While the National Research Act and the commission were being brought into existence in the summer of 1974, the House of Representatives made an independent move of its own. A bill sailed through the House prohibiting the Secretary of HEW from conducting or supporting research on a human fetus outside the mother if the fetus had a beating heart. This meant that much fetal research would be prohibited as a matter of law, circumscribing the Secretary's powers.

But the Senate now had to pass a similar bill. Senator James Buckley (R-NY) proposed a matching ban. But Senator Edward Kennedy (D-MA), in turn, proposed what he chose to call a "perfecting" amendment to Buckley's. It proposed prohibiting live, ex-utero fetal research, but not permanently, as in the House bill. It asked for a prohibition only until the commission finished its two-year task of considering the ethics of fetal research and delivering its recommendations to the HEW Secretary.

Ramsey noted that this "enabled senators and congressmen to pass the ball to the commission and avoided their having to take decisive stand on a controversial public question."[10] Kennedy had reopened a door, with his "perfecting" amendment, that many thought would be best permanently shut.

The commission was sworn in on December 2, 1974. Not only did it have as its task the future of ethics and practice on fetal experimentation, it also was to spend four months on the same issues for psychosurgery. The difference between the two subjects was great and still is. Psychosurgery had a long listing in case law, whereas fetal experimentation does not. Did the commission then enter this loophole with their own desires? Here is what Ramsey said:

> The recommendations of the temporary commission . . . will still terminate in the secretary of HEW . . . Perhaps, then, policy will be

> made in much the same way as it was in the past if these bodies accumulate prestige enough to dampen congressional intervention.[11]

Ramsey went on to say that the Secretary had to report to the public if he did not agree with the commission's recommendations. Here, Ramsey saw an outside hope that the public would be drawn into public policy. However, against that possibility, he wrote hinting that even inclusion of the public could be used as a mere smokescreen for the commission to cater to the desires of the pro–fetal research doctors:

> That would mean that [private] determination of medical ethical issues is coming to an end, and the public is now deeply involved in debate over these issues. That may be a good thing—or not. For I have said in the course of this account that I, for one, expect no better rulings on fetal research to be put forth in the United States than those in the original NIH guidelines. . . ."[12]

Let us see whether Ramsey's prediction has been borne out.

The Commission and its Search

Chosen to chair the commission for the Protection of Human Subjects of Biomedical and Behavioral research was Dr. Kenneth J. Ryan, then chairman of the department of obstetrics and gynecology at Harvard University Medical School. In 1976, Mrs. Randy Engel, director of the U.S. Coalition for Life, did a profile of Dr. Ryan. At that point in time, (two years after the commission met), Mrs. Engel was mainly trying to strengthen the Coalition's charge that the March of Dimes, which has favored Ryan with many grants, is not only *not* neutral on abortion as it publicly maintains, but that it is deeply involved via its research objectives, in selective abortion of babies prenatally diagnosed for genetic defects.

Mrs. Engel correctly traced Dr. Ryan's involvement with eugenic abortion to 1972, when he was Professor and Chairman of Obstetrics and Gynecology at the University of California School of Medicine, La Jolla. At that time, Ryan was a signatory to a statement on abortion generated by the Association for the Study of Abortion. This white paper was published in the *American Journal of Obstetrics and Gynecology* that same year.[13] As Mrs. Engel wrote[14]:

> The statement signed by one hundred professors of obstetrics suggests that "in view of the impending change in abortion practices generated by new state legislation and federal court decisions," it will be expected that doctors perform abortions "simply because the patient asks that it be done."

Mrs. Engel did not omit Ryan's chairmanship of the commission:

> As chairman of the National Commission for the Protection of Human Subjects of Biomedical and Behavioral Research, Dr. Ryan was instrumental in engineering the Commission's approval of live fetal experimentation unrelated to the health or well being of the preborn child who currently enjoys *less* protection than most laboratory animals used by institutions receiving federal monies.[15]

The year that HEW published its regulations based on the commissioners' recommendations, 1976, was the same year that Dr. Ryan was given a $100,000 grant from the March of Dimes "to determine if induced abortions . . . are associated with subsequent increased risk of miscarriage, prematurity, congenital malformations and various complications of pregnancy which threaten the survival of the fetus or mother; and that such effects may vary with the method by which prior abortions were induced."[16]

Dr. Ryan set out to determine abortion's role in maternal and fetal health by monitoring women who had had previous induced abortions as well as by monitoring first-time clients of abortion. For his trials, he was using the new abortion agent prostaglandin, which can produce a live fetus, ripe for harvest of tissues and organs. Ryan had, in fact, published a paper in *Contraception* that logged the efficacy of the method for second-trimester abortions.

With his very large sample of 25,000 women and March of Dimes grants totaling $580,000, Ryan "studied" the question and announced that only women who have had two or more induced abortions are increasingly likely to suffer spontaneous loss of the next fetus. Mrs. Engel argued that this study and its conclusion supply evidence that Ryan and the March of Dimes, his patron, have tried to promulgate abortion as comparatively safe. The official position of the March of Dimes is that it is neutral on abortion, and that it is in the business of funding scientific work only, even if abortion happens to be the subject of the research. Studies of abortion methods, such as the one conducted by Ryan, are of course scientific at base. What must be held up against this plea of neutrality by the March of Dimes is that it is the premier foundation in the United States that has funded and then widely supported prenatal screening for defects, a practice that predicates a willingness to abort. We shall return to the March of Dimes later to examine it more closely.

For our purposes of studying Ryan, who was head of the Commission on the Protection of Human Subjects, it is clear that he was not at all inimical to abortion, and was to perform a massive amount of abortion research. His political role in the U.S. abortion forum is also undeniable. A question can be asked, and was by Mrs. Engel: Was Ryan trying to supply an American "soft" study on abortion to supplant the foreign critical ones? Those studies, from a multitude of countries, including England, Wales, Germany, France, Sweden and Hungary, had already established that even first-time abortion is linked to complications such as future cervical incompetence, premature births, still-births, sterility and a number of other serious health consequences.[17] Nor did the Ryan study touch on the psychological consequences associated with abortion, on which there is a wealth of material from the scientific community itself. Nor did it mention the effects of abortion on various ethnic groups: for instance, one study has reported that induced abortion among black women is indicated as a cause in the rise of infant mortality rates for the same women in later pregnancies. Nor could Ryan have been innocent of the link between prostaglandin-induced abortion, the method he himself had tested in 1975, and the supply of fetuses for researchers.

Turning to the other commissioners, let us consider just one more, as he was to become the only dissenter to the final recommendations of the commission. He was David W. Louisell, J.D., professor of law at the University of California's Berkeley campus. Just as Ryan had a past that heavily suggested a pro-abortion stance, so Louisell did not. In 1970, he had contributed to a volume named *The Morality of Abortion.* With the editor, John T. Noonan, Jr., Louisell wrote an article titled "Constitutional Balance."[18]

Essentially, the article strove to point out, from case and statute law up to the time of the abortion law relaxations, that the human fetus, whether viable or not, had been accorded rights associated with human personhood under the law. Although we shall take up this whole question of the law and the fetus later, here, because the commission became preoccupied with separating viability from pre- or non-viability, we shall quote just that part of Noonan and Louisell's article applying to that:

> Many of the early cases required that the unborn child have reached the stage of viability at the time the injuries were inflicted in order to maintain an action. The modern trend, however has been to reject viability as a criterion and to allow recovery whenever the injury was received . . . [19]

The makeup of the commission was stipulated by public law 93-348, which commanded that five of the eleven "members of the Commission shall be individuals who are or who have been engaged in biomedical or behavioral research on human subjects."[20] Dr. Vaupel of Duke University saw this as stacking the commission rather than as simply insuring that the researchers had equal time. In his 1980 critique of the commission, he wrote[21]:

> With the specification that 5 of the 11 members be those involved in the research, and given that most likely one of the other six board members might support the research, it is extremely clear that the cards were stacked the very first day. The Commission, thus, appeared to be inherently biased toward experimentation from the onset.
>
> Board members, *in general*, were chosen from elite segments of society. . . . Eight of the eleven members had degrees (M.D., J.D., Ph.D., or B.A.) from either Harvard or Yale. One other had a degree from Columbia, while yet another was a researcher at Johns Hopkins Medical School. That makes a total of nine "Ivy Leaguers" out of eleven Commission members.
>
> Not surprisingly, the lone dissenter (Mr. David Louisell) to the final recommendations . . . was the only member appointed to the Commission who did not have an Ivy League connection or who was not directly involved in the research. . . .
>
> Perhaps more than anything, a sense of "professionalism" characterized the majority of Commission members.
>
> There appeared to be an underlying assumption—a sometimes false assumption—in the appointment process that equated professionalism with rationality, and with a sense of compassion for the victims of human experimentation. History has shown us that this is not always the case. Testimony from the Nuremberg trials is evidence enough:

> "Outstanding men of science, distinguished in their scientific ability in Germany and abroad, are the defendants Rostock and Rose. Both exemplify, in their training and practice, the highest traditions of German medicine. Rostock headed the Department of Surgery at the University of Berlin and served as dean of the medical school. Rose . . . became a distinguished specialist in the fields of public health and tropical diseases."

Vaupel also pointed to an American collaborator of the German doctors by quoting *Medical World News,* June 8, 1973:

> "The most striking thing about the Nazi episodes . . . is the high standing of a number of the doctors involved and of the medical science they represented. One was a former professor at Harvard Medical School, sentenced at Nuremberg to life imprisonment."

In addition to the work of the eleven commissioners, a few studies and investigations were separately contracted for from outside parties, who also had the tinge of being involved in nontherapeutic research. For instance, Dr. Maurice Mahoney of Yale–New Haven Hospital was asked to search the medical literature for examples of live fetal research. At the time, Mahoney was deep into the development of fetoscopy, a technique for prenatal viewing of the fetus. It allows precise withdrawal of blood samples to detect such diseases as sickle-cell anemia. The development of this powerful tool relied upon use of live fetuses in utero whose mothers had already opted for abortion. In fact, *Contemporary Ob/Gyn,* in 1975, while the commission was still in progress, published a congratulatory article on Mahoney's research: "Yale Explores the World of the Fetus"—a title that did not reveal the relationship between fetoscopy and selective abortion of diseased children. The article mentioned this dimension, but not in critical terms.

Battelle-Columbus Laboratories, also engaged in fetal research, was asked to study the role of the live fetus in medical advances. And a study was made by Columbia University, in the person of Dr. Leon Kass, to establish guidelines for determining fetal viability and death.

Dr. Maurice Mahoney, in between his recitation of the examples of fetal research, stood up for the viable live-born infant, stating that "any viable live-born infant should receive the best possible medical care including experimental therapies performed under appropriate safeguards." By "viable live-born infant" he meant the premature baby, who was not being considered as a subject for experimentation. Mahoney was interested in drawing a line for viability, in order to endorse experimentation on the nonviable fetus. He put it in a subtle way: "The most important reason for drawing such a line [of viability] . . . is the desire to avoid injury to a fetus that will survive."[22]

Mahoney also laid another bargaining chip on the table: that experimentation on nonviable but live fetuses, although not benefiting those fetuses, would benefit others. "Fetuses as a class should legitimately benefit from this type of experimentation."[23] Thus not only were fetuses divided into viable and nonviable in order to provide researchers with subjects, but the nonviable fetuses were appointed to martyrdom for the sake of fellow, wanted fetuses who would benefit from what could be done to them in experimentation. This point of view found a curious supporter: Fr. Richard McCormick, a Jesuit from Georgetown.

Fr. McCormick stated in an invited paper submitted to the commission that "morality and public policy are both related and distinct. . . . That is, the common good of all persons cannot be unrelated to what is judged to be promotive or destructive to the individual."[24] But he shored up this compassionate statement by saying that children might be entered into low-risk experiments by virtue of the proxy consent of their parents so that the child might have a chance to participate in the "justice" of making a contribution to society. McCormick extended this idea to the human fetus, which is in an even more reduced, if not totally so, capacity to "choose" such a good than is a child. McCormick was drawing heavily on the idea of proxy consent of the parents to carry out this ideal of "justice." In his favor, McCormick was not for any risky experiments on living fetuses. However, twelve years after he wrote this, his statement on "justice" is usually quoted by supporters of fetal research who delete the rest. Thus a rather esoteric moral argument is drawn in to support fetal research on the premise that the human fetus, although aborted and depersonalized, has some moral obligation to society.

Dr. Mahoney lobbied also for administering drugs to fetuses to be aborted to determine what effects they might have. He reasoned: "The field of fetal pharmacology is one of the most crucial areas requiring research with the living fetus *in utero* and with the fetus that will be or is being aborted. . . . The effect of [an] enormous amount of drug therapy . . . on a developing fetus [is] almost entirely unknown."[25] Opponents of using live nonviable fetuses in utero for drug testing point out that it offends the restriction on the researcher that he must have nothing to do with the abortion decision. Having entered a drug study, a woman would be less likely to change her mind about having the abortion; this is relevant, because studies show that otherwise women often do change their minds about abortion, right up to the last minute.

When the Battelle-Columbus Laboratories came forth with their report on medical advances involving the fetus, it was lengthy and aimed at reducing reservations. Mainly, it treated the development of the rubella vaccine, amniocentesis, Rh vaccine, and respiratory distress syndrome, all of which in some part relied on fetal experimentation. Wrote the authors of the report under "Overall Conclusions"[26]:

> It is apparent from a study of the development of the four selected cases . . . that research on living human fetuses played a significant role in each. The concern here is the estimation of the probable effect that a ban on research involving the use of living human fetuses would have had on the course of the developments. . . . To carry such a restriction to the ultimate would, of course, prevent new procedures for fetuses or pregnant women from reaching clinical usage.

But the Battelle-Columbus report came under fire from one of the commissioners, Dr. Robert E. Cooke. He accused Battelle-Columbus Laboratories of jeopardizing the credibility of the commission with its apology for fetal research by being too pro-experimentation. "The only true objective approach beyond question, since scientists make this analysis, is to collect information and analyze past research accomplishments with the intention of *disproving, not proving* the hypothesis that research utilizing the living human fetus nonbeneficially is necessary."[27]

Cooke also pointed out that in neurosurgery no invasive nonbeneficial research on the human brain had ever been used, and that researchers in neurosurgery presumed, without the restriction of a ban or law, that invasive nonbeneficial research was out of the question. Cooke filled out this analogy by pointing out that, with *no human experimentation,* "great progress has been made in understanding a very complex organ or collection of organs by highly creative animal research."

He accused the Battelle-Columbus report of focusing on what some would consider trivial contributions by nontherapeutic research—"sharpness of needle, etc., in amniocentesis"—and on contributions from therapeutic research, and research on tissues and fluid. "The report is written as though human research is in question and substantial credibility of the report as regards fetal research is thereby lost," he wrote.[28]

Cooke also dismissed the claim that knowledge about rubella was gained from amniocentesis as "utterly false." He pointed to Rh transfusion therapy and said, "Transfusion therapy was for the benefit of the fetus" (neither involving nor justifying nontherapeutic procedures) and, further, that "Rh vaccine required maternal blood samples—not fetal research." Concerning the study of prevention of respiratory stress, he said. "[The Battelle-Columbus report] further implies that without amniocentesis and/or fetal research there would be 'no basis for successful research toward prevention or cure.'" He called this a "gross exaggeration . . . Animal research or research on lungs of dead prematures shed enormous light on RDS and exchange transfusion in living newborns was the giant step in Rh disease."[29]

But Cooke went beyond scientific argument. He pointed out that most of the research cited by Battelle-Columbus "was done before any significant number of legalized abortions were being carried out and practically none of the work in Rh disease or hyaline membrane disease used abortuses." As pointed out earlier, Cooke also maintained that using live in-utero fetuses to be aborted to test the rubella vaccine was also unnecessary.[30]

So the Battelle-Columbus report, to Cooke's mind, made fetal research seem successful in important fields when, in fact, it had not made a contribution therein or had been done on dead fetuses before abortion victims became available. But the fiction created by the Battelle-Columbus report goes on, and obviously without Cooke's critique attached to its claims. The March of Dimes sent this writer a sheet vindicating live, nontherapeutic fetal research by citing rubella and Rh isoimmunization as two of its achievements. Cooke saw this endorsement of fetal research based on false information coming even then; he stated, "[The Battelle-Columbus report] unfortunately has been presented unchallenged in the press as authoritative."[31]

There were two points of discussion that, had they been written into the new regulations, would have put a great squeeze on fetal experimentation. In one report to the commission by John P. Wilson, titled "Legal Issues Involved in Research on the Fetus," the author suggested a "physician advocate" for the fetus involved in nontherapeutic experiments. "Another protective device," wrote Wilson, "is to require two physicians to be present in any research situation, one to perform research and the other to be responsible for the patient. The latter physician, who might be appointed to represent a fetus, an abortus or a premature infant, would be responsible for protecting his patient's best interest; he would communicate the progress of research faithfully to the parents or guardians, make sure that consent is truly informed, and require that every precaution be taken; he could withdraw his patient from the research if the risk of harm became too great."[32] It would have been interesting had that idea come to fruition, for it would have challenged the Supreme Court's decision on abortion and raised several questions. One would be how a fetus, a nonperson under the law, could be aborted because of that nonpersonhood and yet, before or after abortion, be given an "advocate," which implies personhood and legal protection. It could also have spawned a discussion as to whether the advocate might stretch his role from monitoring experiments to ensuring the fetus' actual survival, especially since some experiments were deeply involved in trying out life-saving equipment, not for the fetus undergoing the experiment, but for wanted, future fetuses.

One other potent recommendation also went ignored, although very much lip service was paid it during the commission's seven meetings. This was the so-called "concordance" or "equality" doctrine. In sum, it meant that nothing would be done on a fetus to be aborted that would not be done on a fetus being carried to term. Had this been let into the final regulations, fetal research would have been all but banned.

Our report would be incomplete if it did not include some of Commissioner David W. Louisell's dissenting statement to the commission. In a future becoming more and more loaded with biotechnological capabilities that have in their power the ability to change the very definition of human life as we know it, Louisell's remarks may become important to history. He wrote:

> I am compelled to disagree with the Commission's Recommendations (and the reasoning and definitions on which they are based) insofar as they succumb to the error of sacrificing the interest of innocent human life to a postulated social need. I fear this is the inevitable result of Recommendations (5) and (6). These would permit nontherapeutic research on the fetus in anticipation of abortion and during the abortion procedure, and on a living infant after abortion when the infant is considered nonviable, even though such research is precluded by recognized norms governing human research

> in general. Although the Commission uses adroit language to minimize the appearance of violating standard norms, no facile verbal formula can avoid the reality that under these Recommendations the fetus and nonviable infant will be subjected to nontherapeutic research from which other humans are protected.[33]

Louisell complimented the commission's efforts, as he saw them, to uncover some of the therapeutic goals of fetal research, which of course do exist and are laudable. This could not sway him to buy nontherapeutic fetal use along with the positive aims:

> "But the good in much of the Report cannot blind me to its departure from our society's most basic moral commitment: the essential equality of all human beings. For me the lessons of history are too poignant, and those of this century too fresh, to ignore another violation of human integrity and autonomy by subjecting unconsenting human beings, whether viable or not, to harmful research even for laudable scientific purposes. . . .
>
> " . . . Even if I were to approach my task as a Commissioner from a utilitarian viewpoint only, I would have to say that on the record here I am not convinced that an adequate showing has been made of the necessity for nontherapeutic fetal experimentation in the scientific or social interest. The Commission's reliance is on the Battelle report and its reliance is misplaced. The relevant Congressional mandate was to conduct an investigation and study of the alternative means for achieving the purpose of fetal research.[34]

Louisell also deplored the fact that, at the Commission's last meeting, it began to depart from the subject of fetal experimentation and "without prior preparation or discussion, it adopted Recommendation (12) promotive of research on abortion techniques."[35]

Finally, then, the pro-abortion bias of the majority of commissioners was proven by themselves, it would seem.

Louisell ended by asking that the ban be kept on live nontherapeutic research, and paraphrased poet John Donne: "We may have to learn once again that when the bell tolls for the lost rights of any human being, even the politically weakest, it tolls for all."[36]

In a sense, the commission had done everything but bring a live fetus into the hearing chambers and perform a "beneficial to medical science" experiment on it in hopes of vindicating nontherapeutic fetal experimentation. Were they far away, mentally or spiritually, from an incident revealed in the Nuremberg trials? Dr. Leo Alexander, a medical consultant to the Medical Examiner at the trials, in an article in the *New England Journal of Medicine,* (July 14, 1949,) told the story of an SS judge who put Dr. Waldemar Hoven on trial for the poisoning of several SS officers. Hoven had developed the idea of giving poisons such as phenol or gasoline in the guise of medical injections. The judge, to prove Hoven had perpetrated this on the SS officers, brought several prisoners of war into the courtroom and had the same poisonous injections given to them. They died, reported Dr. Alexander,showing the same symptoms as had the SS men. Wrote Alexander, "This worthy judge was rather proud of this efficient method of proving Dr. Hoven's guilt and appeared entirely unaware of the fact that in the process he had committed murder himself."[37]

It is certainly significant that David Louisell, one of only two nonresearchers on the Commission for the Protection of Human Subjects, was the only dissenter—the only one who saw, he believed, the advertisement for fetal research that the commission had actually been.

After the recommendations were submitted, Casper Weinberger accepted the recommendations as the foundation of "new" regulations, with two exceptions. Weinberger decided to write in that nontherapeutic research on the previable, living fetus aimed at developing an artificial placenta would be permitted. Weinberger added that sacrificing aborted, living fetuses could be done for the health of future premature infants. It is interesting that this permission was rescinded in the slight reworking of the regulations that took place in 1983 and that stand today. No experiments may be done that prolong the vital signs of the previable fetus ex utero. A fetus may not be, then, hooked up to an artificial placenta. But not allowing this may have an element of protection of nontherapeutic research. More and more, technology is able to save very premature babies. Too many artificial placenta experiments might point out that the previable fetuses might, with extraordinary means, be able to make it to viability. If that became clear via improved technology, previable fetuses might lose their research definition as just another piece of tissue.

Weinberger's second addition to the regulations is what critics have called "the wet noodle clause." This was the waiver power he gave himself as Secretary of HEW, and to others who would follow him in that post. The secretary would be able to waive or modify *all* of the regulations with the consent of the Ethical Advisory Board in cases where "the sum of the benefit to the subject and the importance of the knowledge to be gained" outweigh the costs to the subject.

To understand the consequences to the fetus from such a waiver power, let us look at the last waiver granted by the Secretary in 1979-80. This was for the development of fetoscopy. It is interesting that fetoscopy had already been developed in 1975 by Maurice Mahoney at Yale. Mahoney used fetuses to be aborted as he worked out the difficulties before moving on to clinical trials. But in 1979 the Secretary allowed the waiver for what seems to have been useless involvement of fetuses to be aborted in developing something already in clinical use.

Beyond that inanity, the waiver demands that there "be a sum benefit to the subject." Mahoney reported that, in his first seventeen trials on fetoscopy, a few of those subjects died from the test itself. The waiver goes on to state that these sum benefits to the subject should outweigh the costs to the subject. How could an experiment in which fetuses died as a result of the experiment be able to meet this criterion? In the instance, then, of the waiver for fetoscopy, the whole ethical basis of the regulations, and particularly of the waiver, expose themselves as an obfuscating arrangement of legalistic phrases beneath which flow unmistakable heartlessness, recklessness and perhaps even sadism.

The existence of the wavier, which pushes all ethical considerations aside for the sake of utility, exemplifies Santayana's phrase "If it's useful, it's good." Of course, the same philosopher said, "Those who forget the past will be condemned to relive it."

The waiver also offended another rule set down for nontherapeutic fetal experimentation: that animal trials must precede human ones. Maurice Mahoney, who developed fetoscopy first, actually admitted to the commission that this common rubric of science was omitted in his work.

Paul Ramsey had predicted that no improvements in the regulations were likely to be made, even though the commission allowed written public statements in response to its recommendations before they were pressed into regulations. It was Dr. Vaupel of Duke University who, in his 1980 critique, a full four years after the regulations were passed, commented on how much credence was given to the public's remarks. "Public response to the suggested regulations was collected and analyzed. . . . While the public *clearly opposed* forms of nontherapeutic research on living children which would be invasive or harmful, the Secretary was not advised to reinstitute the ban on fetal research."[39] Vaupel had also gotten access to the files at the Office for Research Risks in September 1980. There, he reported, he "came across a letter directed to Dr. Kenneth J. Ryan, chairman of the Commission. The letter was written by Mrs. Barbara Syska, an immigrant to the United Sates from Poland . . . many of her fellow Polish citizens were experimented upon after the Nazi invasion of Poland in 1939. Excerpts from the letter appear as follows:

> Dear Dr. Ryan: July 1, 1977
>
> . . . my purpose in writing now is mainly to express my opinion that the National Commission for the Protection of Human Subjects . . . is failing in its mandate on several accounts . . .
>
> I think that it would be just as shocking to the public and to the Congress who voted to form this Commission as it was shocking to me to hear, repeatedly, a member of the Commission referring to handicapped children as "catatonic vegetables."
>
> . . . However, the most important area in which the Commission fails in its mandate is the role the Commission undertakes. The name of the Commission is clear: The National Commission for the *Protection of Human Subjects* of Biomedical and Behavioral Research. It is neither for the "protection of research" nor for the "advancement of science" but for the "protection of human subjects." At one of the meetings, you, Dr. Ryan, mentioned that . . . all of the members of the Commission agreed that your role is to *protect* not only subjects of the research but the *research itself,* since ultimately with advancement thus achieved, everybody . . . would benefit. *This is not your mandate.* By extending your interest to protection of research you failed in what you are supposed to consider.
>
> The Commission is in its final months of existence. I, as an interested member of the public, can only suggest that if the Commission cannot fulfill its mandate, the Commission should admit its inability to do so and dissolve itself now. This would be a better solution than finishing the task and publishing any further recommendations of which society would have to be ashamed of for years to come.
>
> Sincerely, Barbara Syska [40]

Not only did Mrs. Syska and those others who protested the commission's distortion of its task expose the essential bias of the commission; they also voiced the public's majority opinion against accommodating experimentation on children and fetuses, giving the history of nontherapeutic experimentation documents for today and tomorrow. Additionally, public protest to the commission showed Paul Ramsey to have been right in advance: even with public participation, the ominous mood of the medical research community in America would go inexorably forward, creating a biocracy within a democracy. The medical research community showed itself to be obsessed with its own logic, unable, despite its scientific accomplishments, to doubt the wisdom of its moral aims. It ignored the public's concern for the weakest members of society and exposed itself as a community to be feared. Leaning on the automatic prestige it always gets, it seeded the way for having itself stripped of that unworthy prestige, to lay bare a kind of normally mad, fantastical substrata of society. Wordsworth's harsh words on the "scientific spirit" in "The Poet's Epitaph" come through, but with an extra chill added: "One that would peep and botanize/ Upon his mother's grave."

Just as Congress tried to step in with the ban in 1973 and some in Congress opposed and softened that ban by making it co-terminous with the commission, that pattern goes on today.

In 1982, Congressman William Dannemeyer (R-CA) floated an amendment to the Health Research Extension Act, which authorizes activities and funding of the National Institute of Health. The amendment would have prohibited experimental research on living fetuses "before or after induced abortion" unless such research is done to insure the survival of that fetus. The amendment passed by a vote of 260-140.

At the time of the passage of the amendment, Richard Doerflinger, of the American Bishops' Pro-Life Committee, explained its rationale: The concept behind this language is that a child, whether born or unborn, must not be subjected to any significant risk of harm unless the procedure may benefit that particular child.[41]

Dannemeyer's amendment was opposed by a longtime supporter of live fetal research, Congressman Henry Waxman (D-CA). He insisted that the current regulations sufficiently protected fetuses. He contended that the Dannemeyer amendment was "an ideological statement" that would imperil important research.[42] One Catholic newspaper report by Paul A. Fisher pointed out that "earlier Waxman commended Congressman Doug Walgren [D-PA] for his amendment to the basic legislation which protects laboratory animals from improper care and treatment."

Dannemeyer, in arguing for the amendment, returned to the flimsy "minimal risk" clause of the regulations, saying that this term "could be interpreted to justify virtually any experimentation on a child intended for abortion." He said that to insure that an experiment truly poses only minimal risk, all funding of experiments on to-be-aborted fetuses should be banned. In other words, Dannemeyer seemed to be saying, "If you're *not* subjecting fetuses to more than minimal risk, then prove it by endorsing the ban." As with the situation as it transpired in 1973 when the first ban was enforced, this proposal also brought defenses of fetal research from the scientific community.

In 1982, when Dannemeyer's amendment passed the House, Senator Robert Packwood (R-OR) blocked the legislation from reaching the Senate floor, causing the bill and the Dannemeyer amendment to die in the 1981-82 Congress.

In 1983, Dannemeyer tried again. Waxman won approval of a different amendment, which would have simply turned the existing regulations into law. Dannemeyer had wanted to forbid the waiver power of the Secretary, but Waxman included it.

Senator Jeremiah Denton then announced that he would offer a no-waiver amendment when the bill came into the Senate. The NIH bill was again blocked by opposing forces in the Senate.

The bill to which the amendment, strong or weak, was to be attached was a bill to create a new institute at the NIH, one for arthritis research. Waxman wanted this institute. Finally he compromised and let the Denton amendment, with the ban and the abolition of the waiver, be tacked onto the bill. But, in the end, President Reagan vetoed the bill in his effort to cut back federal spending. With that veto, the amendment too died.

This reporter asked Richard Doerflinger, who acted as Denton's legislative aide in drafting the amendment, if this did not cast a rather ludicrous light on Reagan, who has written passionate letters of support to some opponents of fetal experimentation. Doerflinger, of the National Bishops' Pro-Life Committee, admitted disappointment after so much hard bargaining, beleaguerment and pure fight.

The last revision of the NIH Regulations was in 1983. Could they be revised once more, and would that revision be more permissive or more restrictive? John C. Fletcher, NIH's ethicist, put forward a few thoughts in 1985 that bode ill for opponents of nontherapeutic fetal research. Fletcher addressed experimentation that is aimed at "life-saving in cases of extreme prematurity. To *learn* to do such work and to test the technology would require research with nonviable fetuses, in our view, since it would be ethically objectionable to subject a possibly viable fetus to totally unproven techniques."[43] Thus, fetuses who are *designated* unable to survive (although they *may* be able) would be entered into experimentation to advance the ability of other fetuses to survive. Fletcher expressed his belief that it is desirable to maintain the nonviable fetus on experimental life-saving equipment, although the regulations now forbid experimentation "unless vital functions of the fetus will not be artificially maintained." Opined Fletcher: "In our view, the regulations go too far in an effort to prevent recurrence of nontherapeutic research with nonviable fetuses that had no relevance to potential therapy. The nonviable fetus to be studied to 'develop important biomedical knowledge which cannot be obtained by other means' . . . and which is clearly related to potentially life-saving therapy, should be anesthetized and the fetal experiment terminated at a specific predetermined point."[44] Thus, babies would be subjected to life-saving experiments and then cut off from them when the researcher had gotten the "important biomedical knowledge."

Such an extension of the regulation is among the most controversial that could be proposed, and its very suggestion in 1985 rather proves that the mentality supporting nontherapeutic experimentation on fetuses has not been very much influenced by the regulations. That may be because the regulations are not actually restrictive. That 'minimal risk' was never defined, although it is a crucial key and measure of any experimental work, and that the waiver was ever created, are both signs of ill will. Additionally, the federal government, in its regulations on research on the fetus, is at odds with the states. As of 1985, Charles H. Baron, a law professor at Boston College Law School, reported that twenty-five states have laws forbidding nontherapeutic fetal experimentation.[45] This conflict illustrates that the federal government has advanced a set of regulations that do not fit into what state legislators understand to be rightful protection of fetuses under the law. Whose initiatives then is the government advancing?

One matter was never touched by the commission: Exactly from where do previable survivors of abortion come? During the term of the commission, a new abortion agent hit the scene. The head of the commission, Dr. Kenneth Ryan, had done some trials on that abortion agent himself—ostensibly not to benefit research but for abortion. This new abortion agent had already been spotted by quick-minded researchers as a sure way to get a previable fetus intact for harvest or for experimentation. Yet the commission never touched on the ethics of researchers deliberately triggering an abortion to yield a research subject, or of notifying obstetricians that they preferred fetuses gotten by this method because the fetus would be born with some vital signs. It was only cast as a "General Limitation" and not a regulation that a researcher should have no involvement in the method, timing or procedure of abortion.

4

How Live Aborted Fetuses Are Obtained for Research

> "If I wasn't real," Alice said—half-laughing through her tears, it all seemed so ridiculous—I shouldn't be able to cry."
>
> "I hope you don't suppose those are *real* tears?" Tweedledum interrupted in a tone of great contempt.
>
> —Lewis Carroll
> *Through the Looking Glass*

Between the time when abortion laws in some states were loosened in the late 1960's and the formal Supreme Court decision (*Roe v. Wade*) in 1973, medical researchers were already seizing what theologian Paul Ramsey has disparagingly called "the Golden Opportunity": nontherapeutic experimentation on the living fetus.

Until 1974, the ordinary means of abortion (suction and curretage, or hypertonic saline induction) were unable to yield much that was usable to the researcher.

If one wanted to work on a live fetus, it often had to be a live infant—a premature baby aborted in the third trimester of pregnancy. This was achieved by a procedure called hysterotomy, a miniature caesarean section. Researchers would go abroad, where second- and third-trimester abortions via hysterotomy were more common.

The blow-up over fetal research in the seventies took the viable live aborted baby off the roles of subjects for nontherapeutic experiments, but a way was found to reap the living, nonviable fetus for research.

Before laying bare the circumstances of the discovery, let us trace back a bit further to the late 60's, when there were some experiments on viable, hysterotomy-delivered fetuses.

The debut for such controversial experiments, all aimed at developing technology for treating premature infants, was March of 1968, when *The American Journal of Obstetrics and Gynecology* printed Dr. Geoffrey Chamberlain's report on his work at George Washington Hospital in Washington, D.C. His article was called "An Artificial Placenta: The Development of an ExtraCorporeal System for Maintenance of Immature Infants with Respiratory Problems." This meant that Dr. Chamberlain was trying to find a way to help premature babies to survive. To achieve this helpful and legitimate end, however, he decided to practice and test his equipment on living, aborted babies whom, above all, he could not allow to survive the experiment. That is, he willfully gave experimental therapeutic help to an aborted baby of seven months' gestation but, in the end, did not allow the baby to survive. The experiment was not meant to help that particular infant, but rather premature, wanted infants who would not, of course, be aborted.

The 900-gram infant was obtained by hysterotomy. After delivering the infant, Chamberlain hooked it up alive to the artificial placental unit. His notes were:

> Irregular gasping movements, twice a minute, occurred in the middle of the experiment, but there was no proper respiration. Once the perfusion was stopped, however, the gasping respiratory efforts increased to 8 to 10 per minute. The fetus died 21 minutes after leaving the circuit.[1]

The infant survived a total of five hours. Chamberlain received a professional award for this experiment.

The artificial placenta work is a good example of the futuristic implications of some experiments. The current advertisement is that the artificial placenta will give premature infants with respiratory distress a chance for survival. This is, of course, true and there should be no objection to working toward perfection of the systems using animal models and those babies who would be themselves helped toward survival, even if it be in an experimental milieu. Yet, today we may not see tomorrow. For instance, David Rorvik, in *Brave New Baby,* pointed out that with the perfection of the artificial placenta, embryos brought into being by *in vitro* fertilization could be brought to term in the laboratory. Rorvik cited Aldous Huxley's no-longer-futuristic *Brave New World* by paraphrasing it in his own context: "In the world Huxley envisions, people recall the old days in which babies were ejected from a woman's womb with revulsion. The pain, blood and agony of pregnancy and birth, as suffered in the previous era, are all the proof the Brave New Worlders need that they have pulled themselves up from their barbarous origins into a greater day—a day in which babies are produced on an assembly line in a fully automated 'factory.'"[2] If Rorvik knew of the implications of the artificial placenta research in 1971, surely the review boards of hospitals where workers were mining this territory and the funders of these experiments also knew. That is not to say that the artificial placenta, using animal models, should not have been explored in order to rescue distressed babies. But the omens are bad. No public debate occurred concerning the use of human, aborted subjects in the Chamberlain research. Why then should we trust that factory production of babies will not go forward without serious public debate when the technology is ripened? How will the public know if, combined with the technique of cloning of certain genotypes, a race of laboratory humans could be at the disposal of science, the factory owner and others in need of a submissive type of human being?

Artificial placenta experiments were talked against at the hearings of the Commission for the Protection of Human Subjects, but Caspar Weinberger chose, in the end, to reinstate permission for them in the final regulations in the name of benefit to future infants. In 1980, though, they were again forbidden except if applied for under the waiver. But it may be that by the time the artificial placenta work was banned again in 1980, the experiments had run their course.

For instance, two prominent Canadian doctors in that field, Blanchaud and Goodyer, have written that they accept that they may no longer do that kind of research. Without reference to ethics, Blanchaud and Goodyer said that they learned a lot from the experiments when they were doing them. It is also relevant to note that these two researchers did not stop their own work because of the uproar over these live hookups of previable, living survivors of abortion. Rather, they kept on until they were stopped from the outside. Thus we see that although the research profession is bright, it may not be wise enough to do what it needs to do: police itself.

Not long after the Chamberlain perfusion experiments and others like them, the issue of the previable rather than the viable fetus as a research subject hit the news in England.

A *Cambridge Evening News* report stated that "a storm of protest blew up in England when a Member of Parliament learned that private abortion clinics had been selling live babies for research." Note that the public and the M.P. were outraged because the baby was worked on while alive. But the doctor involved, Dr. Lawrence Lawn, explained to the public that although the baby was alive it was previable—unable to survive on its own, so the public ought not be concerned. It ought to, additionally, be glad that doctors like himself had the foresight to use such a human subject. Lawn allowed himself to be photographed checking the perfusion tank in which we see suspended a fetus in its last hours. Said Lawn, "We are simply using something which is destined for the incinerator to benefit mankind . . . Of course we would not dream of experimenting with a viable child. We would not consider that to be right."

But the most detailed description of the fate of a live, previable fetus came from the United States. In 1973, a Connecticut District Attorney submitted the following testimony[3] of an identity-protected doctor (called Dr. Baker in the report) to the U.S. Supreme Court as part of an appeal of two abortion cases, both of which were dismissed. The testimony was accompanied by the D.A.'s words on behalf of the petitioners, "Your petitioners also respectfully note that the evidence in this record demonstrates that where abortions are freely performed, there is also a tendency to demean life after birth." The testimony on what happened to a previable infant delivered by hysterotomy at Yale–New Haven Hospital is very crucial. Except for the hysterotomy procedure, the vivisection described was not an isolated incident, but routine. It was a premeditated act to allow tissue and organ harvest—and it is still occurring.

The questions and answers that follow are excerpted from the affidavit.

Q: Are you a medical doctor?

A: Yes.

Q: At any time did you ever observe abortions at Yale–New Haven Hospital?

A: Yes.

Q: Would you please tell us what, if anything, you observed?

A: There are two types of abortions that I have witnessed, one is what they call a hysterotomy when the fetus is much bigger and the pregnancy is much more advanced. . . . This fetus is a fairly well-formed fetus and has a beating heart, not necessarily breathing but the heart is beating and it is alive at the time it is taken out. This is put in some kind of a container and, of course, after it has been detached from the womb it obviously dies off in time. I don't particularly witness that moment when they take the last heartbeat, we don't go into the detail of monitoring that.

Q: Can you give any further details as to how the baby appears once the incision is made and from the time it is taken out?

A: The baby appears well-formed, it has all its hands and feet and the mouth and ears and the nose and eyes, and all that.

Q: Doctor, can you tell us what movements, if any, you can observe in such a baby?

A: There are a few purposeless movements of the extremities. . . . Without any purpose, they have this sort of gasping action, sort of moving their limbs about, they call it purposeless, there is no purpose for it, it gives you an idea that some of the musculature is already developed.

Q: Are there movements at the time it is put in the container? [after the umbilical cord is cut]

A: Yes . . .

Q: Was there a case where some type of surgical procedure was performed on a baby after induced abortion?

A: I did not actually observe the operation itself.

Q: Can you tell us anything about it, to the extent that you know?

A: A baby was aborted by hysterotomy. Then it was taken to another room with a medical student.

Q: Do you know why it was taken out of the room?

A: Well, they wanted to get something out of it.

Q: How did you know they were trying to get something out of it?

A: That's what they said. I just overheard it. They were going to get some kind of an abdominal organ, I think it was the liver. I was not very sure.

Q: You overheard this from whom, a nurse?

A: From the doctor.

Q: Was this the doctor that was presumably going to take this liver or whatever it was?

A: Yes, and the obstetrician that was performing the operation.

Q: When it was taken out of the room, did it have any movements?

A: It had some movements.

Q: Were there any excretions at all?

A: Excretions, urine, yes.

Q: Can you describe how the medical student appeared when he returned?

A: He was sort of pale. He said he felt sort of sick in his stomach. That's why he left the room and went back to the operating room where I was.

Q: Do you recall what, if anything, the medical student said?

A: He just said he couldn't stand it.

Q: Do you know whether or not this baby was given any anesthesia when the operation was done?

A: I don't think so . . .

A hysterotomy was not an everyday occurrence. Additionally, it could have had an impact on the woman's reproductive future, just as a Caesarean section can. In no way was hysterotomy colloquial enough to be able to make any large number of previable fetuses available.

Even as the event at Yale–New Haven was entered into the annals of Twentieth Century history, the unsubtle and infrequent hysterotomy was on its way out. It would soon be abandoned because of the advent of a new abortion agent, Prostin F2 Alpha, manufactured by Upjohn Pharmaceuticals.

The *raison d'etre* for this new abortifacient was not only the problems of hysterotomy but the unsafety of saline induction. Saline induction had a naughty way of causing maternal death, a fact the Japanese learned much before the Americans. By 1950, the Japanese had already abandoned the technique and substituted hypertonic glucose induction. In 1974, Christopher Tietze of the Population Council of New York reported that most of the twenty-five maternal deaths occurring in 425,000 abortions came from the saline potion.

So Prostin F2 Alpha's positive profile was that it was safer for the mother. Vomiting, diarrhea, and headaches were side effects, but there was, said the practitioners in the trial runs, no need to fear death. The drug was to be used for second-trimester abortions.

By 1974, Yale University School of Medicine, where the D.A. had taken the testimony reproduced above, was routinely inducing second-trimester abortions this way. Dr. Gerald Anderson reported from Yale in *Contemporary Obstetrics and Gynecology,* July 1974: "Our entire staff agrees on this point; on the rare occasions when a shipment of prostaglandins is delayed and we have to abort with saline, everyone becomes upset."[4] At this time, Prostin F2 Alpha was still simply a new abortion agent.

Upjohn's voice was heard during the trials before the drug was approved by the FDA in 1974. The company reported that there were no live births in the series of trials.

On July 15, 1972, an article was published by Drs. Wentz, Cushner, Austin and Shams, in the *American Journal of Obstetrics and Gynecology.* All were at Johns Hopkins University School of Medicine. Their experiments with Upjohn's product were "paid for in part" by the U.S. Agency for International Development (AID); the Prostin F2 Alpha used in the experiments was supplied by Edward M. Southern, M.D., of Upjohn. Upjohn must have known about Wentz et al.'s findings: After a single injection of the abortion agent in three patients at fifteen to twenty-two weeks gestation and seven patients at thirteen to twenty weeks gestation, "abortion occurred in all 10 patients, with complete expulsion of products of conception in 8. Three patients vomited." The doctors also logged news of another set of trials done by another team who had induced abortion in four patients with Prostin F2 Alpha "with no generalized side effects."[5]

Wentz et al. were mainly concerned with the effects of the agent on the mother, mainly because of previous reports of fever, diarrhea and vomiting. Their aim was to investigate those side effects in their own trials.

But the researchers found out something else en route. " . . . it has not been shown that prostaglandin itself is lethal to the fetus as is 20 per cent saline solution in most cases. Therefore . . . the occurrence of undesirable live births might possibly be noted."[6]

The researchers were apparently recording their doubts that the abortifacient ought to be used at all because of this unseemly quality. After all, a live birth in the abortion process was called even then "the dreaded complication" and certainly perverts the image and the very purpose of abortion. Ten years later, in 1982, *National Right to Life News* carried a report that stated that "in separate studies, [Prostin F2 Alpha] resulted in seven to nine births per 100 abortions, a rate 30 times higher than with saline."[7]

What registered as troublesome to Wentz et al., despite its relative safety for the mother having a second-trimester abortion, registered to other researchers as a virtue and a boon.

In the year of its maiden voyage to clinical use, 1974, blessed with FDA approval, Upjohn's new abortifacient had its extracurricular profile published in the *American Journal of Obstetrics and Gynecology.* Dr. Mitchell C. Golbus and Dr. Robert Erickson, while working on a 1973 March of Dimes grant for storage of amniotic fluid and live fetal tissues gotten through experiments with amniocentesis, made a discovery:

> The occasional delivery of a fetus with a heartbeat suggests that fetal death usually occurs close to the time of abortion . . . Therefore, it seemed likely that the fetal tissues so obtained might be suitable for organ transplants, for growing and attenuating viruses for vaccines, and for basic research. The report on second-trimester [Prostin F2 Alpha] abortions demonstrates that fetal tissues are viable and that representative enzymes are not altered significantly by the abortion technique.[8]

The same researchers reported that samples of skin, lung and thymus from eleven fetuses were minced and put into solutions that would fix them for later use. The small intestines were stored at −70 degrees C for up to four weeks before being thawed for experiments. The enzyme activity was then compared with the values of those obtained by hysterotomy. In this experiment involving fifteen women, "Three fetuses were born alive but died within a few minutes of delivery."[9]

Researchers are strictly forbidden by their own private institutional review boards and by the federal regulations to have anything to do with the abortion procedure. But here we find that the researcher performed the maiden research work on how to obtain the live fetus, himself performed the abortion, and plundered the remains. This process for gaining a live fetus or a freshly dead one by the method of abortion itself has led many researchers who take advantage of it to involvement with the abortion procedures in hospitals where they stand to gain "materials" from those abortions. Researchers are very much alert to and aware of prostaglandin-induced abortions as being crucial to their own work.

Thus, it seems that Golbus and Erickson had read Wentz et al.'s article with separate eyes, ones tuned to the lone sentence in that report that suggested a new source of live fetuses for experiments. With this discovery, a new and deepened relationship between abortion and fetal experimentation was forged. It heralded the concept of the fetus as an organ farm in the real sense. The social contract signed by those favoring legal abortion was now significantly compromised by the self-interest of the research community and remains a completely hidden factor to most Americans today, who still equate abortion with the cessation of the fetus' life during the abortion process itself.

There were a few who sought to expose this new liberality in the process of abortion. Joan Wester Anderson, a freelance journalist, in her article "Beyond Abortion—Fetal Experimentation: New Upjohn Drug Delivers Perfect Fetus for Laboratory Use," reported the following incidents and quotations that pinpoint the aliveness of the previable fetus delivered by prostaglandin abortion.

"Wilhamine Dick, testifying at the Shapp Abortion Law Commission Hearing of March 14, 1972, said Pittsburgh's Magee Women's Hospital packed aborted babies in ice while still moving and shipped them to experimental labs." In a later interview, Ms. Dick added, "It was repulsive to watch live fetuses being packed in ice while still trying to breathe and move, then being rushed to some laboratory and hear a medical student later discuss the experience of examining various organs of a once-live baby." At the time, Magee Women's Hospital did not refute the charge. It only spoke to a point of professional ethics at Magee, Ms. Dick claiming she had many times asked to be switched from her anesthetist's post at abortions to another detail. Chief of Pediatrics, now deceased Dr. Donald Hutchinson, commented only on this aspect of Ms. Dick's testimony. "Magee Women's Hospital has, does and will respect personal morals and ethics of its staff."

Ms. Wester Anderson quoted a *Washington Post* April 15, 1973, report that Dr. Gerald Gaull, chief of pediatrics at New York State Institution for Basic Research in Mental Retardation, "injects radioactive chemicals into umbilical cords of fetuses. . . . While the heart is still beating he removes their brains, lungs, liver and kidneys for study."

She continued, "The *Washington Post* also reported that Dr. Robert Schwartz, chief of pediatrics at Cleveland Metropolitan General Hospital 'severs the cord (linked to the mother) and as quickly as possible he removes organs and tissues.'"

Ms. Wester Anderson correctly observed that "Until recently, experiments such as these were relatively rare, due to the fact that most infants were not intact when aborted. . . . While not all second-trimester infants are aborted by prostaglandins . . . if prostaglandin use becomes widespread, it will increase the number of babies available for fetal experimentation."

Also quoted by Ms. Wester Anderson was Dr. Kurt Hirschhorn of New York's Mt. Sinai Hospital. Hirschhorn is a longtime advisory board member of the March of Dimes and one of its most prominent grantees. He is, among other things, the editor of the March of Dimes Original Birth Defects Articles Series. Hirschhorn spoke with candor about prostaglandin induction: "With prostaglandins you can arrange the whole abortion . . . so [the fetus] comes out viable in the sense that it can survive hours, or a day."

Some interesting background notes on Upjohn's development of Prostin F2 Alpha might be noted. The Kalamazoo Pro-Life Action League, in its publication *Uprise,*[10] reported a 1979 story by UPI editor Patricia McCormack, which "commented on the connection between the Upjohn company and the Planned Parenthood Federation of America, since both were being represented by the same major New York City advertising agency." McCormack was quoted: " . . . the (Planned Parenthood) Federation choice of Manning, Selvage and Lee will place the public relations firm in the position of helping both clients, the Federation and Upjohn, since anything done to preserve abortion-on-demand works to keep up Upjohn's abortion medicine business." *Uprise* went on to report that when the Kalamazoo (Upjohn's headquarters), Michigan, Planned Parenthood chapter "burned its mortgage on Wednesday, 24 October 1984, it was a long-time director of the Kalamazoo based Upjohn Company which set the fire." It was "Richard Upjohn Light, a member of the Upjohn board for more than 30 years." *Uprise* also alleged that "current Upjohn Vice-President for Research and Development, Jacob C. Stucki, is a director of the Kalamazoo Abortion Shop" and that Upjohn's "Executive Director for Corporate Planning and Development, Arthur A. Hilgart, Jr., is the Kalamazoo Planned Parenthood President."

When Prostin F2 Alpha was put on the market by Upjohn, immediately National Right to Life and The American Life Lobby mounted an official boycott of Upjohn Pharmaceuticals. In 1987, Upjohn withdrew that drug from the market. Ms. Jessyl Bradford, spokeswoman for Upjohn's Public Affairs Office, verified to this writer[11] that Prostin F2 Alpha is now being sold only outside the United States. But the withdrawal of the abortifacient is really not much of a victory. Bradford asserted that two other prostaglandin abortion inducers, Prostin E2, a suppository method, and Prostin 15m, administered through the muscles, are still available in this country.

No session of the NIH Commission on the Protection of Human Subjects investigated the ethics of a researcher skewing the commonly held definition of abortion in order to get live research subjects. All that was said was that the researcher may have no part in the abortion decision, its timing or procedure. Yet Dr. Leon R. Kass, M.D. and Ph.D, delivered at that time a paper called

"Determining Death and Viability in Fetuses and Abortuses." Like most of the documents from the commission, it too crashed the gates of traditional meaning. In a spirit of pure accommodation to the necessity of rendering up a class of live fetuses to medical research, Dr. Kass said:

> The decision to have an abortion does not turn a living fetus into a dead fetus. The decision to abort, like the spontaneously occurring "threat" of a miscarriage, makes the fetus at most a "dying" or "condemned" fetus but not yet a dead one. The to-be-aborted fetus is still alive. It is abortion, not the decision, which is the lethal act."[12]

So far, so good, Dr. Kass is still with us; but he takes a turn and winds up over the fence.

> Yet not all abortions are lethal. Not every abortion necessarily turns a living fetus into a dead abortus. For example, where abortion is produced by expulsion or by hysterotomy, some fetuses survive the procedure as living fetuses (sometimes even viable ones). The very term "abortion" is ambiguous: does abortion mean only womb-emptying, or does abortion also mean, necessarily, feticide? In most cases, womb-emptying and feticide go together, but obviously not in all. It is precisely in those cases where abortion means or effects only womb-emptying that the procedure issues in living abortuses that can be used for research. For this reason, "abortion" in this paper will mean only "womb-emptying."[13]

One wonders how many women undergoing abortion expect only "womb-emptying" and not the death of the baby.

The dates are important in all of this. The commission hearings were held 1974-76. Golbus' and Erickson's article was only published in 1974 but was received for publication a year earlier. Surely the commission had to know that there was a mighty ethical question involved in new abortion technology. Nor was the government sphere alone in its tacit protection of researchers' getting live fetuses. For instance, the March of Dimes, in giving Golbus the grant for setting up live tissue banks in 1973, despite its P.R. protestations that it has never funded live fetal research, actually took advantage of a live abortion technique. In funding storage of amniotic fluid samples, with the same grant, the March of Dimes again took advantage of live fetal research, as Golbus and Erickson's collection of those amniotic fluid samples was all from experimental trials on fetuses to be aborted. Thus, we see a leap to capitalizing on nonlethal means of abortion rather than a recoiling from it.

Exactly from where did the NIH commission think previable fetuses for research were to come? Do foundations such as the March of Dimes expect the citizenry not to wonder how live tissues can be obtained from dead fetuses? As it turns out, it is very much in the interest of researchers, the government and private foundations to have the truth about Prostin F2 Alpha safely behind closed doors. In some states, that reason is arrest.

In 1973, California, in a move to bring that state into compliance with the federal ban, passed a law that allowed only research on live tissues from a dead fetus, or on a whole dead fetus. It disallowed categorically any nontherapeutic experimentation on a living fetus ex utero, and charged further that "a fetus born prematurely alive in the course of an abortion be accorded the same rights to medical treatment as any other infant."

This law was passed by both houses of the California legislature and has not undergone any amendments or deletions since 1973 when it was put into the Public Health and Safety Codes of California. The original intent to place it in the criminal codes was softened and it carries no felony charge.

Let us consider Golbus and Erickson's prostaglandin experiment in the light of the restrictions imposed by that law. This writer learned about the California law from R.P. Leavitt of the March of Dimes when asking if that foundation was engaged in live fetal research,[14] I received a categorical "no." I asked about Golbus' amniocentesis trials, all on fetuses to be aborted, which Golbus, in his published articles, said were financed by the MOD and the NIH. Mr. Leavitt said that the MOD only funded Golbus for setting up amniotic fluid sample banks and live fetal tissue banks. The dates for Golbus' articles would point to the possibility that the tissues were gotten from the prostaglandin experiment, which also produced some live fetuses, and from subjects used in the amniocentesis experiments on fetuses to be aborted. Leavitt said that perhaps the MOD does not define amniocentesis trials on fetuses to be aborted as live fetal research, since the amniotic fluid is not the fetus itself! Yet the NIH, in the Human Subjects Commission report, defined amniocentesis research as research on the fetus in utero. Additionally, Golbus and other fieldworkers in amniocentesis delineated clearly that the fetus was very much involved; one of the dangers of amniocentesis is puncture of the skull by the needle intruded into the amniotic sac.

Leavitt also said that Dr. Golbus, in applying for the grant to store amniotic fluid samples, mentioned that he would not be in offense of a newly passed 1973 California state law on fetal experimentation. In a March 22, 1985, letter to this reporter, Leavitt said, "In applying to us for support in 1973, Dr. Golbus wrote that California had just passed a law prohibiting research use of live fetuses, with fetal death defined as cessation of heart beat, and explicitly not defined by "previable" gestational age . . . [Golbus] stated that in his work, 'no procedure will be instituted on any fetal specimen in the presence of a discernible heart beat."

Dr. Golbus, in this communique with his funders, left out the most important part of the California law, one that would make waiting for a heartbeat to cease moot. Considering that Golbus himself reported in his *American Journal of Obstetrics and Gynecology* article that some fetuses in his prostaglandin trials were born alive but died within minutes, and that he was doing that experiment solely for tissue and organ retrieval, why wasn't he concerned that he was very much afly of this portion of the same law: "A fetus born prematurely alive in the course of an abortion has to be accorded the same rights to medical treatment as any other infant." Golbus was right that the law did not distinguish between the viable or nonviable fetus as being a candidate for help. So even the second-trimester fetuses born alive in his prostaglandin experiments should have merited his help. But Golbus was in search of tissue and organs, not live surviving infants.

The March of Dimes, in the person of Mr. Leavitt, did not have a copy of the California law. I asked Leavitt if this penchant of Golbus for liveborn or freshly dead aborted fetuses may not have compromised the March of Dimes grant to him for setting up tissue banks, in that some of the tissues could have been gotten, at the time of expiration of the fetuses, from the same fetuses who may have been born alive and so were candidates for intervention. Leavitt said we cannot infer that Golbus delivered live infants even though Golbus himself reported it.

Leavitt also said that Golbus wrote that he was having good cooperation from obstetricians who provided him with tissues for his bank. This, according to Leavitt's logic, means that Golbus did not have anything to do with any further abortions. Yet it was he who discovered the method to be followed by others. Nor is the matter settled as to whether or not more liveborn but unassisted fetuses supplied the MOD project with live tissues, even if other obstetricians in Golbus' ken supplied them. With a liveborn abortion rate thirty times higher than that of saline, and with Golbus himself taking advantage of an abortion method that does not of itself kill the fetus, how can the cooperating obstetricians be given the benefit of the doubt? In fact, in the following example of another researcher in search of fetal parts, we find a very close relationship between the researcher and the obstetricians performing prostaglandin abortions.

In 1982, Dr. Ernest D. Gardner, Professor of Neurology and Orthopedic Surgery in the Department of Neurology at the University of California, requested and received from the National Institute of Health a $2,357,352 grant for a project titled "Developmental Neurobiology in Primates."[15]

The opening passage of his application discussed how he acquired his fetal subjects, the problems surrounding that, and the special arrangements he made. "We have made the necessary, approved arrangements with obstetricians and pathologists, but in our original application, we completely underestimated the difficulties. (a) Fetuses aborted between 14 and 18 gestational weeks by the prostaglandin method are often normal, but we must have a well-organized arrangement for collecting these fetuses . . . Those [normal fetuses] obtained immediately after death will, in the case of smaller specimens, be fixed by immersion or the brains will be removed directly for Golgi stains." Gardner said the protocols he likes to have followed for freezing and fixing the organs have been circulated by him "to physicians in the Sacramento and Davis area." He also mentioned that he was well protected in all of this because he operated on a closed circuit. "Pathology services for the majority of private hospitals in this area are provided by a single corporation . . . This provides easy access to the private medical community."

Finally, in outlining his travel expenses, Dr. Gardner admitted what some might call "an interest in the method of the abortion," which researchers, ethically, are not supposed to have: "If an unusually well-preserved specimen is expected (e.g. from abortion by hysterotomy or hysterectomy), then project personnel may travel to outlying hospitals to await a normal specimen. They must, of course, retrieve promptly any previously fixed specimens."

In 1975, just a year after Golbus and Erickson's report on live abortions via Prostin F2 Alpha, Kenneth Edelin, a Boston physician, was indicted for manslaughter. He was delivering a live fetus by hysterotomy, but then suffocated the fetus while the fetus was still attached to the mother. Edelin was convicted by a jury; jury members said they were impressed by a photo of the fetus, which they said "looked like a baby." Juror Paul Holland said that the survival of the live aborted fetus should have been left to the baby itself. The District Attorney agreed.

Edelin's conviction was overturned by a Superior Court, which deemed that because the fetus was in the previable range, Edelin had not killed a person and that, further, there was no law to define what he had done. Said Edelin of how he had held the fetus motionless in the womb for three minutes as he watched the clock on the wall, "To allow the baby to survive would have been contrary to the wishes of the mother."

There turned out to be a connection between Edelin's case and researchers working in prostaglandin abortions. That same year, Yale–New Haven was using the prostaglandin method in fetoscopy trials by Mahoney and Hobbins. When Edelin was picked up for manslaughter, *Contemporary Ob/Gyn* called Yale–New Haven and talked to Dr. John Hobbins. The journal reporter asked Hobbins if the Edelin controversy of producing a live infant would change anything at Yale, as Hobbins "is involved in the prostaglandin-induced abortion program there." Said Hobbins, as adamant as Edelin had been, "The Edelin decision hasn't altered anything we're doing."[16]

Thus we see that despite Wentz et al.'s question as to whether Prostin F2 Alpha should be unleashed on account of its producing live births, despite the Edelin conviction, despite California law, researchers chose to go on risking liveborn abortions. For them it was not at all a risk, but an advantage.

When the powers of prostaglandin were unleashed, Mitchell Golbus, like Cortez surveying the horizon, was right to indicate that they would be optimum for organ-transplant work. Today, the portfolio on this matter is coming into its own.

Until recently, one of the major funders of research into transplanting whole fetal pancreases was the Kroc Foundation, the MacDonald's medical research foundation, disbanded after the death of founder Ray Kroc, due to his heirs' decision to not continue funding medical research.

> In the Kroc Foundation's 1979 report on its medical research programs, Dr. Josiah Brown reported: "In seeking an improved method to treat diabetes due to absolute insulin deficiency (juvenile onset) transplantation of insulin producing tissue is a promising approach. We have elected to use fetal pancreases as the donor tissue

> for the following reasons: (1) Fetal tissues have a great capacity for growth. (2) After transplantation of fetal pancreases, insulin-producing islets of Langerhans grow and develop but exocrine . . . producing elements atrophy, resulting in a pure endocrine organ. (3) Small size will enhance storage by cryopreservation (freezing) and a bank of donor organs permanently stored can be developed.[17]

An article in *Diabetes,* August 1982, gave a frank discussion of why the fetal pancreas may be the optimum candidate for transplant: "Ample islet tissue is readily available for the study of the effects of islet transplantation in experimental diabetes in inbred animals where tissues from many donors can be pooled, but this is not the case clinically since there is a shortage of suitable donors. The use of fetal tissue may overcome, at least in part, such a shortage."[18]

For the researchers out on this frontier, the question is medical, not moral: can the fetal pancreas maintain normal capacity for proliferation and, second, can the fetal pancreas overcome the immunity problems of the recipient? The research goes onward and upward while the public remains unadvised that pancreases from aborted babies, which had to be harvested fresh for the pancreas to be usable, will be the silo for this new and dramatic moment that is coming. There is even some evidence that those close to medical research don't know what is on the drawing boards.

For instance, Gerald James Stine in his interesting book *Biosocial Genetics: Human Heredity and Social Issues* included a section on diabetes. He stated rightly that the cure for diabetes would entail changing the DNA so the disease no longer occurs. This being unfeasible, he mentioned, "Another approach is that of transplanting a normal pancreas into a diseased patient." But then he wondered, "Even if science could overcome *all* the transplant problems, where would one obtain the millions of pancreases should everyone want the transplant?"[19]

It has been the Australians who have pioneered human fetal pancreas transplants. A few of the Kroc Foundation researchers were from Australia and New Zealand. In 1984, Australian researchers produced a white paper titled "Ethics in medical research involving the human fetus and human fetal tissue." They drew up this document exactly because they were about to be able to launch work on the transplants. The document is interesting, and, in its own way, honorable.

In the May 12, 1984, *Medical Journal of Australia,* where it was published, Dr. Robert Jansen of the Royal Prince Alfred Hospital in Sydney pointed out in "Comment" that "The question of using aborted fetal tissue for research is, many would say, inextricably bound up with the morality or immorality of inducing abortion." Jansen said that the doctors presenting the paper wanted to attempt a separation of the two. He said that the Medical Research Ethics Committee of Australia had neither the duty nor the privilege "to comment on the ethics of abortion, which itself has nothing to do with medical research; but nor could it ignore the fact that the practice of inducing abortion exists and is lawful."

This attitude reflects approximately the one taken by American researchers. But only a very thorough investigation into chronology and characters could delete the possibility that researchers did not push for abortion, for surely they must have understood clearly what the benefits might be for them. At any rate, the Australian researchers felt entitled to use aborted fetal subjects for experimentation.

Immediately they also came to grips with the fact that they were going to be getting their stuff of experimentation from previable, living fetuses. And here they articulated what has never been articulated in the United States: "A separated previable fetus . . . shows some signs of life at the time of delivery. Although such signs do not indicate a capacity to survive to the point of sustaining independent live [sic], we believe that tissues should not be obtained from a previable fetus while a heartbeat is still apparent . . . "Another section explains why: "Human experimentation that causes no discernible harm, pain or discomfort is generally legitimate. In the case of a live but previable separated fetus, the fetus is in a lethal situation and experimentation can add no further risk. However, there is little information available on the sensory awareness of immature fetuses and dissection of a previable but live fetus cannot be assumed to be without neurological impact on the fetus. Dissection of such a fetus could therefore be justifiably regarded as unethical and offensive."

In the last section, the Australians made explicit their decision not to make it ethical to ransack a live fetus for a pancreas or other tissues or organs. There is no such explicit stricture in the American regulations, which do not really say that a previable infant cannot be vivisected, only that no procedure be applied that directly stops the heartbeat. In fact, the image provided in the U.S. government regulations is of a live fetus being worked on in any number of ways. Also, the U.S. regulations are only pertinent to federal grants, while the Australian ones are systemic to Australian research in general.

Dr. Josiah Brown of the University of California told this writer[20] that, feeling ready to advance to human trials of fetal pancreas transplants, he applied for an NIH grant. He was denied, he reported, because the NIH wanted to see more animal experimentation. Dr. Brown, a softspoken man, obviously quite eager in his work and proud of it as well, received instead a grant from the Kroc Foundation. I asked him if he thought the public should be told that pancreas transplants with aborted fetuses for donors is coming our way. He said he wouldn't know how to go about informing the public and said that since he had already been cleared by the U of C's Institutional Review Board, he did not see any need to inform the public.

Brown also said that as the time for the human trials to begin will draw near, researchers will begin setting up pancreas banks, in order to match them to recipients. Yes, he said, prostaglandin abortions are good for pancreas retrieval, but dilation and evacuation is even better because the fetus is even fresher. He did not say it is ever alive and he said that pathologists with whom he is connected extract the pancreas only after the fetus is dead.

Because researchers have promulgated the attitude that as long as the fetus is dead, there should be no objection to salvaging usable parts, there is a tendency to believe that no one would object to use of the dead aborted fetus (freshly dead or otherwise) for such purposes. But *Science* magazine, when reporting in 1983 Australian prospects for fetal pancreas transplants, said in "Fetus as Organ Donor"[21]: "The issue [in Australia] isn't the fetus's right to life; rather, it is whether science has the right to use the organs of an aborted fetus once it is dead." Even without any mention of live-aborted fetuses who often end up as research subjects, there was a question in Australia as to the legitimacy of use of the clinically dead fetus.

In the same article, Dr. Kevin Lafferty was quoted. Lafferty, on loan from the Australian National University in Canberra and working at the University of Colorado, became the reigning king of fetal pancreas transplants. In the *Science* article, Lafferty was quoted as saying, "Right-to-lifers are concerned that this may somehow legitimize abortions. That's like saying that kidney transplants legitimize car accidents." But he added, "Ethically, I myself am not in favor of abortions."

Other researchers are more reserved than Lafferty in proclaiming that fetal tissue transplants present no ethical problems. The American Paralysis Association (APA) has spent much money exploring animal research that suggests that human fetal brain tissue could be transplanted into paralysis victims.

In September 1983, the APA held a colloquium on the subject of the ethics involved in such a wonder cure. *"Could we* use embryonic cell transplants to correct CNS [Central Nervous System] disorders and *should we?"* This was asked by Dr. Vernon Marks, who led the meeting.[22] Invited to the colloquium was Father Paul J. Murphy, S.J., a retired professor of theology at Boston College. In his remarks,[23] he said, "There is no distinct medical morality, rather there is the universal morality of human behavior applied to medical circumstances. . . . At the present level of medical competence [the transplant of human embryonic tissues or cells to the brain or spine] must be characterized as extraordinary patient treatment and experimental. It is also a procedure that requires serious surgical invasion of critical human organs." Father Murphy then went on to remind the meeting, "Abuses have already embarrassed the medical history of this country" and he cited the macabre Helsinki severed heads incident and the Yale–New Haven experiments.

Father Murphy went on to say that he saw no problem in using dead, spontaneously aborted fetuses for such transplants. "But there looms a severe moral problem in the use of fetuses procured by deliberate abortions—it is the stimulation of a crass commerce in aborted fetuses. . . . To the degree that the proposed transplantation of embryonic cell tissue for the correction of nervous system disorders becomes partner to commerce in abortuses, it becomes a partner to the coarsening of humanity itself and to the grave loss of reverence for human life in its most helpless and dependent stage."

Also present at the meeting was Mr. William A. Carnahan, of the Washington, D.C., law firm of Le Boeuf, Lamb, Leiby and MacRae, and former Deputy Commissioner and General Counsel to the New York State Department of Mental Hygiene. He raised a most interesting question: Should the fetus be treated as an organ in which case the mother could donate it as she would a kidney, or should it be treated as a dead body, in which case the mother can donate all or part of it? He asked this by way of asking a larger question: Do embryonic cell transplantations fall within the public policy underlying anatomical gifts?[24]

A call to Mr. Carnahan revealed that none of these matters has become a factor in deciding law. From the contrast among the theologian's perspective, that of a researcher and that of a lawyer, it is easy to see that while researchers or lawyers may incept procedures or enact laws to underwrite those procedures, those concerned with the ethical side of things may remain completely unsatisfied.

As with pancreas transplants, the number of freshly aborted babies needed for brain tissue transplants is overwhelming because there are so many who suffer from paralysis.

But already laboratories buzz with trials, and, in the case of fetal pancreas transplants, some have already been tried. They occur behind closed doors, not really secret, heralded in fact by a news report or so, but not by any semblance of choice on the part of the public. It is a strange image, that of the diseased and the disabled, so familiar with a position of weakness, benefiting from the very weakest member of human society. Could anyone blame them if they celebrated a chance to be well again? Would it be both a cure and the advent of biological Darwinism? The use of the human fetus, denied life and aborted, strangely becomes a mirror to the future. Will society choose to see a sign of medical wonder progress in that face in the mirror or the face of millions of victims of a practicable but most questionable form of human use and experimentation? Will society ever be made massly aware that the abortion procedure has been skewed by abortion procedures that do not kill the fetus but deliver it alive in some measure, not to be saved but to be used for the rest of us?

In fact, to save a live victim of abortion is being declined as a choice. In the January 14, 1985, *Newsweek,* a special issue on abortion, Dr. Richard Stavis, director of the neonatal unit at Bryn Mawr (PA) Hospital admitted that a live birth by prostaglandin abortion would not inspire his staff to take heroic means to keep the baby alive. He said he would put the baby in an isolette, "keep it warm, give it oxygen and observe it. But we would not actively intervene to protect that baby from dying."[25] His reason? Because he would have to hurt the baby with tubes and needles; he said that to place tubes in a fetus that has no chance of survival is abusive. "It is subjecting the fetus to an experiment. To me, that is cruel."[26] So this is where we are today. A baby will be said to be unable to survive, maybe because the baby has been aborted and maybe, as Dr. Stavis protests, because the baby would require being prodded with needles. Many wanted, premature babies have pulled through exactly because of that kind of "experiment," which is essentially therapeutic. On the other side of the strange contemporary but post-modern reality, if helping a baby to viability is "cruel," what is the vivisection of a previable baby aborted by prostaglandins? What is simply waiting for death before beginning to harvest organs? These are the kind of mind-challenging puzzles we are being asked to solve. Maybe we have opened a Pandora's Box comparable to the one opened when the atom was split. In both cases, we seem to have cut loose from the ancient version of that story, in which hope stayed behind, the lid being closed in time to prevent its flight.

5

Abandonment of the Fetus as Patient and Client

Some would like to believe that fetal experimentation is a subject wholly apart from abortion on demand. But the evidence seems to suggest that they are first cousins. As abortion obliterated the Hippocratic and legal traditions that included the fetus in the human community, so fetal experimentation has used that obliteration to seize and widen its province. As abortion on demand introduced a dehumanization of the unborn person, so fetal experimentation has concluded that it may utilize the unborn because they have no enfranchisement. As the medical profession, for the sake of reaping the fiscal advantages from abortion, let go of its tradition of "do no harm" and of applying only therapeutic measures to its patients, so in fetal experimentation the medical profession has visited both harm and exquisite untherapeutic regimes on the living fetus.

Thus, it seems instructive to trace the former respect and inclusion of the fetus in society up to its abandonment by the law and by physicians. This will show us the safe place where we and the fetus were, a place that seemed immune to cynical inroads and guerilla raids on traditions achieved over hundreds of years of struggle. This will, brutally, find us where we are now: what has come to be denied the fetus may lead to the erosion of our own rights.

Yet there is paradox, irony and a glimpse of a hopeful horizon, not sponsored by morals or anything as bright as the rights of man or the dignity of every human being, but rather by the ego and accomplishment of medicine itself. Some of the selfsame practitioners of fetal experimentation of the cruelest sort have recently taken up the surgical cause of the in-utero fetus, calling this "young one" (the literal meaning of fetus") both a patient and a person.

Abortion on demand marked a signal and profound departure from the Hippocratic tradition's interdiction of a physician's inducing an abortion. From the oath's text: "I will neither give a deadly drug to anybody if asked for it, nor will I make a suggestion to this effect. Similarly, I will not give to a woman an abortive remedy. In purity and holiness I will guard my life and my art." Nontherapeutic experimentation on the human fetus capitalized immediately on the abandonment of that honored, even sacred, proviso. The reader will notice that the oath ties giving an abortion agent to giving death-dealing drugs to "anybody." So, it is significant that some analysts of the Supreme Court's abortion decision say it will be inevitably linked in its logic to the open sesame of "euthanasia." That last word must be put into quotes because it has been distorted in its modern use. Originally it meant "a good death," derived as it was from the Greek words "eu" and "thanatos." Its letter meant to give comfort to the dying and the family and friends of the dying. Today, it means exactly what the oath forbade: so-called "mercy" killing by a second or third party.

Before the abortion decision of 1973 and the majority of the medical profession's accommodation to it, the fetus was a patient equal to the pregnant mother. This equality was neither mystical nor rhetorical, but was derived from the physician's intimate knowledge of the fetus from a scientific point of view, and also from the philosophic ideal of not judging the relative value of human life. Thus it was no accident that in 1972 Dr. A.W. Liley, the father of fetal medicine and of fetal surgery, on the eve of the abortion decision in Australia, delivered his eloquent, lasting, and lonely lecture, "The Foetus as a Personality."

This was a special plea for his colleagues to respect the fetus. But even the amount of testimony given by Liley on the autonomy and real life of the fetus in the womb from conception on could not prevail, although it was not at all refuted. Hammering against the gates of the Hippocratic tradition's commitment to the fetus as a patient was a diverse horde of comers, eager for the amputation of the unwanted fetus from the rolls of patients—and of humanity. In that horde some doctors led the charge. Accommodating abortion was a happy farewell to the demands of the oath's restrictions, its inner liberty and its profound and visionary human rights plank.

In the late 1940's, after the debasement in which the German deathcamp doctors had wallowed [and without much prodding from the Nazi regime], the

Hippocratic Oath was news. The revelations at the trials at Nuremberg brought about an eagerness that the oath and its tradition be reiterated. All of its principles were recast in the 1948 Declaration of Geneva.

Less than thirty years later, the tradition was brought to its knees. *Intellect* magazine reported[1]: "Much of the Hippocratic Oath has been dated for some time. It is especially unsuited to today's rapid social and moral changes." That was the brief for on-demand abortion. The article went on to report that Brown University medical students now write their own general medical oath. It has no proscription against administering an abortion. The Brown student receives the image of healer without the worrisome problems that could accrue from forgoing some (or quite a bit of) income from abortion.

As to "today's rapid social and moral changes," it is pertinent to remember that during one period in ancient Greece, philosophers such as Aristotle felt that abortion was an intelligent, indeed the most intelligent, method of birth control. Nevertheless, the physicians—the ones who tied their conscience to the oath and not to reigning opinion—still kept to their rules. And until the 1950's, the medical profession remained more adamant about who was a human and a patient than either philosophy or religion.

Getting back to the Brown students: They pledged "to consecrate my life to care of the sick, the promotion of health and the service of humanity."[2] There was no mention of abortion nor of the old forbidding of giving death-dealing measures to the dying. In highblown replacement language, the Brown students allowed themselves to judge who should live and who should die. One author, Corleton B. Chapman, in *Physicians, Law and Ethics,* saw the change as positive in that now the physician could be primarily responsible to the patient. "One can discourse learnedly on ethical obligations to society, as AMA leaders seem to have done in the past, as a means of avoiding altogether mention of the more binding patient-centered obligation. Such practice brings to mind . . . the warning that ' . . . along with rational convictions about moral behavior there must always go, in some form or other, an identification with the particular person . . . who [is] affected by this behavior, *if the situation is to be morally alive.*' "[3] To apply this in such a way as to allow abortion, the Brown student and other emerging doctors have to eschew the fetal patient and see only one, maternal patient.

The situation at Brown is no anomaly. In *The Abortion Holocaust,* William Brennan quoted Dr. Carolyn F. Gerster, a Scottsdale, AZ, cardiologist, who reported that Brown is not unique. Gerster said that the Hippocratic Oath has been abandoned by almost every medical school in the country. She added that this occurred only once before, "during the twelve years of the Third Reich."[4]

Dr. Gerster also reported the situation at Northwestern University. At its medical school, graduates entering medical practice usually recite the Geneva Declaration, but minus two passages: "I will maintain the utmost respect for human life from the time of its conception" and "Even under threat I will not use my knowledge contrary to the laws of humanity."

A small group of students in the 1982 180-member graduating medical class protested these deletions and asked to be allowed to recite the entire Geneva Declaration "as a means of counteracting the heavy participation of their medical professors in abortion," wrote Brennan. The students wrote what they named a "Modest Protest"[5]:

> The Geneva Oath was first composed in 1948 as a response to the atrocities of the Nazi Holocaust. The doctors living in 1948 were frightened to learn that their German counterparts were actively involved in many of Hitler's mass extermination programs. In fact, many German physicians easily acquiesced to societal and institutional pressures for a "genetically pure" Aryan Race; thus paving the way for later campaigns directed against "inferior humans," such as the Jews and Poles.

At Northwestern, the fact that there is a kind of civil war within the medical profession was vivified by the "Modest Protest." As the dissenting students read the full Geneva Oath, the other members of the class stayed silent, bringing to mind the word "collaborationist" as it was used for these who fell into line with the Nazis. After relating the fray at Northwestern, author Brennan cited Dr. Andrew C. Ivy, American medical scientific consultant to the prosecution at the Nuremberg War Crimes Trial: "The moral imperative of the oath of Hippocrates I believe is necessary for the survival of the scientific and technical philosophy of medicine."[6] Perhaps, then, with Ivy's insight, the 1982 graduation ceremony at Northwestern was, in large part, a funeral.

The Hippocratic Oath figured very prominently in the discussion that preceded the Supreme Court's abortion decision. Some came to bury it and not to praise it. One was pro-abortion attorney Sarah R. Weddington, who was asked "why a discussion of the Hippocratic Oath had not been included in any of the voluminous briefs submitted to the Court" (Brennan's words). She replied, "The Hippocratic Oath does not pertain to that" (woman's constitutional right to an abortion).[7] The Supreme Court itself finally finished off the Oath by giving it more the cast of the sidewalk phrase, "the Hypocritic Oath." The text of the *Roe v. Wade* decision included a reference to the oath by mentioning "evidence of the violation of almost every one of its injunctions" at some time or other by the medical profession. It also disparaged it as a mere "Pythagorean manifesto" and pointed to its "uncompromising austerity."[8] This last is regrettable thinking, for that strict austerity was probably a burst of freedom for the physician, who was forbidden to favor any one set of humans over another for treatment. Hasn't it been a mark against the American medical profession that, in the South, before the civil rights victory, a black person could die rather than be treated by a white doctor?

The Hippocratic Oath's desertion by liberal forces is especially curious, as the oath is tied to a favorite cause of the liberal tradition, human rights. Anthropologist Margaret Mead called the oath the greatest breakthrough in human rights:

> With the Greeks the distinction was made clear. One profession, the followers of Asclepius, were to be dedicated completely to life under all circumstances, regardless of rank, age or intellect—the life of a slave, the life of the Emperor, the life of a foreign man, the life of a defective child.[9]

Others have embellished Mead's insight, one being former Oak Park, Illinois, public health director, Dr. Herbert Ratner:

> Hippocrates, the father of medicine, was to incorporate the rights of the patient, as well as the obligations of the physician, into the Oath . . . It is the Oath . . . which is the prime protector of the purity of medical art. By imposing on its members an obligation to remain resolute against the assault of a sick society, the Oath, properly constituted, becomes the one hope of preserving the unconfused role of the physician as healer.[10]

From the 1950's on, much histrionics was practiced by doctors trying to loosen the abortion laws. One doubts if they had in mind the "constitutional rights of women to privacy over their own bodies" as the impetus for their support. The obstetrical and gynecological professions have long been on feminism's list of oppressors, and this writer remembers the huge tide of women wanting to supplant those doctors with self-examination, midwived childbirth, and even self-performed abortion. Obviously, some doctors were afire, as early as the 1950's, with one of their own internal directives: fees. Of course, they didn't say it that way, but tried to invoke some medical imagery. Consider the verbal quackery of Dr. Robert Laidlaw, who in 1955 spoke at an abortion conference held in New York. Wanting abortion to be equated with any other legally allowed medical procedure, he likened abortion surgery to operating on a ruptured appendix.[11] Later, in 1968, Dr. Alan F. Guttmacher likened abortion "to operating on an appendix or removing gangrenous bowel."[12]

These examples of pro-abortion sophistry are taken from Brennan's aforementioned volume, which never fails to match contemporary departures from classic medical mores to the conduct of the Nazi doctors. In his historical mirror, Brennan brought forward Dr. Ella Lingens-Reiner, who "once pointed to crematorium chimneys and asked Dr. Fritz Klein: 'How can you reconcile that with your Hippocratic Oath?' Klein replied, 'When you find a gangrenous appendix, you must remove it.'"[13] Does this suggest that Guttmacher and Laidlaw read Klein, or that cruelty has a way of conjuring the same base imagery?

Novel pronouncements such as those of Guttmacher and Laidlaw have spawned some even more bizarre ones. In these, pregnancy is defined as a disease. In 1980, at the National Abortion Federation Convention, Dr. Jane Hodgson invoked the image of pregnancy as an epidemic.[14] "We have laws regarding other epidemics. We have mandatory immunizations, but we have no law prohibiting motherhood before the age of 14." Her "cure" for this new public health menace was compulsory abortion "in the very young—say, those less than 14 years.'"

This proposal would greatly interfere with the voluntary ideal of abortion and one that is supposed to represent a woman's right to choose. Again, this writer remembers that the feminist movement in its earlier moments in the 1970's included teenage girls in its ranks, who were equally awarded sisterhood and the title of "woman." Teenage pregnancy as well as teen live births in the U.S., according to a recent *New York Times* report, are the highest in the world, often double or triple those of other Western countries. This phenomenon may inspire more appeal to it as an "epidemic" with a regular epidemology solution: immunization, in this case, by abortion. Richard Doerflinger in a March 17,

1985, *Our Sunday Visitor* article, "The Roots of Force: Abortion Policy in the United States," recorded that in 1983 "the keynote speaker at a convention of PP [Planned Parenthood] physicians went further. . . . Dr. Lise Fortier suggested that every pregnant woman be compelled to sign a document detailing the dangers of pregnancy and the health benefits of abortion. 'Indeed,' said Dr. Fortier, 'if one were to push logic to an extreme, since abortion is so much safer than childbirth from a strict medical standpoint, every pregnancy should be aborted.'"

What may be happening, suggested Doerflinger, is that abortion may be on the verge of becoming a policy of force, and taken, for some women, completely out of the range of choice. Doerflinger rightly saw this as a challenge to liberal pro-abortion forces and fairly noted that pro-choice forces have already come out against one judge who ordered an abortion for an adolescent girl late in her pregnancy. The question, however, is whether either the women's movement or the ACLU would be able to win such a battle over voluntariness. Now that abortion is entrenched, the hardline forces such as Planned Parenthood, as well as eugenic forces, are beginning to come out from their fortress, and with their very separate agendas. It may come to pass that the women's movement and the ACLU will be taking on these proponents of force as they have taken on pro-life forces until now.

Forced abortion in some segments of occupied Europe became common under Hitler, who many like to say had no pro-abortion program. Brennan, the recorder of pertinent historical analogies and equalities between the past and the present, cited "A document submitted at the RuSHA (Race and Settlement Main Office) trial held in Nuremberg." The document read:

> It is known that racially inferior offspring of Eastern workers and Poles is to be avoided if at all possible. Although pregnancy interruption ought to be carried out on a voluntary basis only, pressure is to be applied in each of these cases.[15]

It turns out, based on the above, that even the Nazis were not as forward in calling for compulsory abortion on some groups as are certain elements in the contemporary U.S.A.

Stuck up against the withdrawal from the Oath by the medical profession on the subject of abortion is its leavetaking from the tradition's ideal of therapy.

Just as pregnancy is now seen as a "disease" or "epidemic," the fetus to be experimented on has been described as mere "tissue." Both of these descriptions are supposed to be the entree to nontherapeutic abortion and nontherapeutic experimentation.

Before abortion became legal, no surgical procedure could be done on any patient if it was not therapeutically necessary. The feminists had hammered hard in their early years against unnecessary hysterectomies and mastectomies. Any doctor performing an unnecessary operation on a patient is legally liable for malpractice. Yet, this hallmark was summarily swept aside in the medical profession's performance of what it euphemistically calls "therapeutic abortion."

Some pleas have been made against this mislabeling of abortion surgery. The clearest was presented in *Psychiatric Annals,* September 1972, by Dr. Samuel A. Nigro, then a senior instructor in child psychiatry at Case Western Reserve University School of Medicine in Cleveland, and director of in-patient child psychiatry consultation for Rainbow-Babies and Children's Hospitals of Cleveland. Dr. Nigro took pen in hand to try to burn the medical profession's assent to abortion as a "therapeutic" procedure.[16]

First he upheld the right of all to express philosophical differences on issues; then he immediately stated that medical procedures must be "documented by scientific evidence that goes beyond clinical impressions or philosophical preferences." Here he seemed to be referring to a woman's feeling that she medically needs, for one reason or another outside of a serious health threat to herself, to have an abortion. Nigro cited Sections 2 and 3 of the Principles of Medical Ethics of the American Medical Association, which stated that in the absence of scientific evidence, the technique must be regarded as unethical. Thus, the abandonment of the Hippocratic Oath was supplemented by an explicit default of coded medical ethics.

Dr. Nigro also took up what he called "The Emotional Skew": "This is evident in two ways: the need to call abortions 'therapeutic' and the need to deny complications."

Nigro then quoted L.H. Bartemeier, who wrote in *The American Journal of Psychiatry,* 1967: " . . . the term 'therapeutic abortion' is a misnomer; it appears to have been devised to circumvent the laws of the states. No carefully conducted clinical investigations have demonstrated the therapeutic value of these surgically induced procedures." Thus, curiously, we find that women, who have had such a long and bitter argument against doctors for nontherapeutic and invasive procedures, have allowed doctors to perform nontherapeutic surgery (abortions) on them, have themselves called them "therapeutic," and have promoted this lapse of all medical ethics as a right to be shared in by all sisters. This, in turn, opened the door to medical researchers to expect from women a generous consent to experiment on their fetuses as well. They even learned how to beg to the rejection of the fetus by the mother as a way of propagandizing that they, in nontherapeutic use of the fetus, do what the mother refused to do: they allow the fetus a chance to participate in the community and in the gaining of important biomedical knowledge by becoming a subject of research. The fetus, as we heard Gaylin and Lappe say, "could be ennobled" by research as it could not be from abortion and its underlying maternal rejection.

Before letting go of Dr. Nigro, an incident he cited is worth passing on. C.V. Ford, et al.,wrote an article in *The Journal of the American Medical Association,* 1971.[17] The point of the article was to claim therapeutic efficacy for abortion. Nigro reported the upshot of the article: The study had "such elementary deficiencies that the competence of the editorial board of *JAMA,* ultimately responsible for its publication, was in question before the judicial council of the American Medical Association."[18] Nigro went on to say that "unwillingness" to continue a pregnancy has been chosen to suffice and substitute for medical or psychiatric necessity.

What is a physician to do in the face of a Supreme Court decision that legalizes abortion on demand, and, in the realm of fetal experimentation, what is a researcher's response to a permissive atmosphere on fetal experimentation? The answer to that also lies in history, and points up that some physicians have defied laws and regimes in order to protect their old and sacred contract with their patients.

In 1949 Dr. Leo Alexander, instructor in psychiatry at Tufts Medical School and director of the Neurobiologic Unit at Boston State Hospital as well as a doctor on duty with the Office of the Chief Counsel for War Crimes in Nuremberg, published an article titled "Medical Science Under Dictatorship."[19] Little did Dr. Alexander know how his article might be invoked today.

One section of the article deals exclusively with resistance by one nation's doctors under the boot of the Nazis.

> It is to the everlasting honor of the medical profession of Holland that they recognized the earliest and most subtle phases of the attempt [to propagandize "euthanasia"] and rejected it. When Seiss-Inquart,

> Reich Commissar for the Occupied Netherlands Territories, wanted to draw the Dutch physicians into the orbit of the activities of the German medical profession, he did not tell them "You must send your chronic patients to death factories" or "You must give lethal injections at Government request in your offices," but he couched his order in most careful and superficially acceptable terms. One of the paragraphs in the order of the Reich Commissar concerning the Netherlands doctors of 19 December 1941 reads as follows: "It is the duty of the doctor, through advice and effort, conscientiously and to his best ability, to assist as helper the person entrusted to his care in the maintenance, improvement and re-establishment of his vitality, physical efficiency and health. The accomplishment of this duty is a public task." The physicians of Holland rejected this order unanimously because they saw what it actually meant—namely, the concentration of their efforts on mere rehabilitation of the sick for useful labor, and abolition of medical secrecy.
>
> Although on the surface the new order appeared not too grossly unacceptable, the Dutch physicians decided that it is the first, although slight, step away from principle that is the most important one. The Dutch physicians declared that they would not obey this order. When Seiss-Inquart threatened them with revocation of their licenses, they returned their licenses, removed their shingles and, while seeing their own patients secretly, no longer wrote death or birth certificates.
>
> Seiss-Inquart retraced his steps and tried to cajole them—still to no effect. Then he arrested 100 Dutch physicians and sent them to concentration camps. The medical profession remained adamant and . . . would not give in. Thus it came about that not a single euthanasia or sterilization was recommended or participated in by any Dutch physician. . . . It is the first seemingly innocent step away from principle that frequently decides a career of crime.

Alexander did not write the article for a mere recounting of history. After his chronicle, he moved in on the medical community of the U.S.

> The question that this fact prompts is whether there are any danger signs that American physicians have also been infected with Hege-

> lian, cold-blooded, utilitarian philosophy and whether early traces of it can be detected in their medical thinking that may make them vulnerable to departures of the type that occurred in Germany. Basic attitudes must be examined dispassionately. The original concept of medicine and nursing was not based on any rational or feasible likelihood that they could actually cure and restore but on an essentially maternal or religious idea. The Good Samaritan had no thought of nor did he actually care whether he could restore working capacity. He was merely motivated by the compassion in alleviating suffering. Bernal states that prior to the advent of scientific medicine, the physician's main function was to give hope to the patient and to relieve his relatives of responsibility. Gradually, in all civilized countries, medicine has moved away from this position, strangely enough in direct proportion to man's actual ability to perform feats that would have been plain miracles in days of old. . . . Physicians have become dangerously close to being mere technicians of rehabilitation.[20]

Stunning indeed, up against Alexander's heartfelt warning to the American medical community in 1949, is a 1977 *Villanova Law Review* article, which was printed in a spirit of critique of the "utilitarian" attitude and values redolent at the Commission on Human Subjects, which proffered the regulations on fetal experimentation to the secretary of HEW. The article was titled: "Cost-Benefit Ethics: The Utilitarian Approach to Fetal Research." It was written by Juliana Geran Pilon, then visiting Professor of Philosophy at California State College at Sonoma. Referring to the sheer amount of paper generated by the commission, Ms. Pilon said that it was worth plowing through, "for documents such as these have a way of reflecting the *zeitgeist*."[21] In her view, the *zeitgeist* prevalent in today's society is utilitarianism, and to that pragamatic index, she felt, the fetus was sacrificed once in abortion and again in fetal experimentation:

> A close examination [of the report] provides reasons for serious concern: the prevalent attitude . . . is that *wanted fetuses "as a class" should not be denied the fruits of research performed at the expense of unwanted fetuses.* Since the ominous moral implications of such a position were left virtually untouched in the few papers sympathetic to a more principled point of view, the result is a most

> disturbing document based on a "cost-benefit ethics" that openly defies traditional morality.

She then pursued some of the proponents of nontherapeutic fetal research who spoke or delivered papers at the commission. First she took on Maurice Mahoney, the Yale doctor who at the time was actively involved in live fetal research with his development of fetoscopy. "In effect, Dr. Mahoney suggests it is a privilege not only to benefit from such research but also to be actively involved in it as a participant."

She then took on Dr. Marc Lappé and Rev. Joseph Fletcher:

> Dr. Marc Lappé echoes this belief but first he defines the utilitarian equation at stake: The "costs" of doing fetal research are to be counterbalanced by the good resulting from such research. When the fetus involved in research is an abortus . . . the ultimate fate of the research subject is *death.* Therefore, the beneficiaries of such research are not "fetuses as a class" but fetuses minus the already-doomed research subjects. The doomed fetuses, however, are presumably still better off for having served science. . . .
>
> Rev. Joseph F. Fletcher . . . simply suggests that legislation on fetal research is merely a matter of the greatest good for the greatest number.

Ms. Pilon came closest to Dr. Alexander's warning of twenty-seven years earlier, when the shadow of Nazism was longer and more penetrating, when she looked at the permissions granted by the final regulations for many different kinds and degrees of nontherapeutic fetal experimentation. Referring to the oft-stated clause that "important biomedical knowledge" be the required trade-off for entering the fetal subject into experimentation, she said:

> But what is "important" medical knowledge? Important to whom? To the experimenter on a lucrative grant? To "future generations"? To the wanted babies? To the "racially pure"? As for the condition that such medical knowledge be unavailable "by alternate means," this conceivably could justify nontherapeutic research on any selected group of people, since no other group, by experimental defini-

tion, could provide the knowledge (whether this be the terminally ill, the mentally ill, the diabetic, etc).

Just as Alexander's words had a definitely ominous touch as to the drift of the medical profession, as to those first signs of giving in, so did Pilon close her paper with a black curtain:

> In conclusion, the utilitarian bias evident in the papers presented to the Commission has infiltrated the recommendations of the Commission, at the expense of a principled ethical stand. Judging from the arguments involved here and their implications, the worst is yet to come.

In 1977, experimentation on the fetus meant the current, controversial use of the aborted baby. Today, experimentation has sponsored two major new trends. The first one is the prospective use of live fetal organs from aborted babies for transplants. The second is the use of prenatal diagnostic techniques founded by fetal experimentation and aimed, under the guise of helping parents to have normal children, at aborting the defective. As Alexander said, and as both of these trends exemplify, the physician has chosen to become a technician, armed with spare parts (and munificent grants), or in the case of prenatal diagnostic techniques, with an overload of gadgetry that in the end can be used to sponsor the abortion of a fetus found to bear some greater or lesser defect.

As much of fetal experimentation is based on the utility of the research profession's (and the public's) notion that any and all means must be invoked to produce "cures" for disease and imperfection, we must go back to Alexander's search for the early warning signs of deterioration of the medical profession's classic task. He felt that he was seeing the medical profession, even in 1949, responding to incurable illness with an attitude of hostility:

> The essentially [utilitarian] rational attitude has led [the medical profession] to make certain distinctions in the handling of acute and chronic diseases. The patient with the latter carries an obvious stigma as the one less likely to be fully rehabilitated for social usefulness. In an increasingly utilitarian society these patients are being looked down upon with increasing definiteness as unwanted ballast. A certain amount of rather open contempt for the people who cannot be

> rehabilitated with present knowledge has developed. This is probably due to a good deal of unconscious hostility, because these people for whom there seem to be no effective remedies have become a threat to newly acquired delusions of omnipotence. . . . From the attitude of easing patients with chronic diseases away from the doors of the best types of treatment facilities available to the actual dispatching of such patients to killing centers is a long but nevertheless logical step. Resources for the so-called incurable patient have recently become practically unavailable.[22]

Alexander blamed the rise of this aversion to the incurably ill to a shortage of funds put forth by society and the state rather than on the medical profession itself. Yet he of course noticed that the medical profession had heeled too easily to the scarcity by accommodating itself in 1949 to a certain amount of "hostility" to the incurably ill. Today, in this respect, things are somewhat drumming to a different, but not essentially so, beat.

Today, the research profession within the medical profession has latched upon transplants and spare parts procedures to undercut the fact that cures cannot be found at this point for diabetes, for paralysis, or for heart and organ failure. Rather than only continue to search for authentic cures, they have turned also to the human fetal subject, with its special live qualities, to shore up that inability to "cure." Have they, in so doing and without consulting the public, overstepped their bounds and their classical duties? They may now offer a pancreas transplant or a brain tissue, they may be able to save society the sight and cost of persons bearing defects or debilitating diseases, but have they not also given society a moral burden to bear in that the source of these measures, which are not at all cures, is a fellow human being? Has the medical research profession taken the decision to hide behind the plurality of American society, making our traditional diversity of opinion on controversial subjects the shield over the fact that they are obsessed with gadgetry and that this obsession is founded on a feeling not of humility but of arrogance and omnipotence?

If fetal experimentation does not fit into the medical profession's classic presentation of itself to the public, why is this phenomenon not known beyond the gates wherein it has been raised to a lucrative and ongoing enactment? If fetal experimentation of the nontherapeutic stripe is classic cohesion to the Hippocratic tradition of "do no harm," if it is neither taboo nor forbidden game, why is there such an effort to construct a rationale for it that includes a bizarre insistence that the fetus undergoing abortion has a further responsibility to medical progress, or what passes for it? Can the medical research profession say that it is eager to stand before the public with its log of the use of fetal bodies, that it is ready for the television cameras to come into their laboratories where live fetuses may be aborted, left to die, packed (while alive and moving) in ice for further use, or, if dead, then packed when freshly dead to allow the culling, mincing, storing and handing out of the remains? Wasn't it only recently that an anti-smoking ad showing a *plastic* fetus with a cigarette dangling in its mouth (as a symbol for the mal-effects of the mother's smoking) was turned down as too shocking by two of the major networks?

Finally, it is ironic in the extreme that a backup man to the research profession's eagerness for live fetal tissues and organs spoke clearly on the physician's departure from his traditional role. When Upjohn Pharmaceuticals was deluged with letters to have its new abortion drug, Prostin F2 Alpha, taken off the market because it often produced live abortions, W.N. Hubbard, then Vice-President and General Manager of Upjohn, related the company's view. Hubbard was to write the brief on abandonment of the Hippocratic tradition by doctors and their new subscription to utilitarianism, often masked as "quality of life." "If we are to have each human life fulfill its potential, then we will have to reduce [the] discrepancy between productivity and consumptive demand . . . *For the first time, the medical profession is involved in the inhibtion of life, and here we look to the most effective and convenient means* . . . [italics added]."[23] Hubbard, at least, was frank. He was also inaccurate on two counts: First of all, as a matter of history, it was not the first time that the medical profession killed its patients. Second of all, in the case of the medical researcher scanning the horizon for live or freshly dead fetuses, Hubbard refused to look in the face the fact that what he called "the fatal inhibition" of life, by means of the abortion agent his firm produces, requires some fetuses to go through a live sequence and by all accounts of science, one painful and degrading, before death.

The Abandonment of the Fetus by the Law

When a researcher performs any kind of nontherapeutic experimentation on a fetus up for abortion at any stage of development it is not at all a measure of the researcher's scientific creativity or acumen. It reflects, rather, his or her belief that the fetus abandoned to abortion holds no claim on the researcher for protection. The researcher, in so doing, leans with all of his weight on the

Supreme Court abandonment of fetal rights in favor of the "constitutional right of privacy" of the mother.

What the researcher inherits in the act of nontherapeutic experimentation on the fetus is his own share in the legal abandonment of the fetus by the law.

The rude beginning of nonprotection of the fetus occurred in Rome, where the father as *pater familias* held the despot's position, able at will to order an abortion for his wife or to order any other measure. From this point on, however, Western civilization began to improve the prospects for the unborn child.

By 1798, the fetus was ensconced as a member of society with fairly elaborate rights. In that year, in the case *Thellusson v. Wooford,* attorney J. Buller replied to the contention that the fetus is a nonentity:

> Let us see, what this non-entity can do. He may be vouched in a recovery . . . He may be an executor. He may take under the Statute of Distributions. . . . He may have an injunction; and he may have a guardian. . . . Why should not children *en ventre sa mere* [in the womb] be considered generally as in existence? They are entitled to all the privileges of other persons.[24]

Almost two hundred years later, the fetus was still protected by constitionality, *even if the parents died.* In 1938, in *Industrial Trust Co. v. Wilson,* a Rhode Island court held that a posthumous child could begin to share in the proceeds of her father's trust upon his death rather than upon her own subsequent date of birth.[25] A New York surrogate court said in 1941: "It has been the uniform and unvarying decision of all common law courts . . . that a child en ventre sa mere is 'born' and 'alive' for all purposes for his benefit."[26]

At the turn of the eighteenth century, there was some movement abroad in the law to make "quickening" the criterion for a felony that caused "the miscarriage of any woman." This mirrored the viability standard of *Roe v. Wade* as a basis for providing protection to the fetus in the limited range of viability indicating a potential life. But in 1887 physicians themselves moved to make the courts widen the felony charge to include anyone attempting to abort a woman's baby at any stage of pregnancy. The medical profession came forward with compelling medical proof that the fetus at any age has life. Said Isaac M. Quimby in the *Journal of the American Medical Association,* "This fallacious idea that there is no life until quickening takes place has been the foundation of, and formed the basis of, and has been the excuse to ease or appease the guilty conscience which has led to the destruction of thousands of human lives."[27] Not only did protection of the fetus against abortion at any stage become a regular feature of most law, but statutes were enacted carrying criminal penalties for parents who did not support even their unborn children. Thus, for instance, a father could be convicted of not giving adequate support to an in-utero child.

One of the most revelatory historical facts surrounding abortion and the women's movement of today and its position on birth control is the work of Margaret Sanger, famous for her advancement of birth control in this century. Initially, one of her main reasons for promoting contraception was to end abortion. To women who used abortion as birth control, she made it clear that she had no sympathy for that solution to unwanted children. In *My Fight for Birth Control,* she wrote, "Birth control does not mean [to them] what it means to us. To them it has meant the most barbaric methods. It has meant the killing of babies—infanticide—abortions—in one crude way or another."[28] (Sanger eventually embraced abortion.)

Another advocate of contraception at that time was Dr. William J. Robinson, who wrote in *Birth Control or The Limitation of Offspring by Prevenception* (1929), "I can truthfully say that one of the principal reasons, one of the strongest motives that makes us advocate contraception so persistently and assiduously is because we want to do away with the evil of abortion as far as we can; for we do consider abortion a terrible evil."

There is also the point that parents are not at liberty to bring harm to their children. In their article "Constitutional Balance" in *The Morality of Abortion,* John Noonan and David Louisell wrote[29]:

> Over a period of about 2500 years there has been built up a defense by the state in behalf of children, born and unborn, against the aggressive and the proprietary instincts of their progenitors. The problem of the "battered child" today is evidence, if evidence is needed, that the state must still by law restrain the freedom of conduct of parents. . . . The statutes on abortion [before the Supreme Court decision overturning them] prevent the mother from treating the child in her womb as "her thing."

Noonan and Louisell did not overlook the fact that the new "constitutional right" of the mother to take the life of her fetus is connected to a woman's right to self-determination. But Noonan rejected this by pointing out that the claim that a woman is free to destroy the being whom she has conceived voluntarily having sexual intercourse makes sense only if that being can be regarded as part of herself, a part which she may discard for her own good. But at this point the evolution of social doctrine favoring freedom for women encounters the growth of scientific knowledge and recognition of the fetus as a living person within the womb. Noonan and Louisell used the fairly familiar case of the supercedence of the court decision that required a blood transfusion for a child with Jehovah's Witness parents on the grounds that "The state as *parens patriae* will not allow a parent to abandon a child . . . The mother had a responsibility to the community to care for her infant."[30] Obviously, the Supreme Court decision on abortion seems to have tried to evade all of the foregoing status of the fetus under the law by begging to the fact that they could not postulate when life begins and so set it at viability, and legal personhood upon birth. This was aimed, perhaps, at not letting go free all of the kinds of things that Noonan and Louisell cited as real and historical pertaining to protection of the fetus under the law regardless of gestational age.

Noonan also invoked A.W. Liley, the discoverer of the real, autonomous world of the fetus, with individual organs and blood, and whose placenta, despite popular belief that it is part of the mother, is actually secreted by the fetus. "Within his watery world (where we have been able to observe him in his natural state through a sort of closed circuit x-ray television set), he is quite beautiful, perfect in his fashion, active and graceful. He is neither a quiescent vegetable nor a witless tadpole . . . but rather a tiny human being, as independent as though he were lying in a crib with a blanket wrapped around him instead of his mother." Added Noonan, "The medical developments confirm the soundness of the law in terming the fetus as a being with rights not dependent upon his parents."[31]

Also quoted by Noonan was Ashley Montagu, who has emphasized that the prenatal experiences of a child are indeed unique and critical: "The nine months spent by the individual in the womb are fundamental. It is during these nine prenatal months that the individual's foundations are well and truly laid—or not. To an extent rather more profound than had hitherto been expected, the individual's prenatal past influences his post-natal future."[32]

Today the law is in a push-me, pull-you state over fetal rights. Despite the Supreme Court's sweeping negation of the "meaningful" life of a fetus, and of its personhood until birth, the fetus has been making a comeback. For instance, in Canada, women who drink excessively during pregnancy, causing their babies to be born with fetal alcohol syndrome, which permanently skews the facial features and causes brain damage, are liable under the law. The temporary addiction to methadone in fetuses born of mothers taking that drug is also covered as prenatal child abuse under that law. New child welfare acts in Ontario and British Columbia now define a child as under a certain age, such as sixteen, rather than from birth on. Therefore, the fetus, while not explicitly given rights as a person, is included in the description of "child" and so moves directly into the ken of the law.

Additional moves to protect fetuses in utero include a few random but significant cases. In Baltimore, a doctor sought, in a juvenile court order, to have a woman who was seven months pregnant stop taking all nonprescription drugs. A North Carolina industrial plant banned all women of childbearing age from certain jobs under a "fetal vulnerability" policy. (This could be a "fake" fetal protection policy to legitimize discrimination against women, but it might be authentic.) In Maryland, a man sought a court order to prevent his estranged wife from having an abortion; he argued that the abortion would violate the state's child abuse law.

The fact that the fetus is not recognized under the law has dire consequences for wanted fetuses. As Margaret W. Shaw, of the University of Texas Health Center at Houston, wrote in 1976 in "The Potential Plaintiff,"[33] "It is well established in American law that a fetus is not a "person" in the constitutional sense . . . states are under no legal obligation to provide welfare funds or food stamps for fetuses (although they may, if they wish, increase the benefits of a pregnant woman)." As we are sadly aware, the infant mortality rate of the United States is far above that of many other Western nations. That even the wanted fetus is not a person under the law points out clearly that in order to accommodate abortion on demand as flowing from nonpersonhood of the fetus means leaving all fetuses abandoned by what is supposed to be our hard-won tradition of protecting the weak and feeding the poor.

Although *Roe v. Wade* centered on the legal nonpersonhood of the fetus, in practice it seems that the *wanted* fetus is given patient status and protection in some cases. Consider the following report: "Selective Birth in Twin Pregnancy With Discordancy for Down's Syndrome." It was written by Drs. T.D. Kerenyi and U. Chitkara, of the Division of Perinatology, Dept. of Obstetrics and Gynecology, Mt. Sinai School of Medicine, and published in the *New England Journal of Medicine,* June 18, 1981.

First, a few facts. Amniocentesis performed to determine the state of the fetus is problematical when there are twins. In some reported cases, learning that one twin was normal and the other bearing some defect, parents elected to continue the pregnancy for the sake of the normal child, accepting as well the abnormal one. Kerenyi and Chitkara, in their work, decided on another alternative, based on the decision of the parents. From their article:

> Presented with the diagnosis of carrying one normal and one affected fetus, the parents were confronted with the difficult task of making one of two decisions: to induce abortion and lose both fetuses, or to continue the pregnancy. The mother desperately wanted to have the normal child but could not face the burden of caring for an abnormal child for the rest of her life.

The mother's obstetrician made her aware of a report from Sweden in which a twin with a defect was killed in the womb at birth in order to allow the birth of the normal child. The mother, upon deciding that this would be the course she would take, was then referred to the two Mt. Sinai specialists.

Kerenyi and Chitkara first drew off amniotic fluid from the sac containing the unwanted twin; then they used a needle to puncture the heart and draw out the blood, causing cardiac arrest. An ultrasound scan confirmed that movement and heartbeat had ceased, and chromosomal analysis of the blood confirmed that they had indeed killed the right twin.

Twenty weeks later the mother gave birth to a normal baby and a shriveled twin.

This incident, which would be bizarre in any climate except the one we have today, prompts this question: can a fetus be at once a patient and a nonperson? After all, the wanted fetus was *treated;* but how can one treat a nonperson? When Kenneth Edelin suppressed an infant in the womb because it did not die in the abortion process, a Superior Court overturned his conviction by a jury on the grounds that since the fetus is a nonperson under the law until birth (separation from the mother) Edelin had committed no crime on any "person."

What is most ironic is that it has been doctors such as the ones mentioned above, with no antipathy toward killing one patient and delivering another, who are themselves muddying the waters of 'nonpersonhood' by treating some fet-

sues in the womb. The most far-reaching case of raising this severe contradiction occurred in 1983, when doctors began to perform fetal surgery.

Two doctors famous for nontherapeutic fetal experimentation led the way. The ground broken may, in fact, force the law to reestablish the fetus as a person, not by virtue of any moral standard, but because of what medicine can and does do for a fetus in utero. Drs. Mitchell C. Golbus and Robert Erickson were the first doctors to perform fetal surgery at the University of California. Ten years earlier, these same two doctors performed live trials for amniocentesis on fetuses to be aborted. Golbus and Erickson were also among the first to report the possibility of getting live fetuses for research using Prostin F2 Alpha. Golbus was also the beneficiary of a grant from the National Institute of Child Health and Development to do more experimental trials on chorion villus sampling (cvs), an earlier test than amniocentesis, the "virtue" of which is that it enables diagnosis and abortion of a defective child early in pregnancy.

After determining that a fetus in utero had hydroencephaly (a sac of fluid attached to the brain), Golbus and Erickson were able to insert a shunt to drain off the fluid. This, of course, was therapeutic for that fetus. Even though a fetus may survive with other defects that are less life-threatening than hydroencephaly, this was a positive act of surgery and even a positive form of fetal experimentation; the therapeutic thrust of it made the quantum difference.

When Drs. Golbus and Erickson performed this feat, this question immediately arose: can the fetus be a patient if he is not a person? Dr. John C. Fletcher, an ethicist at the National Institute of Health, even tried to suggest that prenatal surgery be abandoned because it could endanger the legality of abortion. Fletcher frankly told this writer that he is for abortion of the defective, which is strange because he has been one of the most eloquent exposers of the parental psychological tragedies that often follow prenatal diagnosis and eugenic abortion.

Not only did Golbus perform the shunt operation, he also wrote a book, *The Unborn Patient*,[34] published with a grant from the Kroc Foundation, which had also financed work on "management of the fetus with a correctable defect." This sounds very much like a retraction of the scheme of things that routinely proceeds from negative prenatal diagnosis to selective abortion. But Dr. Golbus was simultaneously involved in the cvs trials. Cvs leads to selective abortion or, in the case of hydrocephaly and only two other congenital defects, to fetal surgery.

Yet, that very book has been used as evidence that the fetus is indeed a person. *The Unborn Patient,* although hypocrisy of the highest sort, is also eloquent in its defense of the fetus as a patient.

First, in the foreword, the coauthors conceded that amniocentesis was *not* the best of all solutions. Those who have defended amniocentesis against its pro-life critics may now blush to see that some of its very inventors now disparage it, at least while they are promoting fetal surgery:

> . . . rapid advances in amniotic fluid analyses, ultrasonic imaging, and fetoscopy have meant that diagnostic procedures have flourished in a *therapeutic vacuum* [emphasis added]. As a consequence, antenatal diagnosis has acquired in the minds of some the sinister image of a "search and destroy" mission.
>
> *However on the positive side,* around the world a few score investigators and teams with a *positive commitment to fetal survival and welfare* are attempting fetal therapy as the *logical* sequel to fetal diagnosis [all emphases added].[35]

Moving on in this veritable conversion experience, we go to Part III of the book. At its beginning is a stunning quote by Richard Seltzer from *Mortal Lessons.* It is a quote, by the way, with others from literature, that his writer has often seen in right-to-life literature:

> And who would care to imagine that from a moist and dark commencement months before there would ripen the cluster and globule, the sprout and pouch of man?
>
> And who would care to imagine that trapped within the laked pearl and the dowry of yoke would lie the earliest stuff of dreams and memory?
>
> Is it a persona carried here as well as a person. I think it is a signed piece, engraved with a hieroglyph of human genes.[37]

Today, these doctors, who have been party to who knows how many selective abortions and who defended those as humane and in service of helping people to have normal children, now espouse as their mentor Dr. A.W. Liley, who did *only* therapeutic fetal experimentation in his lifetime, through the medium of amniotic fluid, which these doctors subverted into providing information for selective abortion.

Perhaps, after all, the fetus has rebelled. In the cult movie *If,* the oppressed schoolboys looked into the jar holding a caught and unborn fetus, a symbol to them of their own caughtness, and used that fetus to spur their own rebellion. Maybe these doctors, like Dr. Nathanson before them, are finally beginning to respond to the ancient and deepseated call of their profession's tradition to aid unborn life. If their conversion is part hypocrisy today, perhaps it will be authentic soon.

The fetal surgery they pioneered has already affected the law. In 1981 a man who wanted his wife to abort became incensed when she wouldn't. He thrust his hand into her vagina and pushed upward, severing the uterine wall, causing the baby to pass into her abdominal cavity. The baby died, and Robert Hollis was indicted for first-degree assault against his wife and for first-degree murder of the fetus. The state attorney sought the death penalty.

The state attorney general actually used *Roe v. Wade* in his attempt to convict Hollis, begging to the decision's idea of state interest in the life of a fetus approaching viability. Although the judge sympathized, he ruled for Hollis on the grounds that the existence of laws permitting abortions meant that fetuses not born were not "persons" and therefore Hollis had killed "no one." However, an appeals court reinstated the case and this judge reasoned that because *science can now diagnose and treat the fetus in the womb,* even before being close to viability, the traditional requirement that a fetal homicide victim be proven viable was now outmoded. In a September 1984 *Ms.* magazine article, "The Fetus and the Law—Whose Life Is It Anyway?" Janet Gallagher, herself an attorney, wrote of this incident: "Kentucky feminists worried that the case might cause confusion and undermine women's right to legal abortion, but disentangling this from the public outrage over the brutal and horrifying assault on a pregnant woman seemed an impossible task."

Eventually the Kentucky Supreme Court reversed the appellate court's conviction of Hollis for murder of the fetus and upheld only the conviction for first-degree assault on his wife. Although relieved, Ms. Gallagher noticed that the case was extremely significant. "The Hollis case and others like it have created plausible, sympathetic openings for antiabortion forces to renew their insistence on legal fetal personhood." Ms. Gallagher did not seem to understand that it is what has transpired on the operating table and not in pro-life caucuses that may cancel the Supreme Court decision, which got where it was going because it denied the whole legacy of biological, legal and practical information on the fetus.

While this news of resurgence of fetal rights is potent, there is an opposite tide surging against the fetus, this time against the fetus with some measure of defect, from a serious one to an innocuous one. Very keen on keeping the fetus in the ranks of nonpersons are the outspoken geneticists and genetic counselors who make their living and cull their lucrative grants from eugenic abortion of the defective.

Some in this powerful, vociferous group would even like to see a woman prosecuted for child abuse if she brings a defective child into the world.

The tools they wield were forged from live nontherapeutic fetal experimentation, which enabled fetuses to be invaded by apparati, and the information gotten then used to get rid of them. This trend has its own set of rationales, procedures and economics. Proponents of eugenic abortion have also spent time and grant money to persuade the insurance industry to consider payment for prenatal diagnosis, leaning in turn on widespread availability of genetic screening services. The possible, futuristic result? That no woman, no couple, would be able to say they did not have both availability of and payment for genetic services. Conceivably, insurance might not be available in the event of birth of a defective child.

6

Extermination of the Handicapped Unborn

> In the extermination camps natural death was completely eliminated. There the lethal machines operated with absolute efficiency, leaving no uneconomical residues of life. There the venerable proposition, All men are mortal, had already become an understatement. If this proposition had been inscribed on the entrance gates to the gas chambers, instead of the usual misleading, "Shower Baths," it would have aroused jeers; and in this jeering laughter the voices of the victims would have joined in an infernal unison with the voices of their guards. For the truth contained in the old proposition was now more adequately expressed in a new proposition—"All men are exterminable."
>
> —Gunther Anders, "Reflections on the H Bomb" in *Man Alone*

One of the most startling and alarming results of fetal use and nontherapeutic live fetal experimentation is their intrinsic link to the rise of the twin forces of prenatal diagnosis and eugenic abortion of the afflicted unborn. Fetal skin biopsies and cell cultures were used to gain important genetic, cellular and metabolic information about the causes of a range of maladies. Once the causes of these "defects" were identified through biological and genetic investigation, live, unborn, to-be-aborted fetuses were then unsparingly used to develop the mechanical means to draw fetal cells out of the amnion, or blood from the fetus itself, thus introducing two powerful prenatal diagnostic techniques: amniocentesis and fetoscopy. (In some instances, cell culture and prenatal diagnosis have been used to learn treatment techniques for an affliction, but, as those closest to the work admit, most birth defects are as yet unable to be eliminated or even ameliorated through treatment of any kind.)

Development of prenatal diagnostic techniques required nontherapeutic invasion of the fetal body. All of this private information, and all of the ruthless practice of devices aimed at abortion for "fetal indications" was then turned on afflicted fetuses as a class by the promotion of eugenic abortion. One of the most familiar, encouraging arguments for nontherapeutic fetal experimentation was that it would "benefit fetuses as a class."

Present eugenic abortion is not limited to the most severely afflicted, say, those who would die in the first year of life because of their affliction, or perhaps those born without even a brain. Eugenic abortion is sanctioned for the whole gamut of afflictions: the mentally retarded in all degrees; the hemophiliac; the child with osteogenesis imperfecta; those with Tay-Sachs disease, which, unlike most of the above, results in death by four years of age; all types of mongolism; persons who have mixed sexuality; etc. Or, to put it another way, anything less than perfect is now apt to be named "defective." Dr. Kenneth Garver, of Magee–Women's Hospital, himself an example of the intrinsic confusion of the modern eugenicist, spoke to the fact that the word "defective" is indeed relative, and in the eyes of the beholder.

In a 1978 interview with reporter Kris Mamula of *The Steel City Star,* Garver said he hoped amniocentesis would not ever become a standard procedure for all pregnancies, rather than only for "high risk" ones. Said Garver, "This would indicate that our population is attuned against birth defects of any sort." In this remark, Garver, himself a genetic counselor, seemed to level the blame for genetic discrimination on the "population," with total disregard for the fact that his profession (one that is not even forced to undergo any licensing procedure) has brought genetic search-and-destroy missions to fruition and to public consumption. Garver washed his hands of the societal outcome of prenatal diagnosis and eugenic abortion through the handy rhetoric that the genetic counselor is neutral and that couples themselves make the final decisions. When asked which birth defects should be allowed in a society, Garver tried to evoke an image of himself as indulgent of a range of defects, but his customers as not always so, mindless of the reality that it is he who makes the means available, and who labors in the same hospital where the eugenic abortion will be performed. Said Garver, "To me, a cleft palate is not a serious abnormality but to a couple with a child with a cleft lip, it could be. I think there should be no lines drawn from the standpoint of any formal policy. Each couple has to make that decision."

Also, "each couple's decision" may be the result of very much noxious and obfuscating advertisement by the biomedical/genetic counseling cadre hotly involved in pushing eugenics today. These eugenicists, having learned from their forbears' excesses in the second and third decades of this century, are subtle. They do not speak of getting rid of anyone—not in public, anyway. Rather, they tout natural selection of the fittest via their new doctrine of aiding normal births, using advertising slogans redolent with democratic images. Thus the eye and the mind are focused on the healthy, happy birth; the critical faculties are dulled against realizing that the eugenics machinery has taken a private stand against the "defective" and wishes to spread that consciousness among us all. The eugenicists' rhetoric is especially heavy on "individual decision" and "voluntarism." In the aura of the democratic camaraderie inspired by these phrases, what is unrevealed is that the most relentless and merciless among them are working toward a goal for "no survivors." There is coercion in their agenda, brought about by deletion of their private opinions in their public brochures, in the deletion of important information, and by their working through mainstream institutions without full public realization of their goals.

Earlier in this century, eugenicists were stopped in the U.S. but were not stopped in essence. As Richard Doerflinger pointed out,[2] Hitler adopted the U.S. state eugenics laws as models for his own catacylsmic obsession with human perfection. Today, there is a relationship between the capturing of prenatal diagnosis into the stable of regular medical procedures and the rise and implementation of many opposites of the Hippocratic tradition—namely, eugenic abortion, infanticide, and euthansia.

Eugenics: is there any place for it in a civilized society, given that a society is judged successful on how it treats its weakest members? Is eugenics ever and always not the same dirty little pseudoscience that codifies what is properly human and what is not, that begs to a misbegotten notion of humanitarianism in executing the afflicted under some compassionate, twisted title? Can eugenics ever be anything but what it is, whether backed up, as today, by biology and not by purely social Darwinist "theories," although these burrow today beneath the science?

It might be instructive to draw back the curtain of time for a moment in order to ask if the eugenicists of today are not still that misguided and dangerous gang who sit, as they did yesterday, elite and outrageously protected by their medical and scientific credentials?

In 1915, as Germaine Greer recorded in *Sex and Destiny,* there was an outpouring of philanthropic zeal, not unlike the concern for human suffering we hear often phrased by eugenicists today. In that year, she wrote, "the *Medical Review of Reviews* selected men from the bottom strata of life, gave each a banner to carry, and directed them to parade in the crowded districts of the city . . . [with] these large-lettered warnings:

> I am a burden to myself and the state.
> Should I be allowed to propagate?
> I have no opportunity to educate or
> feed my children. They may become criminals.
> Would the prisons and asylums be filled
> if my kind had no children?
> I cannot read this sign.
> By what right have I children?
> Are you willing to have me
> Bring children into the world?"[3]

Has anything changed?

Prenatal diagnosis and a platform of "no survivors": The 1960's and 70's

No sooner was prenatal diagnosis routinized than it was assigned to a program of "no survivors" for the chronically and incurably ill in the womb. One typical example of this "no survivor" mentality is the work of Dr. Henry L. Nadler. In 1968, Dr. Nadler, of Children's Memorial Hospital in Chicago, by "reading" cultured amniotic fluid fetal cells, successfully diagnosed Down's Syndrome in the womb at ten weeks. This was done with fetuses scheduled for abortion. In 1969, Nadler was given a $28,600 grant by the March of Dimes to "find a safe and simple method of amniocentesis."[4] The MOD also held a hope for widening the reach of amniocentesis: Nadler would be searching in the amnion fetal cells for the cause of cystic fibrosis, whose victims live till their early twenties, and may accomplish, despite their afflictions, very much.

The year before Nadler got this grant, he betook himself to an institution for the retarded, Dixon State School, in Illinois where, supported by state and federal funds, he took "skin biopsies from five mongoloid children, 11 children with 18-trisomy syndrome, and four children with D_1 trisomy syndrome."[5] These he compared with skin biopsies from ten normal children done in 1955.

We see in Nadler's experiment the pattern for cracking prenatal diagnosis, one that would become the model: First comes the invasion of the most private genetic material of the afflicted, either from live, in-utero subjects or the living afflicted in society. This private information is used to crack the codes that indicate their malady. Next, through technological "pioneering," the researcher prevents the births of many more afflicted by reading their private genetic information in the amniotic sac surrounding them in utero. This particular wing of science, under the general permission of abortion, has managed to introduce the invasion of genetic privacy without any semblance of a public debate.

By May 12, 1970, Nadler was able to make a stab at preventing the births of children like those in the state institution. He had used their skin biopsies well and in a way maliciously insulting to them. (Did he mention to any of them that, via his research, persons like themselves need not ever be born?) His report on 155 high-risk pregnancies being introduced to amniocentesis appeared on that date in the *New England Journal of Medicine.*[6] (The term "high risk" is one introduced by the medical profession and used to introduce pregnant women to their unlucky status if they are above a certain age, a bearer of a previously afflicted child, etc.)

Nadler wrote his report in the usual language of beneficence. He said that amniocentesis represents a veritable miracle performed by doctors like himself, one that enables couples to have only *normal* offspring. Thus, amniocentesis/ selective abortion becomes positive rather than negative, associated by the researcher with "cure" rather than with eugenic execution of the unfit (in terms of the Hippocratic tradition, killing the patient). Nadler's report, one of the first, showed two things clearly: propagandization of eugenic abortion to the medical profession itself and to the public by using language that disguises its true and basic act; and a policy of "no survivors."

The body count proportionately surpasses that of even the worst tallies of such outrages as the bombing of Dresden. In Nadler's group of 155 "high risk" pregnancies, fourteen were found to be afflicted with various maladies. It might be well to let Nadler's body count[7] settle in on the reader:

Of those suspected for Down's Syndrome (who are trainable and/or educable and have a lifespan to the mid-thirties or beyond), seven were so afflicted and fifteen found to be normal; all seven of the afflicted in this group were aborted. Those at risk for maternal age formed a group of eighty-two. Two were found to be carrying infants with Down's and these babies were aborted. Mothers with previous trisomic Down's syndrome provided eighteen "high risk" pregnancies. One with Down's was found and *not* aborted. So far, one survivor.

Then there are those in the 155 at risk for other diseases. Mothers carrying x-linked recessive disorders numbered seven. In 1970, when Nadler was doing this trial, x-linked diseases could not yet be prenatally diagnosed. However, at the time, amniocentesis could determine the sex of the child. Therefore, where x (male) children were found among the seven "at risk" for x-linked disorders, they were summarily aborted, simply in order to skirt the chance that the child might be affected. (Nadler did not log whether, upon post-abortion examination, these were found to be normal.)

Next came the eight mothers at risk for Pompe's disease. One fetus was found to be affected and was aborted. The list proceeds for others at risk for more diseases; all found to be afflicted were aborted. This means that in Nadler's trials, out of fourteen found to be afflicted all but one were aborted.

By 1972, a eugenics movement in the United States, founded on nontherapeutic experimentation on fetuses in order to establish the methodology and to ascertain the biological or genetic origin of many diseases, was firmly underway. That year, also, pronouncements were already being made. For instance, the National Foundation/March of Dimes and the American Genetics Association sponsored a Symposium on "Advances in Human Genetics and Their Impact on Society." The proceedings were to become Vol. VIII, No. 4 of the *MOD Birth Defects—Original Article Series,* which, in its aggregate, is a compendium of eugenics' most current opinion and agenda.

Dr. Digamber A. Borgaonkar of Johns Hopkins University School of Medicine made the critical point at the symposium that parents are the "sole authority" over the in-utero child. By placing the whole power over the child's destiny in the hands of the parents, Dr. Borgaonkar launched the idea of the "neutrality" of both science and the attending doctor and/or genetic counselor. He wondered why there is controversy "when a couple, after obtaining *proper advice*, choose not to carry on with their unborn child [emphasis added]."[8] Prof. Arthur Dyck of Harvard commented on the notion of "neutrality":

> The assumption that the use and application of amniocentesis is a neutral sphere for physicians and society pre-supposes that for physicians and society, abortion is not a moral issue, and that existing or

> future laws do or will assure that abortions are decided solely by families and physicians. To go that way is not morally neutral . . . if both physician and society should be impartial regarding the use of amniocentesis to prevent diseases by eliminating the diseased, what advocate is left for defenseless life?[9]

In light of Professor Dyck's comment, Dr. Borgaonkar's paen to "neutrality" takes on the color of a propagandistic remark designed to suggest and to hope, upon that suggestion being repeated, that this will be the public and professional belief.

At the symposium, one of the strongest eugenic statements came from Dr. Kurt Hirschhorn, a longtime grantee of the MOD, who was one of the first to define a living, previable survivor of abortion as "a piece of tissue." Hirschhorn, a Mt. Sinai School of Medicine researcher, reviewed the fact that positive eugenics proponent Herman J. Meuller promoted the goal of a human genetic study registry and service for planned breeding of optimum stocks. Hirschhorn also noted that others have favored negative eugenics, which prohibits, sometimes by law, reproduction by those who are considered genetically defective. After reviewing these well-known lines of battle, Hirschhorn cast his own die on the table: "Our currently changing attitudes about practicing negative eugenics by means of intelligent selection for therapeutic abortion must be encouraged. Basic to this change is a more accurate definition of a living human being . . . "[10]

In 1973, '74 and '75, more evidence that eugenics was again burgeoning came from a variety of sources.

At the Fourth International Conference on Birth Defects, held in Vienna in May 1973, supported by a grant from the U.S. Public Health Service, Arno G. Motulsky, of the Division of Medical Genetics, University of Washington School of Medicine in Seattle, delivered his paper "Brave New World?—Ethical issues in prevention, treatment, and research of human birth defects." In retrospect, it was both definitive and prophetic[11]:

First, Dr. Motulsky linked today's investigators to the "management of birth defects" legitimately associated with true science, which he assured us will bring only good. "Research and methods of management of birth defects are intimately tied up with modern biological techniques which according to the 'gloom and doom' prognosticators . . . will lead to the 'Brave New World.'" Motulsky went on to note that the majority of his colleagues are free of the doubts that assail these detractors: "Most researchers in the biomedical sciences and practitioners of medicine have been less pessimistic than many of our confreres in the humanities, social sciences and theology."

Then Motulsky said that the rest of his remarks reflected his own beliefs; yet, he seemed to invoke the majority of his colleagues as having beliefs concordant with his own when he said, "Most of us are philosophic utilitarians, i.e. we want to do the most good for the largest number. We want this goal achieved by consensus rather than by edict and value individual freedom of action." Then Motulsky inserted a sociobiological, behavioristic doubt: "How free we really are, however, is not entirely clear. Data from such diametrically opposed ways of viewing behavior, such as behavioral genetics and Skinnerian psychology . . . question our cherished beliefs of freedom of action." Motulsky had confidence that today's "thinkers" in behavioral genetics and Skinnerian psychology would eventually be able to solve the riddle of his free or limitedly free will. "Considerably more work in human neurobiology, neurogenetics and psychology will be required to settle how fixed our choices really are."

After revealing his dubious mentors and his complete confidence in "science" as the fount of truth, Motulsky moved on to genetic disorders *per se.* He was against worrying too much about the fact that those who are being treated for genetic disorders today will pass them on to their progeny, saying he thought there would be no dysgenic effect on the gene pool and that society would cope. He was a little less indulgent as he moved down the scale to those who are afflicted by ailments that have no complete treatment, such as spina bifida. Motulsky noted that at that time, 1974, spina bifida could not be diagnosed prenatally. He recognized that the triage system—performing spine-closing operations on the least affected cases only—was not satisfactory. Finally, he looked to prenatal diagnosis of spina bifida as a way out of the dilemma: "Hopefully this present state of affairs may be only temporary. Means of diagnosing spina bifida and related disorders *in utero* or even by blood tests on the mother carrying an affected fetus are becoming available." Here, then, we find one of the first pre-announcements of prenatal diagnosis/eugenic abortion as a "solution" to semitreatable illness.

While those committed to the idea that all life is sacrosanct and that man indeed does possess free will might find Dr. Motulsky loathsome, he considered himself a far cry from the "radicals" in the field, whose position he stated in order to part company from it:

> The most serious ethical problem raised by widespread abortion for birth defects is an argument made privately by some physicians and publicly by Crick . . . and Watson . . . The reasoning goes as follows: Why go to all the trouble of doing complicated expensive and possibly harmful intrauterine tests, if inspection and diagnostic tests at birth would be much easier? If a serious birth defect is diagnosed, the infant could be terminated at that time. . . .
>
> I consider infanticide for medical purposes a regressive and loathsome act which officially sanctions the blunting of human sensitivities which already exists in modern societies.

(It should be pointed out that Thomas Crick, one of the discoverers of DNA, held a nonresident-fellow status at the Salk Institute in California, founded and sustained by the National Foundation/March of Dimes.)

Eugenic abortion as a solution to the problem of treatment for spina bifida was heralded one year later in an editorial in *Lancet,* May 11, 1974, titled "Towards the Prevention of Spina Bifida." The editorial stated: "The procedure is therefore applied only to pregnant women at high risk of bearing fetuses with neural-tube malformations or genetic disorders of various kinds. Were prenatal diagnosis to be restricted to this group, we could hope to reduce the birth prevalence of spina bifida by only 10% or less." But, according to the editorial, widening the scope of prenatal screening beyond simply high-risk mothers would bring the diagnosis and eugenic abortion ratio to twelve out of fifteen anencephalic victims and ten out of seventeen open spina bifida ones, a count that the *Lancet* writer found "more encouraging."

In 1974, Dr. Aubrey Milunsky, another grantee of the March of Dimes, advanced one of the most fastidious and merciless briefs for getting rid of those with Down's Syndrome, one of the most frequently targeted groups of the afflicted. Milunsky, a recognized leader of the proponents of abortion of the defective, was akin to the eugenicists of 1920's vintage in the U.S. in that he has sought most actively to influence the social and political climate to accommodate eugenics through law. Dick Leavitt of the information office of the MOD told this writer that the foundation no longer funds Milunsky because of his strong opinions; however, the foundation has not publicly denounced him.

So in 1974, Milunsky delivered his now-famous cost-benefit analysis of amniocentesis, *The Prenatal Diagnosis of Hereditary Disorders,*[12] to the Commission on Human Subjects which met that year to make recommendations for future federal fetal research guidelines.

Although a geneticist by profession, Milunsky donned an actuary's cap. He calculated that "the birth of 7,667 chromosomally defective offspring in one year could ultimately cost society in excess of 2 billion dollars—about thirty-two times the cost of prevention through prenatal diagnosis and therapeutic abortion. . . .In twenty years of present costs . . . this will have grown to about *40 billion dollars.*" Amniocentesis and eugenic abortion for the 7,667 babies then born to the 400,000 mothers over 35 in the U.S. would come to $63.3 million, Milunsky reported. Notice that Milunsky was counting on implementing eugenic abortion for *all* of the defective offspring.

Spurred by a mostly uncontested climate in favor of selective abortion via the newly developed amniocentesis, more researchers forged ahead to develop even more tests for more inborn errors. In 1975, Maurice Mahoney and John Hobbins at Boston City Hospital developed fetoscopy, and used live, to-be-aborted fetuses to harness the mechanics. They also performed the abortions themselves. Earlier, with the blowup over the March of Dimes grant to Peter J. Adam for the live experiments done at the University of Helsinki, the MOD announced that it would cut off grants to practitioners of live fetal experimentation. But when he developed fetoscopy via live nontherapeutic fetal experimentation in 1975, Mahoney held a research grant for an enzyme investigation from the MOD, and later sat on one of its advisory boards. Also, in 1975, in Washington, D.C., the Commission on Human Subjects at the NIH was denouncing any researcher's involvement in the timing or procedure of an abortion connected with any experiments.

What amniocentesis did for chromosomal afflictions, fetoscopy did for disorders of the blood and x-linked maladies, despite the fact that fetoscopy, then and now, carries an 11% risk of causing injury or death of the fetus.

With fetoscopy, sickle-cell anemia, which attacks mostly blacks, can be prenatally read. Not only were high-risk pregnant mothers screened for carrying an infant with sickle-cell anemia, but a program was mounted by HEW to screen the black population at large. Finally, Caspar Weinberger, then Secretary of HEW, was sued by the National Welfare Rights Organization et al. for instituting the mandatory sickle-cell screening program. The charge was no less than genocide. Germaine Greer said of fetoscopy:

> Negative eugenics is not dead: it lingers in the corridors of the

health establishment, emerging in swift guerilla raids on the Hippocratic tradition. It draws off blood from the fetal cord and assesses it for a multitude of rare disorders, some of which, like phenylketonuria, are much less damaging if treated in the newborn, and others, like sickle cell trait, are asymptomatic and untreatable. The baby's permission was not asked, nor was its parents'.[13]

Of carrier screening, she continued:

What can it profit a child to know he is a sickle cell carrier? Will his life be any more manageable if he only dates girls after they have had a blood test? The instrumentality for eugenic measures already exists under the statute that allows states to demand a blood test as a condition for receiving a marriage license. For that too we have the eugenicists to thank. The blood was meant to be submitted to the Wassermann test for syphilis; in law it can be tested for anything at all and any use may be made of the information. . . . It is now less likely than ever that any move will be made to strike it down.[14]

As Greer intimated, the new eugenics, despite its new tie to biology, bears vestigial traces of the old. In fact, the ability of today's eugenicists to lean on science, rather than on social theory, makes eugenics even more dangerous.

It is interesting to note that many of the diseases researchers targeted early on for prenatal diagnosis are those associated with minorities: Tay-Sachs, which afflicts mainly the Ashkenazi Jewish population; thalassemia, which affects Mediterraneans; and sickle-cell, which affects blacks. As the old eugenics was built on the "inferiority" of exactly these groups, we must ask, despite the overlay of biological fact, if there may not be either a conscious or unconscious racism at play. For instance, James Stine in *Biosocial Genetics* quoted Dr. Paul Wolf of Stanford and Sen. John Tunney (CA), who quipped that had sickle-cell anemia been a white disease, a cure for it would have been found long ago. Obviously, society cannot be too careful about genocidal imperatives nestled in the "neutral" medical programs that come our way.

In 1974, when Mitchell C. Golbus of the University of California was working on amniocentesis, the March of Dimes gave him the grant to set up a fetal tissue and organ bank. In 1976 he published the results of a long run of trials meant to ascertain whether the prenatal diagnosis was accurate, verifying his diagnoses by examining fetuses after abortion, and noted that prostaglandin abortion yields the freshest bodies for tests. Years later, the MOD would not say that the tissues and organs used in the grant for a bank were those derived from the bodies of the abortions done for eugenic reasons via his amniocentesis trials. Calls to Dr. Golbus yielded no response. If the "banks" were made possible by the abortion of the afflicted, then a definitely new appearance of biological Darwinism was in evidence. For Golbus said that the use of prostaglandin abortion to check the prenatal diagnosis would make it possible to harvest fresh organs and tissues for many things, including transplant research. Thus, the bodies of the defective, though deemed unfit or too imperfect to survive, sponsored research for the sick, who might ultimately be served by the newest, most dramatic showpiece of medicine: transplantation.

So, by the mid-1970's eugenic abortion had found its practitioners, sponsors and tools. All that remained was expansion. But before profiling its expansion, let us look into any objections to the burgeoning eugenics.

Opponents of Eugenics: Articulate but Few

Criticism of prenatal diagnosis/eugenic abortion as well as exposure of prenatal diagnosis' reliance upon live fetal experimentation is neither copious nor influential. However, the criticism is often poignant and biting, and totally conscious of the eugenic proportions of what passes for "neutral" prenatal counselling. One such critic, a powerful man himself in science, Dr. Leon Kass, went on record in Desmond Zwar's provocative book *New Frontiers in Medical Research.*[15] Kass, executive secretary of the Committee of Life Sciences and Social Policy, National Research Council, at the National Academy of Sciences, reflected on his luck: "I was conceived after antibiotics, yet before amniocentesis, late enough to have benefited from medicine's ability to prevent and control fatal infectious diseases, yet early enough to have escaped from medicine's ability to prevent me from living to suffer from my genetic diseases. To be sure, my genetic vices are, as far as I know them, rather modest . . . myopia, asthma and other allergies, bilateral forefoot adduction, bowleggedness, loquaciousness, and pessimism, plus some four to eight as yet undiagnosed lethal genes in the heterozygous condition—but, taken together, and if diagnosable prenatally, I might never have made it. . . ."[16]

He also saw clearly the weird and portentous interplay of social history:

> It is ironic that we should acquire the power to detect and eliminate the genetically unequal at a time when we have finally succeeded in removing much of the stigma and disgrace previously attached to victims of congenital illness, in providing them with improved care and support, and in preventing, by means of education, feelings of guilt on the part of their parents. One might even wonder whether the development of amniocentesis and prenatal diagnosis may represent a backlash against these same humanitarian and egalitarian tendencies in the practice of medicine, which, by helping to sustain to the age of reproduction persons with genetic disease, has itself contributed to the increasing incidence of genetic disease, and with it, to increased pressure for genetic screening, genetic counseling, and genetic abortion.[17]

Finally, Kass broached the question that has haunted our epoch since the development of the atomic bomb: should science pick and choose what it develops? But the question, although it seems to have answered itself in our time, should continue to be asked, as Kass himself did:

> The moral question of what decision and why "does not disappear simply because the decision is left in the hands of each pregnant woman. . . . We physicians and scientists especially should refuse to finesse the moral question of genetic abortion and its implications and to take refuge behind the issue, 'who decides?' For it is we who are responsible for choosing to develop the technology of prenatal diagnosis, for informing and promoting this technology among the public, and for the actual counseling of patients."[18]

Kass expressed his belief that widespread prenatal diagnosis coupled with eugenic abortion already sponsored the phenomenon of children suing their parents for "wrongful life" because the children were permitted to escape eugenic abortion. Cases thus far brought before the courts here have failed to reap monetary damages on the grounds that the court has no way to compare the life of the survivor to not being born at all. However, Kass pointed out that in Germany the courts have already awarded damages to plaintiffs in these suits. What sponsors such bitterness on the part of a person whose parents may have chosen the traditional value of the sacredness of every life? Kass reflected:

> A child with Down's syndrome or with hemophilia or with muscular dystrophy born at a time when most of his (potential) fellow sufferers were destroyed prenatally is liable to be looked upon by the community as one unfit to be alive, as a second-class (or even lower) human type. He may be seen as a person who need not have been, and who would not have been if only someone had gotten to him in time.
>
> The parents of such children are likely also to treat them differently, especially if the mother would have wished but failed to get an amniocentesis because of ignorance, poverty or distance from the testing station . . . In such cases, parents are especially likely to resent the child. They may be disinclined to give it the kind of care they might have before the advent of amniocentesis and genetic abortion, rationalizing that a second-class specimen is not entitled to first-class treatment. . . [19]

Kass's statement is of absolute importance. It points out, especially to foundations such as the March of Dimes, the largest "pusher" of genetic screening in the U.S. today, that their rhetoric of being "neutral" on abortion, and of working toward cures for genetic disease, cannot absolve itself of the hydralike social rise of a consciousness about genetic inferiority that has been directly sponsored by prenatal diagnosis/eugenic abortion "options." "Options" have a way of becoming the standard. T.V. was once an option, as were radio, telephone, etc. For nations, nuclear arms were also optional at the start. Now, these are personal, social and political commonplaces. But the March of Dimes, with its poster children and its past success, especially with polio vaccine, insulate it from becoming a target of debate on the rise of eugenics in the U.S.

Prenatal diagnosis and eugenic abortion also embody the danger of eliminating the constitutional mandate of equality of all citizens, or at least of setting up a double standard. Kass told of a Maryland case. Parents of a Down's Syndrome infant refused to allow surgery on the child for an intestinal obstruction present at birth. The physicians and hospital sought an injunction against the parents' decision. Kass wrote, "The judge ruled in favor of the parents, despite what I understand to be the weight of precedent to the contrary, on the grounds that the child was a mongoloid, that is, had the child been 'normal' the decision would have gone the other way. Although the decision was not appealed to and hence not affirmed by a higher court, we can see through the prism of this case the possibility that the new powers of human genetics will strip the blindfold from the lady of justice and will make official the dangerous doctrine that some men are more equal than others."[20]

Kass also pointed out the distinction between individual feeling and the universality of human rights: "For what it is worth, I confess to feeling more than a little sympathy with parents who choose abortions for severe genetic defect. Nevertheless . . . in seeking for reasons to justify this practice, I can find none that are in themselves fully satisfactory and none that do not simultaneously justify the killing of 'defective' infants, children and adults."[21]

Finally, Kass said that in 1983 the rubrics of prenatal diagnosis/eugenic abortion were already being extrapolated beyond biological indications:

> But once the principle, 'Defective should not be born,' is established, grounds other than cytological and biochemical may very well be sought. Even ignoring racialists and others equally misguided—of course, they cannot be ignored—we should know that there are social scientists, for example, who believe that one can predict with a high degree of accuracy how a child will turn out from a careful, systematic study of the socioeconomic and psychodynamic environment into which he is born and in which he grows up. They might press for the prevention of sociopsychological disease, even of 'criminality,' by means of prenatal environmental diagnosis and abortion. I have heard that a crude, unscientific form of eliminating potential 'phenotypic defectives' is already being practiced in some cities, in that submission to abortion is already being made a condition of the receipt of welfare payments. 'Defectives should not be born' is a principle without limits. We can ill afford to have it established.[22]

Kass has scientific credentials. Others who do not have often fared badly in attacking the eugenicists. Randy Engel, pro-life activist and journalist, for her documented and continually unafraid attack on the March of Dimes, has been treated as though she is the only objector. Fr. Edward Bryce, of the Catholic Bishops' Pro-Life Committee, recommended that Ms. Engel "be sued for libel" for her vigorous attack on the MOD, when hers is not at all the only one to date. Her material is composed exactly of Kass' concerns, except that she has chosen a target. Finally, Fr. Bryce, very far from Kass' point of view, chose to deflect rational criticism of amniocentesis by saying that it "is not evil in itself." This seems to be a facile and even puerile response to the legal and social evidence that gathers and mounts up daily on the outcome of this "safe and simple" test, as it was first described by the MOD in Nadler's developmental, ground-breaking grant. By Kass' assessment, amniocentesis and other prenatal diagnostic techniques, when coupled with eugenic abortion, may become a spiral that could reach out for any of us and our neighbors.

Nat Hentoff, a preeminent civil libertarian and journalist, in the March 1985 *Atlantic Monthly,* described how the University of Oklahoma Health Services Center ran a five-year experiment on newborn infants with spina bifida. A team of physicians, nurses, physical and occupational therapists, a social worker and a psychologist "decided, in each case, whether to recommend 'active vigorous treatment' or to inform the parents that they did not consider them obligated to have the baby treated . . . "[23] Hentoff, his prose showing appropriate moral courage, explained how the decision was made on each infant. "To determine which infants were to be given death tickets, the medical team relied in substantial part on a 'quality of life' formula: QL = NE x (H+S).

"QL is the quality of life the child is likely to have if he is allowed to live. NE is the child's natural endowment (physical and intellectual). H is the contribution the child can expect from his home and family. S is the probable contribution to that handicapped child from society."[24]

Hentoff noted that an infant loses part of his chance for survival "if his parents are on the lower rungs of poverty. If, moreover, he is poor and has been born during the Reagan Administration—which prefers missiles to funding for the handicapped—the baby has been hit with a double whammy."

Hentoff reported that a civil rights lawyer, Martin Gerry, investigated this classically eugenic Oklahoma "experiment." He found that parents were not told about the quality-of-life formula, that is, they were led to believe that whether their baby received treatment or not was solely based on medical criteria.

This brings us to the subject of eugenic coercion (and therefore, unconstitutionality and illegality) by members of the medical profession and their sponsors, who see their thought and activity as not coercion at all, but evocations of humanitarianism, logic, justice (especially for the poor), and patented ethics.

The corridors through which the eugenicists course are redolent with a ripening agenda, which would finally reorder perception and law to fit their plans. Some quotes from the 1978 March of Dimes–sponsored *Birth Defects* reveal that by then a full house of prenatal diagnostic techniques was in hand,

and eugenic zeal was at a high due to the 1976 passage of the Genetic Diseases Act. The latter mandated publicly funded genetic screening, a dream come true for eugenics proponents.

Anne Harrison-Clark, lobbyist for the MOD, showed that the MOD and eugenicists at large will no doubt use current social and environmental problems as a tool to expand their own agendas.

Ms. Harrison-Clark said[25] that the MOD supported the Genetic Diseases Act, which, under the term "voluntarism," sanctions eugenic abortion. (Due to its non-profit status, the MOD may not lobby for legislation that is pro-abortion.) The semantic key is "voluntarism," as the act did not mandate abortion for genetic diseases, only screening.

This writer asked Ms. Harrison-Clark whether the MOD had ever spoken out against corporate poisoning of Americans; I asked her because I'd noticed that the 1983-84 grant list included many grants for investigating environmental and workplace causes of birth defects. Their emphasis at the MOD on this subject seemed to complement a 1984 *New York Times* article, which stated that, since 1954, birth defects in the U.S. have *doubled*, mainly because of workplace and environmental attacks on citizens' genes. My thought behind the question to Ms. Harrison-Clark was that MOD investigators' work might cause the MOD to present evidence at hearings conducted on the effects of these mountingly dangerous conditions.

Instead of testimony, the MOD had taken a stand by supporting the Genetic Diseases Act, which puts the burden for corporate poisoning on the victimized family and the fetus by ensconcing prenatal screening and possible eugenic abortion as the "solution" to this monstrous problem. Ms. Harrison-Clark also informed me of protests from scientists and the EPA to the *New York Times* that the article's figure was overdrawn. Ms. Harrison-Clark seemed to concur with that criticism.

Yet, we have something with which to compare MOD's response to the ever more endangered species we are becoming because of corporate irresponsibility's attack on our DNA, and so on future generations. Lois Marie Gibbs, then president of the Love Canal Homeowners Association, wrote the preface to *Who's Poisoning America—Corporate Polluters and Their Victims in the Chemical Age.*[26] She spoke, as a mother and an activist, of the infringement on their reproductive safety that the poisoning of Love Canal meant:

> The decisions we have had to make have changed too, from the

> normal concerns of every day life to: where can we move that's safe? Will my baby have leukemia? Will my daughter ever have a normal pregnancy, a normal baby? The fears and uncertainties of the past two years have created many stresses and anxieties.

However, Ms. Gibbs, unlike the MOD, did not see the solution as prenatal diagnosis/eugenic abortion to identify those who have been poisoned so that they need not be born. Ms. Gibbs was interested in stopping the cause:

> The only way we will avoid new Love Canals, and more disasters like those described . . . is if people force the government to implement laws requiring industry to properly dispose of their toxic wastes, which now pollute our land, air and water. Pressuring the government and the corporations to take these steps is the responsibility of all of us: taxpayers, consumers, victims.

Incidentally, the MOD has a special grant category for "Reproductive Hazards in the Workplace." Its grant list in this category for 1983-84 included forty-five separate grants representing hundreds of thousands of dollars, dealing with environmental contaminants, industrial contaminants, exposure to certain anesthesias, tobacco, the soil fumigant DBCP, the uranium that miners pull out of the earth, video display terminals, and much more. Certainly, the MOD could write a book of its own, one that, with the MOD's enormous credibility, could injure corporate America.

Instead, the MOD response is illustrated by a grant to Ronald D. Hood, Professor, Department of Biology at the University of Alabama. Dr. Hood received $10,000 for 1983-84 to "develop a quick, inexpensive screening test using fruit flies to identify agents that can cause embryonic maldevelopment."[27] The grant list included a grant to the Laboratory for Embryology at the University of Washington in Seattle to compile a directory for all known poisonous agents. This kind of measure would only be logical if it intended to attack the cause, rather than the result. Too, MOD's support of genetic screening and prenatal diagnosis as a response to corporate poisoning rather than any concerted, outraged testimony to the EPA or perhaps a resounding support for OSHA, raises the logical question: does not the merciless poisoning of Americans by a plethora of agents constitute a convenience for the MOD and other eugenics pushers to spread the practice of eugenic abortion, using public fear as a device for implementing their agenda?

There is more than one point of entry for the raising of eugenic consciousness. The environment is one, and sets the public wondering on issues ranging from sterilization to eugenic abortion as a 'natural' defense against assaults from the outside. Eugenic forces, however, do not confine their efforts to one theater. One of their most tenacious tentacles has been reaching into the special care nurseries of obstetrics departments in hospitals.

Nat Hentoff, in the *Atlantic* article cited earlier, told how *Newsweek* in 1973 wrote about the starving of untreatable, afflicted infants at Yale–New Haven Hospital in 1971, the news of which was first carried by a *New England Journal of Medicine* report in that year. Although titled "Moral and Ethical Dilemmas in the Special-Care Nursery," it revealed, from the perpetrators' own pens, that they had starved the infants. (Readers can see by the title of that article how these "scientists" have deftly learned to incorporate a veneer of debate into a *fait accompli.* At one point, *Newsweek* referred to the infants as "vegetables."

Sondra Diamond took issue both with the word used and with Drs. Duff and Campbell, the perpetrators, in a letter to *Newsweek:*

> I'll wager my entire root system and as much fertilizer as it would take to fill Yale University that you have never received a letter from a vegetable before this one, but, much as I resent the term, I must confess that I fit the description of a "vegetable" as defined in the article. . . .
>
> Due to severe brain damage incurred at birth, I am unable to dress myself, toilet myself, or write; my secretary is typing this letter. Many thousands of dollars had to be spent on my rehabilitation and education in order for me to reach my present professional status as a Counseling Psychologist. My parents were told, 35 years ago, that there was "little or no hope of achieving meaningful 'humanhood' for their daughter [afflicted with cerebral palsy]."
>
> Have I reached "humanhood"? Compared with Doctors Duff and Campbell, I believe I have surpassed it!
>
> Instead of changing the law to make it legal to weed out us "vegetables," let us change the laws so that we may receive quality medical

> care, education, and freedom to live as full and productive lives as our potentials allow.

Hentoff noted that in 1977, Ms. Diamond wrote an epilogue to her spirited objection to *Newsweek,* this time in *Human Life Review.* Wrote Hentoff: "She told of being taken to the hospital with third-degree burns over 60 percent of her body when she was in her early twenties. 'The doctors felt that there was no point in treating me because I was disabled anyway . . . They wanted to let me die. My parents, after a great deal of arguing, convinced the doctors that I was a junior in college and had been leading a normal life. However, they had to bring in pictures of me swimming and playing the piano.' "

It is interesting that Ms. Diamond, in her first letter to the world who never wrote to her, spoke about the law. That her interpretation of it and that of some of the mega-propagandists of eugenic abortion of the defective are diametrically opposed points out that the eugenicists have no use for Sondra Diamond and her kind.

Here, we must turn to Dr. Aubrey Milunsky, MB.B.Ch, C.P., D.C.H., of Harvard Medical School, Eunice Kennedy Shriver Center and Massachusetts General Hospital of Boston. In a book he edited from the proceedings of a symposium he held in 1978, called *Genetics and the Law II,*[28] Milunsky, mentioned earlier for his contribution of the cost/benefit analysis of amniocentesis vs. life for Down's Syndrome victims, went straight to the point:

> Notwithstanding the fact that prenatal diagnosis will never be able to approach all the recognizable genetic disorders known (over 2800 at the present time), the steadily growing list of conditions that are diagnosable will undoubtedly increase the public awareness of the opportunities for the prevention of fatal genetic disease or serious mental retardation. The dawning public realization of opportunities for prevention will inevitably, I believe, encourage the philosophy concerning the "right" to be born of sound mind and body.[29]

Milunsky was worried that the poor are underutilizing genetic screening, noting that it is most frequently used by middle- and upper-class clients. Milunsky was hoping, in his wish for what he called "justice" for the poor, that funds and mandatory screening would be forthcoming once the drain on public finances was more widely promulgated as the result of allowing the afflicted to be born. Thus, it is proper to conclude from the quote above and from the one following that Milunsky might also have had a class imperative—an old imperative at that—up his sleeve.

> Philosophically, genetic disease is clearly not a public health hazard. There is no need to worry about any contagious phenomenon. Legislative actions, however, may develop when public policy concerns reach into the fiscal arena and spawn taxpayer burdens.[30]

Milunsky believed that laws might be enacted to forbid the afflicted from being born. His analogy was society's growing "interest in both the number and the quality of children born—witness the family-planning clinics, court decisions ordering medical care of children against the wishes of their parents, laws on child abuse, etc. It is also an established public policy posture to minimize illness in the community—for example, compulsory vaccination for rubella or smallpox, fluoridation of water supplies . . . "[31]

Milunsky's hankering after legal coercion not to birth a defective child was expanded upon at the same symposium by Margery Shaw whose topic was "Preconception and Prenatal Torts."

Ms. Shaw noted that courts have not awarded damages to plaintiffs (allowed to be born with a defect) in their pleas for wrongful life. She saw two obstacles to legal acceptance of the "wrongful life" concept:

> There are two obstacles to a recognition of negligence actions against the parents of wrongful conception by genetically defective gametes, resulting in birth of an abnormal child. The first is the concept of "wrongful life" . . . This concept embodies the argument that an infant in wrongful life cases claims he should never have been born, which to some is a logical and legal absurdity but to me is perfectly valid reasoning. The second stumbling block is the public policy of favoring intrafamilial immunity. In order to preserve and promote family harmony, courts have been reluctant to allow spouses and children to sue each other. But intrafamilial immunity has been eroded in other settings, and some conditions may be burdensome enough to the defective infant and to society that the parental right to reproduce becomes instead a privilege to produce, insofar as possible, healthy infants.[32]

Pushing for mandatory prenatal screening as a prod to eugenic abortion, Ms. Shaw ended her talk by hoping that legislators would see the light:

> The fetus that is obliged by his parents and obstetricians to become a live-born infant should be protected by the state under the *parens patriae* doctrine. Courts have ordered blood transfusions to pregnant women who refused them, acting on behalf of both the mother and her fetus. States have required Rh and VD testing of pregnant women in the interests of the fetus. But courts and legislatures should not stop there. They should, through tort law and statutory law, take all reasonable steps to insure that fetuses destined to be born alive are not handicapped mentally and physically by the negligent acts or omissions of others. The pace [toward this] is quickening, and perhaps, when we meet for the Third Symposium on Genetics and the Law, we will see the gap closing between science and technology on the one hand and legal responses on the other.[33]

Ms. Shaw was sponsored for this work by a United States Public Health Service Medical Genetics Center grant.

By 1985, although no law had been enacted to make it a crime to bear a defective child, the expansionist agenda had gone forward. First was the effort, nearly complete, to substitute chorion villus sampling for amniocentesis. Although many critics assailed amniocentesis and subsequent eugenic abortion as assaults on many traditions, the biomedical/foundation support for it did not seem troubled. However, privately, the criticism seems to have taken root. The proponents of prenatal diagnosis/eugenic abortion merely searched the research horizon for a prenatal diagnosis method that would be out of reach, supposedly, to critics.

In 1982, at a symposium sponsored by the March of Dimes, in Birmingham, Alabama, John C. Fletcher, an ethicist, gave this report on the controversiality of amniocentesis:

> Critics of prenatal diagnosis believe that the most weighty objection is the option created for abortion of an affected fetus. Many moral reasons for the critique exist, but 2 themes predominate . . . 1) medicine's basic purpose—to save life—is violated by abortion, and 2) certain genotypes are set apart as deserving of abortion and

> thus treated unjustly or unequally. . . . Abortion is a ground for a serious objection to prenatal diagnosis, because it involves the termination of the pregnancy at a stage of development when it is difficult to distinguish a morally relevant difference between the affected fetus and a newborn with the same degree of handicap. Many commentators have wondered what the differences were, in the realm of moral reasoning, between the 2 states of early human existence.[34]

Fletcher, who told this writer he personally is for eugenic abortion of the defective, wrote an editorial after the dramatic shunt operations in-utero were performed on hydrocephalic victims that allowed them to survive. Fletcher suggested that these life-saving operations be weighed heavily, as they might influence legal moves to make the fetus a person and therefore shut down eugenic abortion (and all abortion?) Fletcher was very perceptive in his remarks. He saw that medicine's own strides were tearing down the semantic wall between the fetus and the newborn. A way to shore up the distance, making eugenic abortion safe from association with the possible growing impetus toward rights for second- and third-trimester fetuses, is to harness a technique for prenatal diagnosis that could be done early enough in pregnancy to avoid the association. He said, stressing the importance of the earliness of chorion villus sampling: "The 'turnaround time' for patients who now participate in prenatal diagnosis can be up to three weeks. Many difficulties, anxieties and problems could be helped by swifter methods of analysis. The use of automated methods will shorten the time now required for analysis of cultured cells."[35] And he concluded, "Early abortion (well before twenty weeks) is clearly more acceptable, in my view, than abortion at a stage when the fetus has a degree of brain function that implies sentience, a recognizable human body, countenance, and extensive movements."[36]

Fletcher's paper at the convention was followed by an amazing one on "Legal and Ethical Considerations" by Father R. C. Baumiller, a Jesuit from Georgetown who is also a March of Dimes grantee and a genetic counselor himself. His article in April 1983 *Hospital Practice*[37] revealed that parents counseled by him often request that the baby they have elected to abort be baptized. Baumiller also told of an Islamic couple who, the wife being over thirty-five and therefore susceptible to bearing a child afflicted with Down's Syndrome, sought him out because he was a priest/genetic counselor. The father did not want the amniocentesis done. Baumiller felt under pressure; he wrote,

"My personal beliefs and philosophy were to be used coercively against the wife. I felt this to be unfair and suggested that someone familiar with the Koran or with Moslem theology would be better able to answer their question. The discussion was settled by a Moslem obstetrician who told them that the procedure, which would have come late, was not reasonable since abortion could no longer be done according to Islamic law. A normal child was subsequently born."[38]

At any rate, Baumiller, at the 1983 conference on birth defects, revealed the depths of moral confusion that close association with eugenics can produce. In one paragraph, referring to early diagnosis, which the MOD has funded in research, Baumiller said: "I suppose denying life to something that appears less than human is easier to condone, but such denial is hardly based on firm philosophic principles."[39] So Fr. Baumiller recognized some absolutes. But he then mended any potentially broken fence between himself and his patrons: "Why has the shift to a granting of greater moral status to the fetus occurred? It has happened due to the work of groups such as are gathered at this meeting. It has happened because the March of Dimes Birth Defects Foundation has supported research and education."

Rather, it could be said that the MOD research and education on early human development has backfired onto their eugenic abortion component, as they do encourage both simultaneously. Baumiller did not see the move toward cvs as a "conscience free final solution that is for the time out of reach of *medical* objections."[40] Too, Baumiller was careful to dissociate himself from pro-life critics. He cited Dr. Margery Shaw's Human Life Symposium held in Houston the same year. It was "invaded" by a few protestors, about whom Fr. Baumiller said, "Outside of a few shrill out-of-place polemicists, the *invited* [emphasis added] scholars acted as just that, *scholars.*"[41]

Professional zeal and the elitism of the closed club of the eugenicists seem to deteriorate their critical faculties for understanding the objections to eugenics, and, as evidenced by Baumiller's dilemma, awards strange praise to the eugenicists in the MOD.

As eugenic abortion is again being sought via yet another prenatal diagnostic test, cvs, so again will the fetus to be aborted pay the human price of the test's development. All of the workups done on cvs equipment were performed on fetuses to be aborted, a point substantiated by the NIH, which funded only a study comparing the success rate of CVS with that of amniocentesis in diagnosing defects. This, said NIH ethicist John Fletcher, is because of the equality doctrine implicit in the federal regulations (but not written into them) that nothing be done on a fetus to be aborted that would not be done on one carried to term. However, as with all other prenatal diagnostic techniques, the fetus to be aborted is often used for "practice" by obstetricians wanting to learn the technique, the equality doctrine aside.

The next horizon for the eugenicists is cystic fibrosis. For many, many years researchers have been trying to understand what prenatal sign could denote a child with cystic fibrosis. The low level of a certain enzyme is now believed to be the indicator, and attempts at prenatal diagnosis are under way. A breakthrough in identifying cystic fibrosis could be a strong sign that eugenics is speeding up the "defects" ladder to include screening for and elimination of more and more "defective" children before birth.

Cystic fibrosis is a disease of the lungs. As early as 1976, science was concerned with the possibility of expunging it through eugenics. An international conference held at the Israel Academy of Sciences and Humanities that year in Jerusalem offered an early profile of the agenda. Curiously, there was at the conference a clear understanding that the lot of those with cystic fibrosis was steadily improving. Wrote C. R. Denning:

> The natural history of cystic fibrosis has changed considerably over the past 25 years. In 1955, 50% of CF patients were expected to live until 4 years of age; whereas in 1975, 50% of patients are expected to live to at least 17 years of age . . . Many factors have, no doubt, contributed to the increased life expectancy. Some of the more obvious ones include a better understanding of the pathophysiology of the disease and, therefore, more effective treatment methods, a concerted effort by the Cystic Fibrosis Foundation (CFF) to establish a network of specialized care, teaching and research centers throughout the U.S. . . . and a massive educational program also sponsored by the CFF.[42]

What would seem to be positive, however, turns quickly negative in the perspective of the writer, Ms. Denning, who saw in the longer life expectancy nothing but trouble.

> The experience gained from this has, however, demonstrated clearly that as the life span increases, so do the psychological and

> social problems of the patient and his family. At times they reach such severe proportions that the responsible physician may well ask himself if his comprehensive medical program, albeit successful, is too high a price to pay for the tremendous emotional upheaval it has produced in a given family. . . .[43]

This would obviously be true of many, many diseases that afflict individuals. Is not this type of reasoning about the results of the longer life span of CF victims equivalent to a red light and a prophecy? Science is such today that with the appropriate clues and zeal, diabetes' prenatal signs could be cracked, even perhaps some forms of cancer, blindness, etc.

Denning went on to speak of the denial of the results of stress by families, who, she said, practice denial in order to "sustain the beliefs and hopes required to live with such a disease." From there, Denning became downright malevolent, especially when some other testimony is held up against her remarks. "Denial enables the diseased person to live his life within the framework of the social reality of everyday life. This is done by acting normal, trying to be like everyone else. It appears to us that, for the most part, patients with CF try to be conventional and deny as much of their disease as possible."[44]

Here again, Denning's remarks must be carefully scrutinized. Beethoven, after becoming deaf, continued to compose, an almost superhuman adjustment to the deafness. Dr. Denning would conclude that, as with the CF victims making a play for whatever it is they *can* grasp, "The chronically ill will injure themselves, in physical reality, in an effort to achieve the anxiety-reducing social reality of being normal. Since there is no accepted established role, no way of participating in life as a chronically ill person, people in this position strive to be normal to enable themselves to escape both the wrath of the disease and of society."[45] This, in Dr. Denning's judgment, was not far from mental aberration. For families, she made the mental health comparison very strong: "The psychopathology associated with CF has often been enumerated—communication breakdown, overprotection by mothers, withdrawal of fathers, etc. While these phenomena are true, they are also the classic explanation for all pathology in mental health (e.g. schizophrenia, alcoholism, homosexuality.)"[46] But Denning did say that in CF victims' families, these symptoms lead not to mental illness but to a way of coping. Yet, she introduced a negative psychiatric profile of "coping."

After citing deleterious results of the longer lifespan of CF victims, Denning went on into deeper waters. She spoke of surveys indicating that "this group of people, living with increased stress, could be expected to have a higher rate of divorce than the general population."[47] Then there is the change in the families' view of their reproductivity. "After the birth of a CF child, families are forced to re-evaluate their entire future."[48] Denning's survey found that the 25% risk of bearing another child with CF influenced a full 54% of the families polled to restrict family size. But, 38 out of 103 families said that if the fetus could be identified in the womb for having CF, and they were able to abort, that they would, 39 said they could not, and 26 found the idea too hypothetical to try to answer at the time—not exactly a eugenic mandate.

In 1976, no scientific findings promoted any hope of prenatal diagnosis for CF. Before the 1985 finding that the lower enzyme content in amniotic fluid portents CF, already in 1983 there was, *in advance of the breakthrough,* a government plan for carrier and prenatal testing for CF. This was presented in "Screening and Counselling for Genetic Conditions" in February 1983, a report prepared by the President's Commission for the Study of Ethical Problems in Medicine and Biomedical and Behavioral Research. The National Institute of Health's *Research Highlights* bulletin was reprinted in this larger report.

In 1983, the focus was on carrier screening, that is, zeroing in on families known to carry CF. This, the report concluded, was a stopgap measure, but the only one available in lieu of a prenatal test. "The availability of a prenatal test would eliminate some of the difficulties that arise when only carrier testing is available; in the latter case, test results may be used to select mates or to decide whether to forego childbearing but not to determine the outcome of a particular pregnancy. . . . some potential sickle-cell screenees found that the availability of carrier screening without prenatal diagnosis was more harmful than helpful since they did not wish to make decisions based on carrier status alone."[49] The experience with the outcome of sickle-cell screening of carriers, namely the suit brought by the national Welfare Rights Organization against Caspar Weinberger in the mid-seventies, has made the government tread carefully with screening agendas, always injecting the rhetoric of voluntarism and neutrality. But the yen for the appearance of a prenatal (called *prospective*) test is obvious in the remarks quoted in the government report. These remarks came from Dr. Arno Motulsky, et al., and called again for the familiar "no survivors" policy:

> Under a scheme of prospective diagnosis, the case reduction is 100% (i.e. no cases with the disease are born), as opposed to the less

> effective reduction which can be achieved with retrospective diagnosis (i.e. following birth of an affected child). Considering only the economic aspects, the saving to society by not having to bear the high costs of supporting patients with cystic fibrosis for the relatively large number of years which they can now survive will probably be substantially greater than the continuing costs of the programs for premarital screening, for intrauterine diagnosis and for selective abortion once the use of automated devices is introduced.[50]

Adjunct to Motulsky's blunt remarks, the government writers were careful again to say that cost-benefit analysis, although a relevant consideration, should not be chosen over "the fundamental value of genetic screening and counselling [which] lies in its potential for providing individuals with information they consider beneficial for autonomous decision-making." However, as with fetal experimentation of the nontherapeutic sort, the question is whether or not even families have a right to expunge the life of a person known to be bearing a chronic illness that is nevertheless treatable up to a point. Although the government writers continually inject careful language that assures "autonomy," etc., this all takes place in a text that seems to point to prenatal diagnosis/eugenic abortion for CF when possible. The report recited beautifully all of the prospective woes that could arise from this plan, but the authors seemed to think that it should be up to families to take the test or not during a pregnancy at high risk for CF, and thus that it is not the job of either science or government to take either a pro- or anti-eugenic stand against prenatal diagnosis of CF.

By 1985, the iffy status of CF prenatal diagnosis was nearly settled. The definitive research identifying a lower content of the enzyme alkaline phosphate in amniotic fluid as an indicator of the presence of CF, said Ms. Sherry Keramidas,[51] Associate Medical Director of the CF Foundation in Rockville, MD, was done in Europe. Americans did try to crack it. For instance, Henry Nadler was given $108,000, a very large grant for the 1983 MOD grant list to try to find a prenatal diagnosis for CF. Keramidas said he "flopped." Although, said Ms. Keramidas, European studies do not absolutely establish that the test for the lower content of the enzyme does always yield an accurate prenatal diagnosis, the results of many studies were presented in 1985 to the American Society for Human Genetics. Many people who heard that review felt, she added, that clinical use of the test was now justified.

The CF Foundation keeps to a cautious position on the prenatal diagnosis of the disease it has done so much to ameliorate, if not cure. The CF Foundation used high-risk volunteers to undergo the test; but with the volunteers' consent, because of the experimental nature of the test, they did not reveal the results to them. Also, the CF Foundation has advised people not to terminate a pregnancy on the basis of the test, because the Foundation does not yet believe that the test is absolutely definitive.

On the other hand, the California branch of the Cystic Fibrosis Foundation cooperated with an MOD-funded UCLA School of Medicine team of M. Kaback, et al., in a study titled "Attitudes Towards Prenatal Diagnosis of Cystic Fibrosis Among Parents of Affected Children." The California Consortium of Cystic Fibrosis Centers holds a registry of CF victims and their families.

One of the main parts of the study concerned the reproductive plans of parents who had already had a CF child, and so, statistically, have a 25% risk of having another. 48% said that CF in their child caused them to change their family size; 11% were not sure, and 40% said no, the birth of a CF child had no effect on their family plans for more or fewer children. Of those who said that the CF victim born to them did influence their reproduction, 60% of these had no further children and many of these had gone the way of sterilization of one member of the couple. "Of all the parents responding, 78% felt that the development of prenatal diagnosis for CF would provide an important reproductive option for all or most families at risk for CF in their children. The report said that "a clear minority (8%) felt that it would be an important reproductive option for few or no families."[52] However, although this is high, another question related to their own cases yields a much more mixed, less clear result. "When asked if they would have changed their family plans IF PRENATAL DIAGNOSIS FOR CF HAD BEEN AVAILABLE WHEN THEY BECAME AWARE OF THEIR RISK, 129 of 408 parents responding (32%) indicated that their plans would definitely have been changed. Another 24% of respondents indicated uncertainty as to whether or not this would have changed their plans and 44% reported that this would not have influenced any further family planning."[53]

Ms. Keramidas told this writer[54] that very often parents with one CF child adjust best to having another. I asked Ms. Keramidas why the Kaback report did not include any data from the cystic fibrosis patients themselves, especially since many of them are teens and up to twenty-one years of age and perfectly capable for speaking for themselves. Ms. Keramidas said that the couples interviewed were all in the range of thirty-five years old (although up to forty), thus their children were too young to be quizzed. Keramidas said too that this would be most sensitive because one would basically be asking what the child thinks of a test that will prevent others like him or her from being born. Ms. Keramidas pointed out that the prenatal test would allow couples to have more children. This writer pointed out that the price of that gain is eugenic abortion. Ms. Keramidas conceded that this is so, and also admitted that the positive aspect of the family being able to have normal children is not ever expressed by pointing to the means as eugenic abortion. Finally, Ms. Keramidas said that the Cystic Fibrosis Foundation will not speak out against the prenatal test, nor will it support it. All it will do is make sure that labs doing the test are using good equipment and have a good reputation for the accurate culturing of fetal cells.

Let us assume that the studies done by Kaback et al. recently and that of Denning in 1976 prove that there is a market for this CF screening test, which in part there does seem to be. When recording the survey participants' acceptance of a prenatal test for any chronic and incurable disease, the researchers have not often, if ever, revealed to their subjects any of the horrific information on the psychic results of prenatal diagnosis and eugenic abortion. Nor have they included testimony from the disease victims themselves. This makes the studies both abstract and suspect of coercion toward a eugenic point of view. Nor do they report some of the known consequences of prenatal diagnosis/eugenic abortion.

John Fletcher, NIH ethicist, studied twenty-five couples of varying social and ethnic backgrounds. More than half had come for genetic counselling because of the previous birth of a defective child. The rest came because they were older, in the range of risk for bearing a child afflicted with Down's Syndrome. Fletcher found that the desire for a normal child coupled with a willingness to abort any defective offspring resulted in "moral suffering of the highest order."[55] What happened to those who were given a prenatal diagnosis of bearing a defective child wars heavily with the MOD's image of couples using, without consequences, eugenic abortion to have "normal" children in the future. Fletcher reported that in *his* sample all of those told of genetic abnormality opted for abortion. But, in addition, all of the volunteers then asked for and received sterilization! This concurrence of events Fletcher called the appearance of "cosmic guilt," which he said afflicts those who know there is something wrong with their genes.[56]

What also happened after the prenatal diagnosis and eugenic abortion within the family of these people is akin to Greek tragedy. Fletcher found a transformation in the relationships of the parents with their living children, both those who were normal and those who were genetically defective. One parent said Fletcher, reported this: "One day it hit me. What is Johnny going to think about us now? Is he going to wonder, 'What would mommy and daddy have done if something had been wrong with *me*?'" Other parents reported similar aftermaths. Fletcher concurred that the relationship between the parents and children was permanently altered, and referred to philosopher/psychologist Erik Erikson's concept of "basic trust."[57]

Richard Restak correctly related this disturbance of basic trust as one that will pass from the family into society, and spoke of "The Era of the Nonperson," meaning a second-class citizenship, or even "nonpersonship" for those who slip through the net of eugenic abortion.

Not a less disturbing point of information emanating from the halls of the genetic profession itself, and rarely passed on to clients showing up for prenatal diagnosis, is that many families being counselled about defects they carry or about the malformation or disease of a particular child in utero do not really understand what they are being told. One limited example: Charles R. Shaw, a psychiatrist, in an article titled "The Psychiatrist in the Genetics Clinic," cited two workers, Sibinga and Friedman, who "found that there was no correlation between education levels of children with PKU [phenylketonuria] and their understanding or distortion of information concerning the disorder and its etiology. They found that less than 20% of parents had an adequate comprehension of basic facts about PKU, and this was the result of emotional resistance rather than intellectual ability."[59]

What would happen, too, if prospective clients of prenatal screening and/or genetic counselling were informed, as a kind of consumer right to know, that the genetic counselors are not the neutral creatures they advertise themselves to be? One example of a genetic counselor wearing the mask of neutrality is Nancy S. Wexler, who revealed her eugenic biases in a paper titled "Will the Circle Be Unbroken? Sterilizing the Genetically Impaired."[60]

She opened with a story carried by the *Miami Herald* in 1979 about a British couple who wanted their children to be sterilized because the mother, a Mrs. Gooch, suffered from a hereditary disease and could foresee her children passing it on. Wexler commented: "Some recoil in horror, in vicarious identification with the young children who will be altered irrevocably at an early age. . . . But is our horror only sentimentality? . . . Perhaps we should all become Mrs. Gooches, weighing, evaluating, mini-Mengeles dispatching some to the sterilization tables and others into the world of procreation . . . .To entertain the notion of sterilizing all the genetically impaired is to contemplate the end of civilization."

So far so good. Wexler at least was not for the Final Solution. But she was for a partial one. "Eugenic intervention is limited to those in whom one of the 4 to 10 deleterious genes that we carry has had the bad grace to become obvious. But what do we really mean when we speak of the sterilization of the genetically impaired? Certainly we mean the actual process of sterilizing people with reproductive capabilities. But sterilization can also be considered as a metaphor for the eugenic ideal—the systematic elimination of hereditary defects. For some disorders that are detectable prenatally, sterilization is obviously unnecessary, unless a couple refuses to avail themselves of screening, amniocentesis or abortion."

It becomes clear, through the clarity of Wexler's words, that amniocentesis and selective abortion are being used as proxies for the even more controversial issue of sterilization. Wexler went on to explain more clearly how genetic counselors who are eugenicists can look forward to a rising tide of eugenics without the Hitlerian overtones. "Greater sophistication in our understanding of genetic transmission and an eyewitness observation of Hitler's Hereditary Health Laws has tarnished the popularity of eugenics. There are a number of pressures at work today, however, that could bring eugenic considerations back into the limelight."

She went on to name these as the economic pressures of health care delivery. "From the White House to the mayor's office, conservation of dwindling resources is the watchword. Eugenicists ask, 'Shouldn't these precious resources be reserved for those most able to use them?'"

Next, there is the capability to prenatally diagnose more inborn disorders. She envisioned ever more simple and safe methods that will take the "risk" out of prenatal testing: "Imagine being able to walk into a doctor's office and be screened with a simple blood test for a whole host of blighting diseases that could cripple or kill your children. What enormous freedom and what dread responsibility!"

Then there are the wrongful birth suits to discourage parents from bearing an impaired child. But Wexler found litigation against parent by child "saddening." She concluded that the techniques of the genetic counselor can substitute for policies of force by a eugenically minded state and for the courts: " . . . genetic counselors must be as fully informed as possible about the burden of the hereditary disease involved [for any couple at risk]. . . . The counselor has the unique task of representing not only the best interests of the client but also, ideally, those of any future children the client might have. . . . Counselors must have the courage to push prospective parents to consider the reality of traumatic possibilities, to help them imagine how they would feel if the baby were born with a hereditary defect."

It is not difficult to see that Wexler herself saw hereditary disorders as horrendous occurrences. We are supposed to believe that she was governed by compassion. But can we be sure that she was not guided by revulsion? Was her version of informing not tantamount to frightening clients into a feeling that bringing an afflicted child into the world is a form of cruelty on their part and represents a lifetime of misery for the child?

Nor are those entering the advertised neutrality of genetic services told of the "ethical" master, whose thought pervades that of many of those practicing in that area today, especially those who hold to eugenic philosophies: Joseph Fletcher. One cannot open a symposium report without his thoughts being present in bold relief. Just one example from a crowded field of his works is "Knowledge, Risk and the Right to Reproduce." In this article, contained in *Genetics and the Law II,* he wrote, "Since the United Nations has designated 1979 as the Year of the Child, my thought is that if child abuse is part of its concern we ought to recognize that children are often abused preconceptively and prenatally—not only by mothers drinking alcohol, smoking, and using drugs nonmedically but also by their *knowingly* passing on or risking passing on genetic diseases. There are more Typhoid Marys carrying genetic diseases than infectious diseases.

"Another phrase that needs reexamination is 'communicable disease.' Given what we now know, it is tunnel vision, nothing else, to go on thinking of communicable diseases solely in terms of the infectious and not the genetic diseases."

Fletcher asserted that he is on record for the limitation of reproductive rights and in this essay he again rehearsed and recited his philosophic reasoning behind that opinion. "The relativity of rights is as clear in jurisprudence as it is in ethics. Both work by the principle of equity and 'general justification.' If reproductive partners are informed they both carry a dread disease such as Tay-Sachs or cystic fibrosis, yet even so conceive with the intention of bringing every conceptus to birth, their supposed right to reproduce becomes ethically invalid. This is why there is no constitutional right in the law to have children.

This is why the Supreme Court declared that 'neither rights of parenthood nor rights of religion are beyond limitation.' . . .

"Coercive or compulsory control is justified when people refuse to abide by humane standards of reproduction—first as a protection of society's well-being, and second, to prevent harm to potentially misbegotten children. When we limit the freedom of such reproducers, they can conceive again; conceptuses are fungible. When their gonads dysfunction, such persons can resort to alternative modes of parenting with donated gametes, as in artificial insemination . . . Like everything else we do, baby making is subject to the requirements of justice."

Although Fletcher and his like-minded colleagues have conjured up a public holding on to backward absolutes, there is evidence that the public is more than a little suspicious of the scientific community. In *Man Alone: Alienation in Modern Society,* editors Mary and Eric Josephson wrote in their introduction to the section "Science and War":

> The technology which produces machines . . . is but the offspring of a science which, as it developed the means to transform our planet or destroy it, has become ever more remote from the lives of ordinary citizens and perhaps the ultimate factor in their alienation. *To such citizens science appears magical and mysterious in its capacity for and neutrality toward good or evil* [emphasis added].[61]

Society has, in part, become fearful that science, in its harnessing of such knowledge as is contained in both the atom and in DNA, is taking on a creatorial role. Gunther Anders, in "Reflections on the H Bomb," also in *Man Alone,* wrote:

> . . . during the short period of our supremacy the gulf separating us Titans from the men of yesterday has become so wide that the latter are beginning to seem alien to us . . . .Faust strove desperately to be a Titan; his torment is caused by his inability to transcend his finitude. We, who are no longer finite, cannot even share this torment in our imagination.[62]

Why should society go easily into the realm of eugenics, when eugenics may indeed portent the acceptance of euthanasia? In fact, in 1973, just such a portentous article appeared in the *San Diego Law Review.*[63] Tom Riggs noted that *Roe v. Wade* spoke of a protectible fetus in terms of a "'meaningful life.' It seems equally controversial whether a life of pain, with an expectation of an agonizing death, or a life of unbearable mental torment is 'meaningful.' It would appear that a legislative purpose of protecting such a life would be as 'irrational' as was the legislative decision to protect all fetal life irregardless of its stage of development. . . . By the *Wade* analysis, it appears likely that state interference with voluntary euthanasia or suicide is an impermissible violation of the right to privacy."

Obviously, the words 'meaningful life' made the rise of prenatal diagnosis/eugenic abortion easy and actually undebatable, for if the normal fetus is not 'meaningful' life, how much less so the afflicted one? But shouldn't the introduction of *eugenics,* at any stage of life, prompt a public debate? It is probable that eugenic activity was simply well-shielded by the abortion permission at large.

The private debate of scientists is often disheartening. A symposium led by Dr. Joe Leigh Simpson was reported in *Contemporary Ob/Gyn,* Vol. 2, No. 4. One of the participants was Dr. Kurt Hirschhorn, whom we quoted earlier as saying: "Our currently changing attitudes about practicing negative eugenics by means of intelligent selection for therapeutic abortion must be encouraged. Basic to this change is a more accurate definition of a living human being . . . "

In this symposium, Hirschhorn said that he disagreed with moderator Simpson's statement that "It's certainly not unreasonable for society to consider requiring that the development of the phenotype [defect] be prevented."

Hirschhorn replied, "I think that society should not presume to make such important decisions for individual families."

Dr. Harmon L. Smith, a professor of moral theology at the Divinity School of Duke University, seemed to see clearly what was happening. He commented, "The curious paradox Dr. Hirschhorn is speaking about is that we are rapidly acquiring the capabilities to deprive future generations of the very values that helped to bring us such knowledge and power. If you start monkeying around with discrimination against certain phenotypes, you change the very shape of the social matrix. This seems to me an awful big chew to bite off."

Hirschhorn, in a move to skirt the bio/medical profession's willingness to do what Dr. Smith had just described, tried to shift the matrix of danger away from his own set, saying, "The danger is in the fact that the government is getting more and more into genetics. If we recall the eugenics experiments in the 1930s and 1940s in Nazi Germany, we see how dangerous government control of genetics can become." Hirschhorn said that by allowing only families to decide, the danger of repeating the situation in Nazi Germany would be avoided. But by whom is the family guided if not by eugenicists wearing the helping masks of obstetricians, genetic counselors, etc.? These professionals want eugenics promoted under the veil of voluntarism rather than heralded by the red flag of public policy—probably because public policy would be clearer and bring reprisals and shutdowns.

The German medical profession in the 1920's, before Hitler's rise to power, was practicing execution of the defective, which they considered to be merciful, but which was ideologically informed by a little book called *The Useless Eaters,* a cost/benefit analysis and eugenics monograph. Hirschhorn believed that only a government can sponsor totalitarianism, but Dr. Leo Alexander, the U.S. medical examiner at the Nuremberg Trials, said, "Dictatorships can be indeed defined as systems in which there is a prevalence of thinking in destructive rather than in ameliorative terms in dealing with social problems. The ease with which destruction of life is advocated for those considered either socially useless or socially disturbing instead of educational or ameliorative measures may be the first danger sign of loss of creative liberty in thinking, which is the hallmark of democratic society."[64] Alexander made a point that Hirschhorn could not, by virtue of his own approval of negative eugenics—that Nazi Germany was an end point of a eugenic mandate, not a beginning.

Reflective of Dr. Alexander's prophecy is the Wisconsin Clinical Eugenics Center of the University of Wisconsin's university hospital. The program there, described in a report by Thomas Marzen, Staff Counsel for Americans United For Life,[65] is surely Orwellian, yet real. There, after high-risk pregnancies are identified, a team moves in on the family, and an amniocentesis is done. While waiting for the diagnosis, the family is not left alone. Rather, they are attended to by a "genetics associate." Renata Laxova, the acting director in 1982, was quoted by Marzen from a journal article of hers, as to what happens after the eugenic abortion which occurs 75% of the time when a disorder is found. "Parents are asked if they wish to see, hold the fetus (frequently they do), and whether they wish to receive photographs as well as copies of the autopsy report." (Ms. Lacova is a March of Dimes grantee.)

The absolutist mentality of this eugenics center came forward in 1981 when the state of Wisconsin wanted to withdraw all public funds to state-funded institutions performing abortions. The Eugenics Center at the University Hospital would have had to go elsewhere for funds. Marzen recorded how Barbara Lyons, legislative director of Wisconsin Citizens Concerned for Life, saw the lobbyists flow in from the University. Lyons reported, "They lobbied for one thing. They wanted an exception for eugenic abortion—abortion of the handicapped." Among those who lobbied for the eugenics exception, Marzen continued, was the wife of Dr. Benjamin Peckham, the head of the obstetrical department of the hospital. Marzen quoted Lyon: "Mrs. Peckham introduced the lobbyists for the eugenics exception to the Republicans in the legislature. One of the lobbyists took a legislator to a state institution for the retarded in order to show her how bad off they all were."

Nor is this absolutism, which does not shrink from inciting fear and revulsion to get its way, an anomaly. In *Brave New Baby—Promise and Peril of the Biological Revolution,* author David Rorvik recorded the practice of Dr. Karis Adamsons, once of Columbia University. "If necessary, we will take the mother to visit a group of incompetents [mongoloids and other retarded or deformed children] to help her realize what will happen if she insists on going through with the pregnancy."[66] Then there is the letter sent out in March, 1975, by Dr. Jay Cooper of the March of Dimes Arizona Tay-Sachs Prevention Committee to area physicians. He was advertising amniocentesis:

> Couples who would otherwise be at high risk with each pregnancy for a genetic disorder in their offspring can be assisted in this way to selectively have only unaffected children.[67]

The brochure, aimed at parents as well as physicians, pointed out the great expense of Tay-Sachs care, and inspired fear about the expense of long-term care by saying, "Unfortunately, few hospitals will accept children for long-term care, and when they do the cost is generally prohibitive." Parents who are prey to this kind of one-sided propaganda should be made aware of the fact that, also in 1975, Dr. A.W. Liley, the first pioneer to *treat* a fetus through the amniotic fluid, said in *The Los Angeles Times* that there might be some ways to prevent Tay-Sachs without recourse to abortion. But, he said, as long as abortion remains the outstanding "cure," little progress can be made to real prevention or cure of the disease.

This was echoed by Joshouha Lederberg in *The Genetics of Human Nature*[68]*:*

> . . . the availability of abortion poses serious ethical problems for the exploration of more conservative therapeutic measures! These will be uncertain in the early stages and are therefore sure to result in a considerable residue for still damaged children either from insufficient control for the disease or as a side effect of the treatment. For these reasons, prenatal diagnosis and abortion will probably preempt other approaches to genetic therapy . . .

Parents who, out of anguish and many other emotions, are more and more finding themselves with no apparent choice but prenatal diagnosis/eugenic abortion, certainly will be made to feel sure that they are expressing an "individual" choice. But that individual choice should be meticulously informed as to how their decision also feeds into the social, political and human results of eugenics. By overemphasizing "individual" choice, proponents of prenatal diagnosis/eugenic abortion are neatly squelching primary and important information, and thereby encouraging families to believe that their parental choice does not have tremendous power, in the aggregate, to change the very definition of human rights and equality.

From available grant lists for fetal and general research, from both the NIH and the March of Dimes, it is easy to see that there is a continued effort to track the causes of many kinds of disease. The conceptual powers are already in place, the technology is well-established and it seems only a matter of hard work and time before more and more codes of specific maladies will be prenatally read. At the same time, the funders of research are not inimical to searching for cures—enzyme therapies, etc. There seems to be little differentiation between working on the two from any philosophic point of view. As yet, we have no cures for most diseases, and this sounds the alarm because the biomedical profession has been much more successful at discovering the causes, but then imposes its curious notion of cure: prevention of the birth of that person with the malady. Grants are now funding work toward identifying genes that control personality factors, if indeed this is possible. Grants are given to identify environmental/industrial/drug poisons that harm an unborn child. Once it is known what crosses the placenta and causes birth defects, prenatal diagnosis/eugenic abortion (rather than blowing the whistle on those who irresponsibly attack our genetic material) will probably be the ascendant choice of action, and already is to a great extent. In referring back to our main topic of fetal experimentation, it will be the fetal body, often one afflicted by a disease whose cause is yet uncracked, that will be picked and cultured for clues leading to ever more prenatal diagnostic capability.

Nor is research expansion the only type of horizon-widening for present-day eugenics. In 1979, the Genetic Associate/Genetic Counselor conference held in Williamsburg, VA, had as one of the main topics financing for genetic counselling. The professionals invited the Blue Cross and Blue Shield Association to discuss third-party funding. That is, the genetic counselling professionals were looking for a patron and a way of burrowing their ideology into the consciousness of more Americans. The March of Dimes and the Bureau of Community Health Services were also present at that meeting.

What came out of that meeting could be prophetic and negatively dynamic: a report prepared by Blue Cross and Blue Shield, and paid for by the March of Dimes, called "Genetic Services Benefit Study," completed August 31, 1983. The Preface to the report relates, "As a result of this meeting and subsequent discussions, it was decided that the constituents of the March of Dimes, the Bureau of Health Care Delivery and Assistance and the Association [Blue Cross/Blue Shield] might benefit from expanded coverage for genetic services".

The Blue Cross/Blue Shield Association, in "Project Recommendations," said, "Our research and discussions with genetic services providers suggests that the population affected by genetic disorders is large. The screening, diagnostic, treatment, counselling and educational services provided to the at-risk and affected populations are necessary for their *improved health and well being* [emphasis added]. While data on the true cost of the uncovered services is not consistently available, many believe that a significant portion of the population in need does not have full access to services because of financial limitations."

Curiously, although genetic "disease" is so big a problem according to the "genetic services providers," it is interesting that the Association found that "Only ten of the Plans responding to our survey felt that increased demand for genetic services coverage would come from employers (purchasers)." Part of the problem is that it would drive up the price of plans and employers don't want to pay.

Blue Cross/Blue Shield recognizes that a high percentage of their plans already cover prenatal diagnosis; in fact, between 80% and 100% do. What is at question now is the expansion of genetic services to "less commonly covered services." These include the services that would widen the catch of eugenics: medical history and pedigree, genetic counselling, skin sampling, photography (of faces and bodies), a birth defects information system covering persons with carrier or actual disease status. Present coverage for these ranges from 0% to 73%. There would be screening of relatives, now covered very sparsely by 18% to 31% of plans, and other outreach screening for newborns. Special dietary formulas for victims of some diseases such as PKU is the one noneugenic, paid treatment recommendation in the report.

The Blue Cross/Blue Shield Association is going to encourage this expansion by promoting a pilot program among plans in their ken. These plans will be told, interestingly, to confine this pilot-test coverage to "comprehensive centers of genetic services which are generally associated with large universities or other teaching hospitals." This mainly means the March of Dimes, because it operates its funded genetic-screening programs mainly out of these kinds of institutions.

The insurance industry, then, has now come under the spell of those who try to promote an epidemology idea of genetic affliction, as witnessed by the genetic professionals convincing Blue Cross and Blue Shield that "the population affected by genetic disorders is large." Based on its own investigation, the Association now agrees. Ms. Gail Caplan of Blue Cross/Blue Shield told this writer[69] that the Association has begun to receive data from the two university genetic centers involved, the Regional Genetic Groups located at the University of Rochester, N.Y., and the Laboratory of Medical Genetics at the University of Birmingham. The March of Dimes has funded the data collection from the two centers for Blue Cross/Blue Shield to study.

Ms. Caplan, who was the Project Specialist, would not comment on the eugenics/social impact that could be a result of the study. Asked too about the insurance industry's experience with costs versus benefits of prevention of genetic maladies versus lifetime treatment, she said emphatically that the Association had not yet looked at this, but that such a study was going on at Johns Hopkins University. Their study involved the reimbursement of genetic services and, said Caplan, related that to a look at the total cost of genetic disorders. Ms. Caplan said she had been in touch with Johns Hopkins and was anxious to see the results of the study without meaning that this would necessarily bring about a cost/benefit policy on genetic affliction in the Association.

While the Genetic Services Benefit Study's Preface says that it was the Genetic Associate/Genetic Counselor profession approaching the insurance industry through Blue Cross/Blue Shield, Dr. Kenneth Garver, at Magee–Women's Hospital, told this writer[70] that the insurance industry (without naming any particular company or group) had put to the genetics professionals the question of what they did think of reimbursing for genetic disease prevention services on such a universal basis that it would make it possible for the industry to severely cut back or delete payment for liveborn defective children, based on the argument that such births could have been prevented through reimbursed usage of genetic services. Garver said that the genetics professionals decried this as unethical. Whether this is true will no doubt be revealed by future events. The close association of the MOD, Blue Cross/Blue Shield and the cost/benefit analysis of insurance costs for genetic services vs. lifetime costs certainly reveals that they have some thoughts in common. The insurance industry itself has already created a curious precedent. The *Catholic League for Religious and Civil Rights Newsletter,* as far back as 1976 ran an article titled "Blue Cross: Fetal Death Good Business."[71]

The article's theme was that a free, unfettered choice on abortion was being compromised by Blue Cross. "Blue Cross refuses to pay for the delivery of a child born to a marriage of less than 270 days, unless the woman has prior coverage. Nevertheless, Blue Cross will pay for abortions and the 270 day limit does not apply. . . . Blue Cross makes it financially easier to have an abortion than to have a child. . . . Incredibly, Blue Cross will not pay for the delivery of a premature live baby, if the delivery occurs within the 270-day waiting period. If, however, instead of a premature baby, a miscarriage occurs within the 170 day waiting period and the child is delivered dead, Blue Cross covers the medical expenses."

The insurance industry's policy benefits structure could certainly, in a businesslike and yet political way, begin to standardize and spread genetic services and public use of those services. But eugenics forces, such as the MOD, long hungry for expanded but "voluntary" genetic services, might be seen by many who have logged that foundation's dip into eugenics, as the mastermind of the reorientation of public consciousness about genetic disease if indeed a cost/benefit mandate in this area comes about in the future.

Eugenics is not new, but subtle tools such as prenatal diagnosis and genetic counselling are. The newer rhetoric about voluntarism, humanitarianism, the relativity of rights and the backwardness of absolutes reveals rather than disguises the element of force behind the eugenic initiative.

One of the most creative and vehement opposers of eugenics was G.K. Chesterton. His words on the subject have ripened over time, and eugenicists today, by means of their reopening of the case for the 'dirty little science,' deserve his polemics. From his *Eugenics and Other Evils:*[72]

> . . . sound historians know that most tyrannies have been possible because men moved too late . . . It is not enough to answer say, with distant optimism, that the scheme is only in the air. A blow from the hatchet can only be parried while it is in the air . . . There exists today a scheme of action, a school of thought . . . a thing that can be pointed out; it is a thing that can be discussed and it is a thing that can still be destroyed. It is called for convenience "eugenics." . . . Eugenics is a thing no more to be bargained about than poisoning.
>
> Most eugenicists are euphemists. I meant that short words startle them, while long words soothe them. . . . Say to them, "The persuasive and even coercive powers of the citizen should enable him to make sure that the burden of longevity in the previous generation does not become disproportionate and intolerable, especially to the females"; say this to them and they sway to and fro like babies sent to sleep in cradles. But say to them "Murder your mother," and they sit up quite suddenly. Yet the two sentences, in cold logic, are exactly the same. When I spoke of people "being married forcibly by the police," another distinguished eugenicist almost achieved high spirits in his hearty assurance that no such thing had ever come into their heads. Yet a few days after I saw a eugenicist pronouncement, to the effect that the state ought to extend its powers in this area.

The absolute skepticism and the wielding of absolute power is the real territory of the eugenicist, supplanting a dark absolute for a bright one. Chesterton put eugenics into the context of a malign and forceful state, one that came into history after his own lifetime in the form of the rise of Hitler in Germany. The truth about the vengeance of all eugenic schemes, the absolute contradiction of its terrible vision, is contained in what Chesterton cited as his conception of the title of its seminal work: *Eugenius: Or the Adventure of One Not Born.*

Epilogue

While writing this book, I encountered some people against fetal experimentation because of absolute moral principles and others opposed to it out of what they called self-interest. That is, the fetus today, which group of us tomorrow? That the rise of nontherapeutic experimentation on this weakest group of humans is a watershed marking a departure from the deepest wellsprings of traditional morality probably would not even be denied by its enthusiasts. They would herald that departure as a breakthrough in their own version of humanitarianism and as a rightful overturning of fatalism as they define it.

Amid all the voices, two rose above all others on both sides of the argument. Is it symbolic that they are physicians unable to "move forward" as many of their colleagues have done? Although it was primarily the feminist movement that pressed for and won legalized abortion, in almost every country there has been a coterie of the medical profession more than eager to coattail on it. This cadre has put aside its own time-honored commitment to the woman and the child as equal patients. It has allowed itself to split hairs and rationalize the use of "live tissue" versus the absolute values of humanness and life. In a word, it has crashed the gates of its own sacred principles. But not all in the medical profession have jumped onto the bandwagon.

The physician is the person who, along with the clergyman, comes to know the innermost secrets and truths of humanity by necessity and by vocation. Those who trade easy adulation or aggrandizement for lifetimes of uncovering the transcendant in the midst of the real usually reap the disdain and anathema of those whom they were meant to serve. Those who show eloquent courage in the face of momentous pressures and of mere fashion deserve their words to be imprinted on the running, crystal stream of civilization itself.

Thus, rather than use this epilogue to say that we will be seeing more encroachments on the fetus either for "healing" or eugenics, it is best turned over to Drs. Jerome Lejeune and A.W. Liley. The first is a French geneticist and the second was a pediatrician in Australia. Each has contributed a classic that ought to be much more widely disseminated than at present.

One of the common bonds of Lejeune and Liley is that their tools were simple ones. Dr. Lejeune observed his Down's Syndrome patients with acumen and compassion. Through this stringent and creative observation, he was able to break through to the cause of that malady. His became the voice against using knowledge of the cause as a tool to exterminate the fetus so afflicted. Lejeune expressed one single thought: that we are commonly bound, the sick and the well, by our shared human nature.

With equally simple tools, A.W. Liley, who died in 1983, explored the world of the fetus in utero. From his journeys with simple instruments, he concluded not that the fetus is a *tabula rasa* or a tadpole, a subhuman or an alien, foreigner, but said with never diminishing wonder that fetal life is conscious, alert to learning and stimuli, already both a person and a patient. It is indeed significant that A.W. Liley delivered the following address to his colleagues on the eve of the abortion decision in Australia. It was a noble attempt to universalize at the moment when all was about to become relative and saleable.

Nothing that I could conclude or offer the reader can compare with an overwhelming desire to share and proselytize the convictions of these two physicians. Their thoughts demonstrate that it is from the fixed point that new horizons are discovered, not that the ever new and novel prove scientific or human progress. In either a dark or bright future, both men will be vindicated. If the future will be dark, then it will be their names that will be remembered as keepers of the flame. If it be bright, then they will have helped make it so.

Appendix A

On the Nature of Men
Jerome Lejeune

Presented on the occasion of receiving the William Allan Memorial Award at the meeting of the American Society of Human Genetics at San Francisco, October 2-4, 1969.

To kill or not to kill, that is the question. [*Unknown*]

The correlation between chromosomal errors and their phenotypic consequences is sufficiently well established to allow us to decipher, however partially, the destiny of an individual just by looking at his chromosomes. For example, if we know that a subject will be developing from a fertilized egg carrying an extra chromosome 21, we know for sure that the individual will exhibit later all the characteristics of the 21-trisomy syndrome, including, among other abnormalities, severe mental deficiency. Hence the very practical point has been repeatedly advanced that if early detection of a chromosomal condition could be achieved (such as made possible by analysis of the cells floating in the amniotic fluid), a decision could be taken whether such a pregnancy would be allowed to go to term or would be interrupted by an induced abortion. Such a problem is so close to us and so obviously important that it has become one of the possible immediate consequences of recent advances in theoretical knowledge and technical capabilities. Without proposing to elaborate a new philosophy of the human condition, it seems appropriate that human geneticists realize that the question "to kill or not to kill," is by no means purely practical or technological. I will deliberately leave out of the discussion the ethical aspects, because I think human geneticists are no better qualified in ethics than are any other scientists. On the contrary, I would focus our attention on the biological aspects related to a mere observation: "What do we know about the time at which a new human being comes into existence?"

Such a query is not new, and here the geneticist is very similar to Diogenes coming out of his barrel and looking for a man. The only difference is that our lantern has been modernized into a microscope, and I would propose that we consider this quest for a man in the light of cytogenetical findings.

The Karyotype of Mankind

Our first statement is such a commonplace observation that we generally do not pay enough attention to it. All human beings now living on this planet share the same karyotype. More precisely, apart from the XX and XY sexual dimorphism, every chromosomal pair is morphologically identical in all of us within the degree of uncertainty inherent in preset methods. On the other hand, the continuous recurrence of "de novo" chromosomal rearrangements (like trisomies, monosomies, or various kinds of translocations) exemplifies the tremendous mutational pressure exerted upon the human karyotype. Furthermore, the heavy and painful tribute paid by each generation to meiotic or mitotic mistakes shows at what cost the constancy of the human karyotype is preserved.

If karyotypes other than the standard human chromosomal constitution were equally good or even better, human races should have split from each other, forming multiple karyotypic systems. This has not happened in our species although many examples can be found in other mammals. Conversely, fortuitous convergence of other karyotypic constitutions toward the human-type pattern becomes exceedingly improbable. We are then left with the interesting but academically uncomfortable conclusion that speciation in plants and animals is a very different process from human race formation, and we are obliged to use quotation marks when we speak about "Darwinian evolution of man."

No matter how we tackle the problem, it follows from the actual findings that the present-day human karyotype must have appeared first in an extremely small group, even as small as one couple, and must have maintained itself constant, simply because it was the very best solution. It follows also that mankind is a biological unit of which races are variations with no precise boundaries. Hence the old idea that human beings are brothers is not an ethical hypothesis or a purely moral goal, but simply a correct expression of plain reality. The recognition of such brotherhood is very comforting, but increases our concern as human geneticists for the destiny of those unfortunate children who do not share equitably our chromosomal heritage.

The Disinherited Children

As we first noted, a question is thus raised: Should these variants of the human condition be allowed to live?

Here, to try to simplify the problem, we could first dismiss the problems raised by grown-up individuals or even newborns. No doubt exists, I suppose, that to suppress the life of an adult, an infant, or even a newborn, is to be classified as homicide, no matter how severely affected the patient should be.

Indeed it could be remarked that some conditions like 13 trisomy, for example, are not compatible with a prolonged extrauterine life. An argument could thus be presented that their suppression would be only equivalent to premature euthanasia. Without discussing the particular topic of euthanasia, a very strong difference must be stressed here: the purpose of euthanasia is to spare seemingly unnecessary suffering to *the patient,* while the goal of the suppression of a disabled child is to prevent suffering to *his family and to society.*

If we definitely are not concerned about the finished individual, what about the beginning of life? When the future human being is still a conglomerate of cells, apparently not yet differentiated, should we consider him as human being or not? Should we reject this cell mass if it does not fit our specifications, or should we respect him and protect him in all possible ways? Such a question, directly raised by the possible detection of a chromosomal error in a young embryo, has to be faced by human geneticists. Surely the answer must be based upon scientific grounds and be as free as possible from emotional or opportunistic reactions.

The necessity of assuming this duty is imperative. Geneticists cannot play Pontius Pilate and wash their hands, saying, “The parents will choose.” Parents are generally not cytogeneticists, but are always deeply emotionally involved. How then could they judge?

The Technical Approach

Challenged with this problem we can try a "technical" approach. Just for a moment let us suppose that the question of being a man or not is either irrelevant or already solved, and look for a "technical" solution. Although the matter seems, and indeed is, considerably simplified by such a bold statement, not all difficulties have vanished. We must first consider that the phenotypes determined by chromosomal aberrations cover an extremely broad spectrum.

At one extreme we can locate—apart from the 13 trisomy already mentioned—the 18 trisomy, the pure triploidies, and a few other conditions which are practically incompatible with prolonged extrauterine life. A second category includes severe conditions like trisomy 21 or Cri du Chat syndrome, which are entirely compatible with a long life expectancy but inflict severe physical impairments and a mental deficiency, although varying appreciably from subject to subject. In technical terms, we must stress that our predictions are quite accurate but are only negative. For example, the presence of an extra chromosome 21 in a fertilized egg gives us the following information: the children who will develop from this egg will never attend a high school and will not be able to live independently. Remarkably enough, we do not know whether the affected individual will be able to read, write, or count and achieve a mental age of seven or eight years, or whether he will have an extremely poor development, with an IQ below 20. Obviously the human geneticists looking at chromosomes have not yet reached the cleverness of the fairies who could predict everything just by looking at a baby in his cradle. However, our "misfortune-telling" is precise enough to know that the child will never be self-supporting in everyday life.

The other extreme of the spectrum is much more troublesome. For example, an XO woman, although sterile and slightly physically abnormal, can spend an interesting life found worthwhile by herself as well as by others. I have in mind the case of an excellent technician I met years ago in a laboratory of human biochemical genetics. The case of an XXY Klinefelter is still more ambiguous. Apart from sterility, a kind of built-in permanent contraception, an XXY subject can have a quite normal life and even can become a highly reputable surgeon–to cite another individual case.

Finally we find quite normal conditions, like triplo-X mothers, fortuitously detected, or XYY individuals who can enjoy a perfectly decent and respectable life. Indeed we know, statistically, that the XXX condition is far more frequent among inmates of institutions for mentally retarded persons, and we are quite convinced that the risk of delinquency is greater for an XYY man than for a "normal" XY (although not greater than for an "abnormal" XY). But what about the condition of translocation carriers, not suffering any detectable genetic damage themselves but able to give birth to children suffering from an imbalanced karyotype? And what about complex translocations which, due to *aneusomie de recombinaison,* can occur in two different although morphologically identical karyotypes, one entirely balanced, leading to perfectly normal adults, the other severely imbalanced, and sometimes lethal or dramatically dysmorphogenic.

Intermingled with all the preceding cases is the cumbersome problem of mosaicism. Every human being is a mosaic due to some mitotic malsegregation in some part of the body; the dividing line between normal and pathologic is a matter of percentage: if 50% of abnormal karotype is considered as deleterious, what about 40%, 20%, 5%, and what about topographical distributions? Obviously here some "technical" judgment has to be made about the human qualities resulting from a given constitution, and careful analysis of the burden imposed upon affected individuals, their families, and society must be made.

The burden to the individual himself is very difficult to assess because only the affected person can tell us about it. The overwhelming majority of patients suffering from a genetic disease (and able to express their feelings) do regret their affliction but do not regret being themselves and alive. The social burden possibly could be easier to estimate, but the suffering of the family will stay outside of any "technical" evaluation. Nevertheless, many precise but very complex questions must be solved. For example: is the Turnerian way of life to be accepted? is the 21-trisomic way of life to be protected? . . . , and the like. Willy-nilly we come to the conclusion that such a difficult matter, that of deciding what is desirable and should be respected and what is undesirable and should be rejected, deals with considerable "technical" intricacies. In such situations the common practice is not to leave the decision to unprepared or to directly involved persons, but to resort to some jurisdiction, or some body of counselors.

Thus the time is ripe to see what kind of facility for research and applied eugenics should be constituted to manage these problems. Indeed, there would be no reason whatsoever to limit the competence of this facility merely to chromosomal aberrations, but its terms of reference should include all inborn errors, either genic or chromosomal. In order to work out entirely this "technical" approach, let us read the minimal statutes that such a facility should have.

Elements of the Statutes of a New Facility for Research and Applied Eugenics

Article I

Considering the disputed issue of mankind's betterment, noting the burden imposed upon society by genic and chromosomal diseases, and recognizing the limitation of the available solutions, a special Institution for Research and Applied Eugenics is created: "THE NATIONAL INSTITUTE OF DEATH."

Article II

Under the scientific scrutiny of a board of specially appointed advisors, the NATIONAL INSTITUTE OF DEATH will:

A. Decree on undesirable genes or chromosomes.
B. Deliver unhappy parents from unwanted pregnancies.
C. Discard embryos not fitting standard requirements.
D. Dispose of newborns not reaching minimal specifications of normalcy.
E. And generally, destroy, delete, or decry any human condition voted against by the above-mentioned board of advisors of the NATIONAL INSTITUTE OF DEATH.

Article III

To prevent any possible error, concern, or prejudice, the advisors shall be chosen from among knowledgeable persons not belonging to any philosophy, society, or race.

The Individual Approach

Leaving the board of advisors of the NATIONAL INSTITUTE OF DEATH to its intrinsic "technicalities," we have to remember that we have set aside the core of the problem: when does man begin? To make a short story long (for the beginning of life is just the brief instant of egg fertilization), we can investigate at what stage of development the future human being can be considered as an individual. The available information is spread over many fields of biology but can be summarized under the two headings defining an individual, that is, unity and uniqueness. It is actually impossible to state firmly at what time these two qualities appear, although we know for sure that it is after fertilization. But it is possible to delineate with the aid of pathological findings, the time *after which* these qualities cannot be appreciably changed.

Unity and Chimeras

According to the classical rules of human genetics, every individual is constructed out of one cell, the fertilized egg. This formal statement had no exception until the discovery of human chimeras in hermaphroditism. For example, in the constitution XX/XY, careful analysis of blood groups shows that the red cells are composed of two subpopulations, each of them carrying a particular array of genes coming from the parents. The primary mechanisms of these chimeras is poorly understood but, broadly speaking, it can be asserted that two fraternal twin zygotes have collaborated to build together one embryo instead of two. Speculations about simultaneous fertilization of a reduced egg and of one of its polar bodies have been made, and diploid/triploid mosaics seem to owe their origin to a rather similar type of accident. Although other mechanisms could as well be postulated, the moment at which the process can occur is very early in development.

First, these events happen at the same ovulation period, for embryos a month apart could not fuse into one. Second, to realize the almost-perfect mixture of the two kinds of cells found in every tissue, the symbiosis must establish itself well ahead of the first general organization of the future embryo. This leaves us with a period of uncertainty not exceeding weeks and, quite likely, as short as a few days or hours if the polar body is involved. This problem of the unity of an individual of chimeric origin is intriguing. Compound animals can be artificially produced, like the mouse manufactured from blastocysts of different embryos, thus having many mothers and many fathers. Such a monstrosity fortunately is not to be feared too much in our species, at least, as long as the good old manners of reproduction will be in use! Nevertheless, it seems likely that natural chimeras in our species are about twice as frequent as XX/XY hermaphrodites. The reason is that if two fraternal zygotes, both XX or both XY, fuse, the individual will be perfectly healthy and never examined. It is entirely possible that some here are not the pure clone they believe themselves to be, but are harmonious chimeras resulting from the full integration of two cellular races. Is it entirely chimerical to think that such a fruitful and peaceful coexistence between populations of cells, carrying different tables of the law of life, hopefully could be a model for human societies?

Uniqueness and Twins

The uniqueness of each is also an old rule of genetics. Without developing any statistical demonstration, it can safely be assessed that the precise genetic constitution of every fertilized egg is unique, has never been realized before, and will never occur again. But at what moment is this uniqueness definitely established? Monozygous twins show that two or sometimes more individuals can emerge from the same primordial genetic information. Nobody, I venture, would seriously argue that identical twins are not individual persons although they share the very same nature. The splitting in two embryos surely can occur at the first cleavage of the egg, but what about the latest stage possible? The observation of double monsters demonstrates that complete separation cannot take place after the finalization of the neural crest. Hence, we are left again with an indeterminate period of assuredly less than one month and probably of two or three weeks at most.

Incidentally, again to break one of the old rules, twins coming from the same egg are not necessarily alike. If a chromosomal error intervenes during or just after cleavage, identical twins can be different. If a chromosome 21, for example, is present in triplicate in one twin and normally diploid in the other, the twin set will be composed of a typical 21-trisomic individual and of his normal co-twin, identical but for the 21 trisomy condition. If the accident prevents the transmission for the Y chromosome to one of the twins there will be one normal male (XY) and a female identical twin with Turner's syndrome (XO). In a case of this type, the XO girl apparently suffered from a very strange psychological disturbance which greatly intrigued the psychiatrists: she pretended she was seeing her brother when she looked at herself in a mirror. For the geneticist, such an intuitive knowledge of a complex situation was not at all troublesome, but a mere affirmation of the facts. But, coming back to our timing problem, in what way can all these remarks help us in answering our basic question: "when does a human being begin?"

The Molecular Approach

During the transmission of life, the link between parents and infants is continuous. Without reviewing the complex machinery of coded molecules, from DNA and RNA to ribosomes and proteins, we can safely assume that at every moment this link between generations is material. Nevertheless, with exactly the same degree of certainty, we know that no one molecule, no one individual atom actually present in the fertilized egg, will have the slightest chance of being transmitted to the next generation. Obviously what is "transmitted" is a form, an accident of the matter, and not matter itself as such. This apparent paradox is the very basis of any reproductive process. For example a statue cannot be built out of void; it needs a material substrate such as marble or clay. During reproduction by molding, the link between the statue and its replicate is at every instant a material one; but what *is* reproduced is definitely not the marble or the plaster but the form, or, more precisely, the information imprinted on matter by the genius of the sculptor.

Applied to biology, this principle of information transfer is perfectly relevant because we know that, if not disturbed and if not deprived of nutrient supply, the fertilized egg on its own will produce a full-blown individual by an extremely complex but entirely deterministic mechanism. In utero relations between the mother and the fetus do not affect at all this fundamental determinism, as is clearly demonstrated by the egg of the hen. By such reasoning, the information specialist reaches the conclusion that the more deterministic and materialistic his conception of life, the earlier a human constitution is entirely spelled out. If man is considered as an accretion of matter such that his very nature is entirely dictated by the information imprinted in these materials, then a new man begins at the precise point the necessary and sufficient information is gathered, that is, at the very beginning.

Even interpretation of his theory in philosophical terms will not lead the information specialist any further. Indeed, it could be argued that all nuclear and cystoplasmic information included in the fertilized egg is only describing the "essence" of the future man, not his "existence." But this reserve vanishes immediately if we accept the fact that existence is essence in action. Hence since any transmission of information is the action of its essence, the future man effectively exists either at the first RNA synthesis, or, if we need a more ostensible starting point, at the first cell cleavage. Whether or not we find that reducing man to the genetic and organistic information of his primordial cell is intuitively satisfactory, no clear direction seems open to pursue the argument.

The Practical Approach

Many could consider that we have spent enough time on pure and unproductive speculations and would stop here, saying, "Wait, let us be practical and see the mere facts."

At the early stages of embryonic development there are only conglomerated cells, rapidly dividing. This little mass even does not look at all like a man; it is just a piece of flesh, a very precious flesh because a human being could sprout out of it—a fact impossible from an ordinary tissue culture or from any somatic part of the body. But there is no "humanity" there, just human cells. In this approach, different landmarks can be used in deciding that "humanity" has been acquired by the "thing." Some will hold that organs must have differentiated; others will require some development of the brain; and others will wait until certain reactions to stimuli occur in the fetus or until any other specified step is attained. It follows that the time factor we are interested in varies largely with this approach, for example from fertilization to viability, or, when the disputation is entirely worked out, to the time at which the "growing thing" will finally be able to pretend that he is a man. Generally the process of birth is accepted as a convenient term for the discussion, but this separation from the mother is not relevant whatsoever to the logic of the argument.

When viewed scientifically, this difficulty in spelling out "practically" at what precise time a mass of cells becomes a man is not surprising at all and definitely is not to be ridiculed. If we dissect the intellectual pathway followed here, it is clear that regardless of the circumlocutions used, what the "practical" view is looking for is in plain words: is there some kind of human "soul" or not? Ensoulment theory has been vividly discussed by theologians but, to the best of my knowledge, never solved. Thus, it is no wonder that "practical" discussants cannot beat specialists on their own ground. Curiously enough, we have seen the "molecular theoretician" coming out with a pure information theory, very akin to physical representation of the "incarnation of the logos" and the "pragmatist" discussing the first symptoms of the existence of the "human soul." It could very well be that such an apparent confusion of disciplines stems from the fact that we all tried to solve an incomplete problem.

For the sake of simplification, we have devoted ourselves to the particular query: "When does man begin?" It appeared to be quite a clear-cut question. But should we not have been better inspired to start with the necessary question: "What is a man?" No dictionary and even no legislation of any country or civilization has ever fully answered this question. Depending upon what different specialists look for in man—his quality, his individuality, his molecules, or his internal or external life—the "technician," the "personalist," the "information specialist," and the "pragmatist" have given their own answers not to the question we asked them, "When does man begin?" but to the unspelled challenge, "What is a man?" Certainly this is the crux of the matter, but such a crux is possibly too heavy to be carried by a human mind.

Here are we left, exactly at the same point we started two thousand years ago. The Diogenes-geneticist returns to his barrel after turning off his microscopic lantern. He has not discovered when and where man could be found! Conclusions from such a circular trip are not straightforward! Nevertheless we human geneticists have to face everyday reality: disabled children and distressed parents exist. No formal demonstration being at hand, each of us has to face the challenge, and I believe our response must be guided by two sentiments only—humility and compassion. Humility because we must recognize we have no ready-made answers, because geneticists have not broken the secret of the human condition, and because scientific arguments are of little help in ethical issues; compassion because even the most disinherited belongs to our kin, because these victims are poorer than the poorest, and because the sorrow of the parents cannot be consoled by science. But should we capitulate in the face of our own ignorance and propose to eliminate those we cannot help?

For millenia, medicine has striven to fight for life and health and against disease and death. Any reversal of the order of these terms of reference would entirely change medicine itself. It happens that nature does condemn. Our duty has always been not to inflict the sentence but to try to commute the pain. In any foreseeable genetical trial I do not know enough to judge, but I feel enough to advocate.

Appendix B

The Foetus as a Personality

A. W. Liley

Presented at the 8th Annual Congress of Australia and New Zealand Counselling Psychiatrists, Auckland, New Zealand, October 1971.

I did not choose the title of this presentation. Had I done so, I would have been more careful in my selection of words. The foetus is part of my province of medical practice, and personality is part of yours. But whereas I am sure that you could all define, describe and even recognize a foetus, I am not so confident that I can define personality. One dictionary offers "what constitutes an individual as a distinct person," but does not define what the "what" is. Another dictionary asserts "the state of existing as a thinking intelligent being." This definition might lead to the inference that personality increases *pro rata* with intelligence, or that some people may not have a personality at all if we followed Bertrand Russell's dictum that "most people would rather die than think and many, in fact, do."

My copy of the late Ken Stallworthy's *Manual of Psychiatry* is more help with the definition that "personality is the individual as a whole with everything about him which makes him different from other people," because we can certainly distinguish foetuses from each other and from other people. With the next sentence—"personality is determined by what is born in the individual in the first place and by everything which subsequently happens to him in the second"—we are really in business. Not only can I tell you what is apparent of what is born in the foetus, but I can also describe the environment in which he lives, the stimuli to which he is exposed, and the responses which he displays. Therefore it might have been more apt to title this presentation "A day in the life of the foetus," and together we can revisit a stage of life which we all experienced but which, superficially at least, none of us remembers.

Such a journey is justified for several reasons. For many centuries interest in foetal life was restricted to anatomical studies by embryologists or to mechanical problems in delivery as they presented to the accoucheur. The legacies of this era are well known—particularly the attitude that, apart from some aimless kicking which began in the fifth month, the foetus was a placid, dependent, fragile vegetable who developed quietly in preparation for a life which started at birth. In the present century, many disciplines have extended their interests to include the foetus, but in fields from surgery to psychiatry the tendency has been to start with adult life and work backwards—knowing what the adult state was, one worked back to what seemed a reasonable starting point to reach that goal. Therefore, in fields from physiology and biochemistry to education and psychology, there has grown up the habit of regarding the foetus and the neonate as a poorly functioning adult rather than as a splendidly functioning baby.

Until recently, the human foetus *in situ* was inacessible to study and this seclusion has had two further unfortunate results. First, much reliance has been placed on animal experiment in spite of the fact that there is more variation throughout the mammalian order in reproductive physiology than in the physiology of any other body function. Second, for want of experimental verification or repudiation, theories have flourished without serious challenge. As a consequence, at one extreme, J.J. Rousseau and his pupils could regard the foetus as a witless tadpole with a mind like a cleanly washed slate—the *tabula rasa*—and at the other extreme some interpreters of dreams considered the foetus a skilled voyeur, spying on his parents having intercourse—a sort of "what the butler saw," through the cervix.

If, with regret, we must abandon such fascinating conjecture, I hope that we can replace it with equally interesting fact, because recent advances in foetal diagnosis and therapy have provided both the technology and opportunity to piece together a new picture of the foetus. Far from being an inert passenger in a pregnant mother, the foetus is very much in command of the pregnancy. It is the foetus who guarantees the endocrine success of pregnancy and induces all manner of changes in maternal physiology to make her a suitable host. It is the foetus who, single-handed, solves the homograft problem—no mean feat when we reflect that, biologically, it is quite possible for a woman to bear more than her own body weight of babies, all immunological foreigners, during her reproductive career. It is the foetus who determines the duration of pregnancy. It is the foetus who decides which way he will lie in pregnancy and which way he will present in labour. Even in labour the foetus is not entirely passive—neither the toothpaste in the tube nor the cork in the champagne bottle, as required by the old hydraulic theories of the mechanics of labour. Much of the behaviour of the neonate and infant can now be observed *in utero* and, by corollary, a better understanding of the foetus and his environment puts the behaviour and problems of the neonate in better perspective.

In his warm and humid microclimate, the foetus is in neither stupor nor hypoxic coma. From the few electroencephalographic studies, he appears to show cyclical activity, the lighter periods of which correspond in the neonate to a drowsy wakefulness from which he is readily aroused by a variety of stimuli. Like all internal organs, the uterus is insensitive to touch, indeed, to all stimuli except stretch. Hence foetal movements are not felt in the uterus but in the maternal abdominal wall, which explains why quickening is not apparent until 16 to 22 weeks of gestation. The foetus has been moving his limbs and trunk since about 8 weeks, but some 10 or more weeks elapse before these movements are strong enough to be transmitted to the abdominal wall. In some 40 per cent of pregnancies, an additional cushion, the placenta, is on the anterior uterine wall, and this phenomenon plus variation in foetal position explains why maternal account or external palpation may be a very erratic guide to foetal vigour and welfare.

Foetal comfort determines foetal position, but comfort presents no problem in the first half of pregnancy when the foetus inhabits a relatively large and globular cavity. He is under no restriction and has no axis of stability. Occasionally these conditions still prevail in late pregnancy—in the presence of polyhydramnios, or with a uterine cavity truncated by a fundal or praevia placenta—and then we see an unstable lie. Normally, however, in the second half of pregnancy, the uterine cavity is no longer globular but becomes progressively more ovoid with the lower pole narrower, and the foetus elongates more rapidly than the uterus. Therefore the foetus tends to be corralled into a longitudinal lie. However, amniotic fluid volume reaches a maximum at about 28 to 32 weeks, and until this time the foetus is far from cramped and under no obligation to lie well flexed. As amniotic fluid volume diminishes and foetal bulk increases from 32 weeks to term, comfort becomes more difficult to achieve. If he chooses to flex his knees, the foetus will present by the vertex as his head forms a smaller pole than his back, thighs, calves and feet, and this disposition corresponds to the polarity of the uterine cavity. If however he elects to extend his knees, he will fit in best as a breech since his tapering trunk and thighs form a smaller pole than his head, calves and feet.

Variations of uterine contour, unusual size or location of the placenta, and the presence of another foetus may all present further challenges to foetal comfort and ingenuity and produce stable malpresentations. Foetal position, whether he lies with his spine anterior, posterior or lateral, is determined by other influences. In late pregnancy, the most important of these are the location of the placenta, which converts the circular cross section of the uterus to an oval, the tone of mother's uterine and abdominal wall, the shape of the maternal lumbar lordosis, and the inclination of the pelvic brim. Maternal movement and change affect maternal position. Braxton-Hicks contractions, and external palpation all disturb the foetus and may provoke him to seek a new position of comfort. He will repeatedly and purposefully seek to avoid the sustained pressure of a microphone or phonendoscope or of a knuckle on prominences.

The mechanism by which the foetus changes ends in the uterus is simple—he propels himself around by his feet and legs. The mechanism by which he changes sides is more subtle—he employs an elegant longitudinal spiral roll and at the midpoint of his turn has a 180° twist in his spine. He first extends his head and rotates it, next his shoulders rotate and finally his lumbar spine and legs—in fact, he is using his long spinal reflexes. Insofar as this is the obvious way to turn over, there would be nothing remarkable about it except that according to textbooks of neonatal and infant locomotor function the baby does not roll over using his long spinal reflexes until 14 to 20 weeks of extrauterine life. However, we have unequivocal films of the foetus using this mechanism at least as early as 26 weeks gestation, and it is apparent that the reason we do not see this behaviour in the neonate is not that he lacks the neural coordination but that a trick which is simple in a state of neutral buoyancy becomes difficult under the new-found tyranny of gravity.

The very early embryo develops in flexion, but beyond this stage there is little evidence to justify the traditional assumption that flexion is fundamental in foetal musculoskeletal development. In midpregnancy with plenty of room, neutral buoyancy and intervertebral discs virtually synovial joints, he can assume postures difficult or impossible for the child or adult. In late pregnancy, as the foetus elongates more than the uterus, he must fold to fit in. Commonly the attitude is again one of flexion, but sometimes he elects to lie with neck, trunk or limbs extended and sometimes grossly hyperextended, a preference he will continue to express as his position of comfort after birth, particularly in sleep, if nursed naked in a warm environment.

Foetal movement is necessary for the proper development of foetal bones and joints. The foetus without muscles—amyotrophia congenita—has the slender bone structure more familiar in the victim of paralytic poliomyelitis. From the characteristic and uniform regulations in different limb segments, it is apparent that the fractures in the foetus with . . . the "battered baby *in utero*," is self-inflicted by the baby's own muscles. The foetus who is severely constrained *in utero* like a pound of deep frozen sausages with extreme oligohydramnios presents an assortment of compression deformities with severe restriction of joint range of movement.

The realization that the foetus himself determines the way he will lie in pregnancy and present in labour by making the best he can of the space and shape available to him puts the practice of version in new perspective, and nowadays fewer obstetricians assume that they know better than the foetus how he will be most comfortable. Of course, in selecting a position of comfort in late pregnancy, the foetus may have chosen a position which is difficult or impossible for vaginal delivery. In this regard he may be accused of lack of foresight, but this is a trait not unknown in adults.

The foetus is responsive to pressure and touch. Tickling the foetal scalp at surgical induction of labour provokes movement, stroking the palm of a prolapsed arm elicits a grasp reflex, and to plantar stimulation the footling breech obliges with an upgoing toe. Being totally immersed, the foetus does not feel wet nor cough or choke with his airway full of fluid. The peripheral sensation of wetness and the irritation of fluid in the airways are dependent on surface tension effects at gas/fluid interfaces, and normally wetness is a new experience at birth. That this experience, however, may be startling if not uncomfortable for the foetus is suggested by the one recorded case of air amniography where the presence of a substantial volume of intraamniotic air led to prolonged loud foetal crying.

Since the foetus lacks an external surface of his own, his temperature inevitably cannot be less than his mother's. Among many other functions, the placenta is his heat exchanger and its performance may be gauged by the fact that foetal temperature is normally 0.5—1.5°C above maternal core temperature. If mother runs a fever the foetus must also. The walls of the foetal world are probably not thermally homogeneous, as thermography shows that the areas of the maternal abdominal wall over the placental site are several degrees hotter than areas over the *chorion laeve*. Although the range of ambient temperature to which the foetus is exposed is limited, his awareness of and reactions to thermal stimulation are intact before birth. If cold saline is run into the amniotic cavity, he shows appropriate motor and circulatory responses.

The foetus responds with violent movement to needle puncture and to the intramuscular or intraperitoneal injection of cold or hypertonic solutions. Although we would accept, rather selfishly, that these stimuli are painful for adults and children and, to judge from his behaviour, painful for the neonate, we are not entitled, I understand, to assert that the foetus feels pain. In this context I think Bertrand Russell's remark in his *Human Knowledge, its Scope and Limitations* rather apt—he relates "A fisherman once told me that fish have neither sense nor sensation but how he knew this he could not tell me." It would seem prudent to consider at least the possibility that birth is a painful experience for a baby. Radiological observation shows foetal limbs flailing during contractions, and if one attempts to reproduce in the neonate by manual compression a mere fraction of the cranial deformation that may occur in the course of a single contraction the baby protests very violently. And yet, all that has been written by poets and lyricists about cries of newborn babies would suggest that newborn babies cried for fun or *joie de vivre*—which they never do afterwards—and in all the discussions that have ever taken place on pain relief in childbirth only maternal pain has been considered. Karelitz in New York has shown that, as judged by the strength of stimuli required to arouse them, the first sleep of neonates is more profound than any subsequent sleep, and this is perhaps hardly cause for surprise when we know that labour may represent very prolonged stimulation and interference with normal foetal activity cycles.

The foetus drinks amniotic fluid in a phasic pattern throughout pregnancy, and measurement by isotopic techniques shows that his consumption has an effective rate of interquartile range 15 to 40 ml per hour in the third trimester. Now the foetus has a much larger number and a much wider distribution of taste buds in his oral cavity than the child or adult, but no-one knows—or can recall—whether the taste or flavour of amniotic fluid varies much or if, for instance, meconium stained fluid tastes worse than normal fluid. However, experimental modification of the taste of amniotic fluid produces dramatic results. Foetal drinking rates crash after the injection of the contrast medium Lipiodol®—an iodinated poppy seed oil which tastes foul to an adult or child and which causes a neonate to grimace and cry. Conversely, de Snoo (1937) claimed that saccharin stimulated foetal swallowing, and our isotopic measurements support this claim with usually an approximate doubling of rate. However, some foetuses drink less after saccharin injection and perhaps, like the author, they find saccharin in concentration bitter rather than sweet.

Foetal swallowing appears the major if not the only route of disposal of amniotic fluid colloid and hence, especially in the second half of pregnancy, has an increasingly important effect on amniotic fluid homeostasis and volume. The foetus who cannot swallow, for example with oesophageal or duodenal atresia has a polyhydramnios. Since foetal swallowing powerfully influences if not regulates amniotic fluid volume, what influences or regulates foetal swallowing? Now the foetus gains nourishment from amniotic fluid, for he digests the constituents of amniotic fluid. His calorie intake from this source may reach 40 calories per day and the foetus who cannot swallow is 'small for dates'. Traditionally it has been assumed that hunger is a brand new sensation after birth, that *in utero* an obliging mother and faithful placenta have supplied baby's every need. However, the sight of babies with gross intrauterine malnutrition makes it rather hard to believe that every foetus lives in a metabolic Nirvana. Could foetal hunger be the stimulus to foetal swallowing? Rather contrary to expectation on this hypothesis in general, large, well-nourished babies swallow at a high rate and small, grossly malnourished babies at a very low rate. We could of course suggest that the malnourished child has passed beyond the hunger pangs and into the state of apathy and anorexia known from extrauterine starvation. However, the fact that the large, well-nourished foetus has a bulimia and the small malnourished foetus an anorexia accords well with endocrine evidence that much of what has been called traditionally placental insufficiency is in fact primarily foetal and of hypothalamic origin.

Foetal hiccups are common and often can be induced by irrigating the amniotic cavity with cold solutions. Foetal hiccups are easily recognized, and mother should be reassured for some have misgivings about these episodic series of clonic movements, especially if there is an epileptic somewhere in the family cupboard.

The foetus is not only experienced in swallowing, but also in many cases in suckling. In the neurological examination of the neonate, the 'seeking' or 'rooting' reflex is elicited by stroking the circumoral area. The baby opens his mouth and turns to the stimulus. This reflex is clearly the mechanism by which baby homes on the nipple and underlines a tremendous importance of feeding to the neonate. Indeed his face and mouth are the one part of his body the neonate can reliably locate in space and the mouth remains one of the chief tools of exploration in infancy. Since the foetus is often lying with hands and feet in close proximity to his face, he may readily elicit a seeking reflex himself. Accordingly, it is not uncommon in obstetric radiology to detect the foetus sucking thumbs, fingers or toes, and thumbsucking has been photographed in the 9-weeks abortus. Incidentally, the common observation in neonates of clenched fists, which would appear to preclude thumbsucking, is not a feature of babyhood really but of high thermal tone in muscle. Careful examination of hand position in x-rays shows that usually the foetus with his low thermal tone in his warm environment has his hands relaxed and his thumbs protruding.

Perhaps nowhere does the notion of foetal life as a time of quiescence, of patient and blind development of structures in anticipation for a life and function to begin at birth, die harder than in the concept of the pregnant uterus as a dark and silent world. Indeed even as great a neurophysiologist as Sir Charles Sherrington (1951) could speak of 'the miracle of the human eye developing in darkness for seeing in light and the miracle of the human ear developing in silent water for hearing in vibrant air.' As anyone familiar with a phonendoscope knows, a pregnant abdomen is not silent, and the uterus and amniotic cavity, especially with any degree of polyhydramnios, may be readily transilluminated with a torch in a darkened room. Given a naked abdomen in sunshine, light intensities would be much higher. With a fibre optic light conduit and photomultiplier, not only can the intrauterine illumination produced by an external tungsten or quartz iodide lamp be recorded, but the shadow cast by the foetus is detectible.

Now, for activation of visual pathways, there is strictly no threshold, for the visual rods respond individually to single photons. Sure enough, Smythe (1965) at University College Hospital found that flashing lights applied to the maternal abdominal wall produced fluctuations in foetal heart rate. However, with the high attenuation in tissue, the abnormal spectral composition and the boring view, what the foetus lacks is adequate illumination and a worthwhile image or practice in cone or macular vision. A birth he can see but does not know what he is looking at. Confident recognition of familiar people and reassurance from the sight alone of mother takes some 4 to 7 months of extrauterine life to acquire. However, before this age the baby can be reassured by a familiar voice alone in the dark, and we have to argue either that auditory recognition of patterns matures more rapidly than visual recognition, or that auditory experience began earlier. The latter seems more likely.

Sudden noise in a quiet room—the dropping gallipot or maternal voice—startles the foetus lined up under an image intensifier, and from at least 25 weeks the foetus will jump in synchrony with the tympanist's contribution to an orchestral performance. By applying intermittent pure tones by hydrophone or air microphone to the maternal abdominal wall, foetal audiometric curves may be constructed by recording the abrupt changes in foetal heart rate. There is dispute among the professionals as to sound energy levels reaching the foetus (a given sound energy produces higher sound pressure levels in fluid) and naturally the state of foetal wakefulness and the maintenance of attention span are very hit and miss. Nevertheless, averaging of foetal electroencephalographic records with repeated stimuli shows sound evoked cortical potentials and demonstrates as does experience with deaf mothers that the foetus is responding directly. Both habituation and conditioning—dare we say learning?—have been noted.

With tympanic membranes dampened by fluid in both middle and external ears, the foetus could be expected to have a relative high-tone deafness, but higher frequencies suffer less loss than low frequencies in transmission through tissues and fluid. Therefore, it is probably that with sound, unlike light, intrauterine spectra are similar to extrauterine. Further, it is worth noting that, unlike most foetal organs which start off in miniature, the structures of the inner ear are very nearly of adult size from initial development. This magnitude of course is necessary because cochlear spectral response obeys simple physical laws dependent on cochlear dimensions. If, for instance, the cochlear grew in proportion to the rest of the body, babies and children would hear in a different frequency range from adults and the communication gap between generations would be even wider than it is already.

However, it is not only external sound which bombards the foetus. The pregnant uterus or abdomen is itself a very noisy place. The loudest sounds to reach the foetus or an intrauterine phonocatheter are maternal borborygmi peaking to 85 decibles. Reaching and below 55 db the content is richer in pattern and meaning—the intermittent voice and the all pervading bruits, pulsing in synchrony with maternal heart beat, of blood in the great arteries supplying the uterus and placental bed. Does this long exposure explain why a baby is comforted by holding him to your chest or is lulled to sleep by the old wives' alarm clock, or the modern magnetic tape of a heart beat? Does this experience explain why the tick of a grandfather clock in a quiet study or library can be a reassurance rather than a distraction, why people asked to set a metronome to a rate which 'satisfies' them will usually chose a rate in the 50-90 beat per minute range—and twins show a strong concordance in independent choice? Elias Carnetti points out that all the drum rhythms in the world belong to one or other of two basic patterns—either the rapid tattoo of animal hooves or the measured beat of a human heart. The animal hoof pattern is easy to understand from the ritual and sympathetic magic of hunting cultures. Yet, interestingly, the heart beat rhythm is more widespread in the world—even in groups like the plains Indians who hunted the great herds of bison. Is this rhythm deeply imprinted on human consciousness from foetal life?

Not only do the human eye and ear, therefore, not develop in darkness and silence, but there is also good reason to believe from experimental work and comparative physiology that they would not develop properly in those conditions anyway. As with other foetal organs, development of structure and development of function go hand in hand. And if the function cannot be subserved without the development of the structure, equally the stimulus of the function is necessary for the proper maturation of the structure.

The mechanism by which a concept of sensory space develops has long been a troublesome optic for psychologists. However, for the amateur dabbler, the subject has received some much-needed simplification by the evidence that the various sensory modalities all feed and share a common space, and that this space in fact is the effective motor space. This synthesis certainly has logical simplicity to anyone who compares, say, the tunnel vision of the jet pilot or freeway driver with the short cone extending just a few yards ahead of the walker on rough ground and encompassing the field of the next few paces. Parallels in auditory function are easily drawn. When does such a concept of space begin? Refined experiment on the neonate suggests that his sensory space is a little ball, that although he may receive visual and auditory signals from more distant sources he is not much interested in anything outside a sphere which extends just beyond his toes—a restriction which very neatly corresponds to his recently vacated home.

This then is our picture of the foetus. He does not live in a padded, unchanging cocoon in a state of total sensory deprivation, but in a plastic, reactive structure which buffers and filters, perhaps distorts, but does not eliminate the outside world. Nor is the foetus himself inert and stuporose, but active and responsive.

Since on the one hand the foetus is exposed to a variety of stimuli, and on the other hand can sense and respond to them, presumably we have the prerequisites for learning of some sort. Is there in fact any evidence or suggestion that the foetus has learned anything *in utero*? Study is understandably difficult, for not only are nature and nurture at least as intricately entangled in intrauterine life as in extrauterine life, but for good measure any but the briefest observation and tests after birth may be compromised by the high rate of learning in the neonate. For instance, babies who have had as few as 10 heel punctures for blood samples in the first 72 hours after birth, for weeks or months afterwards will promptly cry if you thoughtlessly grasp their foot.

That recognition by voice precedes recognition by sight and the world preference in drum rhythms is suggestive of foetal learning, or at least imprinting. What of circadian rhythms? It is known that there is not one physiological clock but numbers of relatively independent clocks, some more stubborn than others. Moreover, that such rhythms are modified, if not determined, by activity cycles rather than of cosmic origin is strongly suggested by the evidence that the diurnal rhythms of the inhabitants of fishing villages, living by the tides, are lunar not solar in periodicity. In this context, it is interesting to reconsider the claim, at least of young parents, that the one thing that shows the foetus is utterly stupid is that many neonates do not seem to appreciate that night is a time for sleep.

We know that maternal movement and change of position provoke foetal movement that if we want a foetus lying still and unsuspecting for some diagnostic or therapeutic procedure it is necessary to have mother lying still and comfortable for 15 to 20 minutes to allow the foetus to find a position of comfort. Further, we must avoid last minute palpations and auscultations. Compare these precautions with the performance and restlessness of many pregnant women in bed—with the leg cramps and heartburn, the subcostal and pelvic girdle discomfort, and for variation a trip or two to the bathroom. The neonate could perhaps be forgiven if, as a foetus, he had gained the impression that night was anything but a time for rest.

A similar *cri de coeur* concerns those young babies who cussedly elect to have their briefest rest periods and shortest intervals between feeds in the late afternoon and at dinner time just when it would be most helpful if they would sleep. For the breast fed baby, a ready explanation arises from the fact that there is a striking diurnal variation in the fat content of human milk—from as high as 9 per cent in the early morning to as low as 1 per cent in the afternoon. Hence the breast fed baby may be short changed on calories on his afternoon feeds. However, precisely the same pattern may be seen in the bottle-fed baby, and we are left with the suspicion that the foetus may have been conditioned to the fact that this time of day represents peak activity for mother and peak uproar in many households.

A question very commonly asked is whether maternal emotion—elation, fear, anxiety, may be communicated to or influence the foetus. Certainly, with monitored foetal hearts, there may be abrupt changes in rate with sudden maternal emotion. Such responses could be mediated indirectly by changes in maternal arterial pressure, or directly by substances, for instance catecholamines, which cross the placenta. It has been argued that since the foetus experiences only the consequences and not the cause for the emotion itself the experience would mean nothing to him. More recently this view has been challenged on the evidence that the pharmacological induction of the physiological responses to fear and anxiety induces the sensation of fear and anxiety also—but this may be just a learned response.

It is apparent that many more questions may be asked but as yet few answers given. What I have tried to do is to provide a background, so that by asking the right questions in the right way we might some time get the right answers. We may not all live to grow old but we were each once a foetus ourselves. As such we had some engaging qualities which unfortunately we lost as we grew older. We were physically and physiologically robust. We were supple and not obese. Our most depraved vice was thumbsucking, and the worst consequence of drinking liquor was hiccups not alcoholism.

When our cords were cut, we were not severed from our mothers but from our own organs—our placentae—which were appropriate to our old environment but unnecessary in our new one. We do not regard the foetal circulatory system, different as it is from the child's or adult's, as one big heap of congenital defects but as a system superbly adapted to his circumstances. We no longer regard foetal and neonatal renal function, assymetric as it is by adult standards, as inferior, but rather entirely appropriate to the osmometric conditions in which it has to work. Is it too much to ask therefore that perhaps we should accord also to foetal personality and behaviour, rudimentary as they may appear by adult standards, the same consideration and respect?

Notes

Preface

1 Quoted in *Les Trafiquants de Bébés à Naître* by Claude Jacquinot and Jacques Delaye.

The New Barbarians

1 John P. Wilson, "Fetal Experimentation: Rights of the Father and Questions of Personhood," *Villanova Law Review,* Vol. 22, p. 390.
2 Code of Federal Regulations 45 CFR 46.209.
3 *American Journal of Obstetrics & Gynecology,* Vol. 146, No. 2, P. 231-232.
4 cf. "Comparison of Spontaneous Contraction Rates *in situ* and Isolated Fetal Hearts in Early Pregnancy," *American Journal of Obstetrics & Gynecology,* Vol. 118, No. 1, pp. 73-76.
5 Ibid., p. 74.
6 John P. Wilson, op. cit., p. 404.
7 He made this statement in an interview with the author at Magee–Women's Hospital, Pittsburgh, Mar. 10, 1985.
8 Ibid.
9 Kim & Felig, "Maternal and Amniotic Fluid Substrate Levels During Caloric Deprivation in Human Pregnancy," *Metabolism* 21:507, 1972.
10 Code of Federal Regulations, 45 CFR 46, revised Mar. 8, 1983.
11 Ibid.
12 *University of Miami Law Review,* Vol. 31, p. 689.
13 Ed Grogan and Dr. James Vaupel, "Critique of the NIH Commission on the Protection of Human Subjects" (privately published, 1980), p. 15.

14 Telephone interview with the author.
15 Code of Federal Regulations, 45 CFR 46, revised Mar. 8, 1983; 46.206 (3).
16 Robert E. Cooke, M.D., "Critique of the Battelle Report," appendix to *Research on the Fetus* (published by the HEW National Commission for the Protection of Human Subjects of Biomedical and Behavioral Research, 1976), pp. 15-157.
17 "The March of Dimes on Research Using Human Fetal Tissues," 1982.
18 Richard D. Lyons, "Physical and Mental Disabilities in Newborns Doubled in 25 Years," *The New York Times*.
19 Dr. Thomas Hill Shepard, NIH grant progress report dated Apr. 10, 1978, pp. 14-15.
20 Quoted in "Is the Laboratory Animal Obsolete—Yes!" (published by Friends of Animals).
21 Telephone interview with the author.
22 Interview with the author at Magee–Women's Hospital, Pittsburgh, Mar. 10, 1985.
23 William Brennan, *The Abortion Holocaust* (St. Louis, Landmark Press, 1983), p. 52.
24 Joseph Fletcher, *Moral Responsibility* (Philadelphia, Westminster Press, 1974), pp. 16-17.
25 Joseph Fletcher, "Fetal Research: An Ethical Appraisal," appendix to *Research on the Fetus* (see note 16), p. 3-3.
26 Ibid.
27 Ibid., p. 3-5.
28 Ibid., p. 3-6.
29 Ibid., p. 2-7.
30 Frederic Wertham, M.D., *A Sign for Cain* (New York: Warner, 1969), p. 150.
31 Dr. Hans Jonas, "Philosophical Reflections on Experimenting With Human Subjects," *Daedalus*, Spring 1969, pp. 242-243.
32 Interview with the author at Magee–Women's Hospital, Pittsburgh, March 10, 1985.
33 George Bernard Shaw, *The Doctor's Dilemma; Complete Plays With Prefaces*, Vol. 1 (New York: Dodd, Mead, 1962), p. 33.
34 *Hastings Center Report*, Oct. 1978, p. 23.
35 Mary Anne Warren, "Can the Fetus Be an Organ Farm?" *Hastings Center Report*, Oct. 1978, pp. 23-25.

36 "A Thymus for Maggie," *Time,* Feb. 2, 1972, p. 54.
37 Ibid.
38 Paul Ramsey, *Fabricated Man* (New Haven, CT: Yale University Press, 1970), p. 152.
39 Paul Ramsey, *The Ethics of Fetal Research,* (New Haven, CT: Yale University Press, 1975).
40 Maggie Scarf, "The Fetus as Guinea Pig," *New York Times Magazine,* Oct. 19, 1975.
41 Paul Ramsey, *Fabricated Man,* p. 2.
42 Willard Gaylin, M.D., and Marc Lappé, Ph.D., "Fetal Politics," *The Atlantic,* March 1974, pp. 66-72.
43 Dr. Steven M. D'Ambrosio, grant application to the EPA, Feb. 2, 1982.
44 Bernard Nathanson, remarks accompanying the film *The Silent Scream.*
45 Paul Ramsey, *The Ethics of Fetal Research,* p. 66.

A Catalogue of Fetal Use

1 Germaine Greer, *Sex and Destiny* (New York: Harper & Row, 1984), p. 222.
2 "The Secret World Trade in Human Foetuses," *The Village Voice, Mar. 21, 1977.*
3 Rex Dalton, "Fetuses, Medical Waste Found in Shipping Carton," *The Daily Breeze,* Torrance, CA, Feb. 6, 1982.
4 Lawrence K. Altman, "Scientists Capture 'Norwalk Agent,' Virus That Causes Diarrhea," *New York Times,* July 2, 1972.
5 Frank Morriss, "Aborted Fetuses Used in Dental Experiments," *The Wanderer,* Mar. 2, 1972.
6 Denis J. Gospodarowicz, HEW grant application for a project titled "Transplantation of Corneal Endothelia: Clinical Implications," Mar. 30, 1979.
7 Anthony A. Pearson, NIH grant application Dec. 31, 1979.
8 "New York Pediatrics Specialist Dissects Living Unborn for Study," *Child and Family,* Vol. 9, No. 3, 1970.
9 John E. Harrington, "Experimentation With Prenatal and Neonatal Human Beings—Part 1," *Marriage & Family Newsletter,* Vol. 3, No. 1, Jan. 1972.
10 Lowell W. Lapham & William Markesbery, "Human Fetal Cerebellar Cortex: Organization and Maturation of Cells *in vitro,'' Science,* Vol. 173, No. 3999, Aug. 27, 1971, p. 829.
11 "Fetal Antigen May Lead to Cancer Screening Test," *Journal of the American Medical Assn.*, Vol. 223, No. 13, Mar. 26, 1973.

12 Val Dorgan, "Foetuses' Experiments," *The Cork Examiner,* Aug. 25, 1983.
13 Turtox-Cambosco catalogue, 1974.
14 Randy Collier, "Allegedly Illegal Experiments on Fetuses Are Probed," *The Arizona Republic,* Mar. 2, 1981.
15 Dr. Maurice Mahoney, "The Nature and Extent of Research Involving Living Human Fetuses," appendix to *Research on the Fetus* (published by the HEW National Commission for the Protection of Human Subjects of Biomedical and Behavioral Research, 1976), pp. 1-23 to 1-25.
16 "'Barbaric' Electric Shock Tests on Live Fetuses," *The Guardian, Human Concern* (published by the Society for the Protection of Unborn Children), No. 11, 1983.
17 "Californie Esthetique" (published by Centre Henri Chenot), Cannes, France, April 1980.
18 "Horror Show," *The Village Voice,* Jan. 22, 1979.
19 Quoted in *National Right to Life News,* Nov. 24, 1982.
20 The information on the NIH research grants was obtained from NIH files under the Freedom of Information Act.
21 *Journal of Investigative Dermatology,* 65:16, 1975, and 71:385-390, 1978.

The Federal Regulations on Nontherapeutic Fetal Experimentation

1 Vance Packard, *The People Shapers* (Boston: Little, Brown, 1977), p. 335.
2 Paul Ramsey, *The Ethics of Fetal Research* (New Haven, CT: Yale University Press, 1975), p. 2.
3 Victor Cohn, "Live-Fetus Research Debated," *The Washington Post,* April 10, 1973.
4 Ibid.
5 Ibid.
6 "Post-Abortion Fetal Study Stirs Storm," *Medical World News,* June 8, 1973.
7 Paul Ramsey, op. cit., p. 7.
8 Paul Ramsey, op. cit., p. 8.
9 Ibid., p. 17.
10 Ibid., p. 18.
11 Ibid., p. 20.
12 Ibid.
13 Vol. 112, pp. 992-998.
14 Mrs. Randy Engel, "The Ryan Grant: Case Study #1—Induced Abortion as a

Cause of Birth Defects" (published by U.S. Coalition for Life, Export, PA), pp. 1-2.

15 Ibid.

16 Dr. Kenneth Ryan, National Foundation–March of Dimes grant proposal April 1976: "High Risk Pregnancies."

17 Mrs. Randy Engel, op. cit., p. 2.

18 *The Morality of Abortion,* John T. Noonan, ed (Cambridge, MA: Harvard University Press, 1970).

19 Ibid., p. 227.

20 National Research Act of 1974.

21 Ed Grogan & Dr. James Vaupel, "Critique of the NIH Commission on the Protection of Human Subjects" (privately published, 1980). pp. 19-21.

22 Dr. Maurice Mahoney, "The Nature and Extent of Research Involving Living Human Fetuses," appendix to *Research on the Fetus,* p. 1-29.

23 Ibid.

24 Fr. Richard McCormick, "Experimentation on the Fetus: Policy Proposals," *Research on the Foetus,* p. 5-1. Fr. McCormick is a major U.S. proponent of the doctrine of proportionalism, also often called consequentialism. Proportionalism's main tenet is that the community will decide if any action is to be sanctioned based on its proportionately "good" outcome. Thus, according to this doctrine, there are no intrinsically good or evil acts. Readers interested in perusing this subject should see *Readings in Moral Theology,* ed. by Charles E. Curran and Richard A. McCormick (New York: Paulist Press, 1979). The important essay on proportionalism in this volume is "The Hermenetuic Function of the Principle of Double Effect." A counter view of proportionalism can be found in essays such as William E. May's "The Moral Meaning of Human Acts," in *Homiletic and Pastoral Review,* October 1978.

25 Dr. Maurice Mahoney, op. cit., p. 1-37.

26 Battelle-Columbus report, appendix to *Research on the Fetus,* p. 15-3

27 Dr. Robert E. Cooke, "Critique of the Battelle-Columbus Report," appendix to *Research on the Fetus,* p. 15-155.

28 Ibid., p. 15-156.

29 Ibid.

30 Ibid.

31 Ibid., p. 159.

32 John P. Wilson, "A Report on Legal Issues Involved in Research on the

Fetus," appendix to *Research on the Fetus,* p. 14-26.

33 "Dissenting Statement of Commissioner David W. Louisell," appendix to *Research on the Fetus,* p. 77.

34 Ibid.

35 Ibid., p. 81.

36 Ibid., p. 82.

37 Dr. Leo Alexander, "Medical Science Under Dictatorship," *New England Journal of Medicine,* Vol. 241, No. 2, July 14, 1949, p. 42.

38 Code of Federal Regulations 45CF46, 46.211.

39 Ed Grogan & Dr. James Vaupel, op. cit., p. 12.

40 Ibid., p. 27.

41 Douglas Johnson, "Congress Tightens Restrictions on Federal Funding of Fetal Experiments," *National Right to Life News,* Oct. 25, 1984, p. 6.

42 Ibid.

43 Joseph Fletcher, "Fetal Research: The State of the Question," *The Hastings Center Report,* April 1985, p. 10.

44 Ibid.

45 Ibid., p. 13.

How Live Aborted Fetuses Are Obtained for Research

1 Dr. Geoffrey Chamberlain, "An Artificial Placenta: The Development of an Extracorporeal System for Maintenance of Immature Infants With Respiratory Problems," *American Journal of Obstetrics & Gynecology,* Vol. 101, No. 3, March 1, 1968, p. 624.

2 David Rorvik, *Brave New Baby* (Garden City, NY: Doubleday, 1971), pp. 83-84.

3 Presented to the U.S. Supreme Court by the Attorney General of Connecticut with his Mar. 14, 1973 petition for rehearing of the appeals of *Markle v. Abele* (72-56 and 72-730).

4 Dr. Gerald Anderson, "Prostaglandin vs. Saline for Midtrimester Abortion," *Contemporary Ob/Gyn,* Vol. 4, July 1974, p. 91.

5 Dr. Anne Wentz, et al., "Intra-amniotic Administration of Prostaglandin F2 Alpha for Abortion," *American Journal of Obstetrics and Gynecology*, Vol. 113, No. 4, July 15, 1972, pp. 793-794.

6 Ibid, p. 802.

7 Jeff Lyon, "The Doctor's Dilemma: When Abortion Gives Birth to Life,

Physicians Become Troubled Saviours," *National Right to Life News*, Sept. 16, 1982, p. 8.

8 Dr. Mitchell Golbus & Dr. Robert Erickson, "Mid-trimester Abortion Induced by Intra-amniotic Prostaglandin F2 Alpha: Fetal Tissue Viability," *American Journal of Obstetrics & Gynecology,* May 15, 1974, p. 268.

9 Ibid.

10 *Uprise* is published by the Kalamazoo (MI) Pro-Life Action League.

11 Telephone interview with the author, Dec. 14, 1987.

12 Dr. Leon Kass, "Determining Death and Viability in Fetuses and Abortuses," appendix to *Research on the Fetus,* p. 11-2.

13 Ibid., p. 11-3.

14 Interview with the author.

15 Grant application dated May 27, 1976.

16 "Will the Edelin Decision Affect Abortion Policies?" *Contemporary Ob/Gyn,* Vol. 5, April 1975, p. 21.

17 *Medical Research Programs,* The Kroc Foundation, 1979, p. 82.

18 *Diabetes,* Vol. 31, Supp. 4, Aug. 1982.

19 Gerald James Stine, *Biosocial Genetics* (New York: Macmillan, 1977), p. 307.

20 Interview with the author.

21 "Fetus as Organ Donor," *Science,* 1983.

22 American Paralysis Association, *Progress in Research,* No. 6, Sept. 1983, p. 1.

23 Ibid., pp. 2-3.

24 Ibid., p. 4.

25 Jean Seligmann et al., *Newsweek* Jan. 14, 1985.

26 Ibid.

Abandonment of the Fetus as Patient and Client

1 "New Oath for Physicians," *Intellect,* Nov. 1979, p. 148.

2 Ibid., p. 147.

3 Carleton Chapman, *Physicians, Law & Ethics* (New York: New York University Press, 1984), p. 124.

4 William Brennan, *The Abortion Holocaust* (St. Louis: Landmark Press, 1983), p. 140.

5 Ibid., pp. 140-141.

6 Ibid., p. 135.

7 Ibid., p. 139.
8 Ibid., pp. 139-140.
9 Ibid., p. 134.
10 Ibid., pp. 135-136.
11 Ibid., p. 126.
12 Ibid.
13 Ibid.
14 Ibid., p. 125.
15 Ibid. p. 29.
16 Dr. Samuel Nigro, "A Scientific Critique of Abortion as a Medical Procedure," *Psychiatric Annals,* Sept. 1972.
17 C.V. Ford, et al., "Abortion: Is It a Therapeutic Procedure in Psychiatry?" *Journal of the American Medical Assn.*, Vol. 218, pp. 1173-1178.
18 Samuel Nigro, op. cit.
19 Dr. Leo Alexander, "Medical Science Under Dictatorship," *New England Journal of Medicine,* Vol. 241, No. 2, July 14, 1949, pp. 44-45.
20 Ibid., p. 45.
21 Juliana Geran Pilon, "Cost-Benefit Ethics: the Utilitarian Approach to Fetal Research," *Villanova Law Review,* Vol. 22, 1976-77, pp. 395-402.
22 Leo Alexander, op cit., p. 45.
23 Joan Wester Anderson, "Beyond Abortion—Fetal Experimentation."
24 John Noonan & David Louisell, "Constitutional Balance," *The Morality of Abortion* (Cambridge, MA: Harvard University Press), 1977, p. 221.
25 Ibid., p. 222.
26 Ibid.
27 Ibid., p. 224.
28 Ibid., p. 234.
29 Ibid., pp. 235-236.
30 Ibid., pp. 234-235.
31 Ibid., p. 252.
32 Ibid., p. 253.
33 Margery Shaw, "The Potential Plaintiff," *Genetics & the Law II* (New York: Plenum Press, 1976), p. 225.
34 Golbus, et al., *The Unborn Patient* (New York: Grune & Stratton, 1984).
35 Ibid., p. xvii.
36 Ibid., opening page of Part III

Extermination of the Handicapped Unborn

1 Gunther Anders, "Reflections on the H-Bomb," *Man Alone,* ed. Eric & Mary Josephson (New York: Dell, 1962), p. 291.

2 Richard Doerflinger, "The Roots of Force," *Our Sunday Visitor,* Mar. 17, 1985.

3 Germaine Greer, *Sex and Destiny* (New York: Harper & Row, 1984), p. 359.

4 Dr. Henry Nadler, March of Dimes grant summary, 1969, p.38.

5 Dr. Henry Nadler, "Lymphocite and Granulocite Enzyme Activity in Patients With Down's Syndrome," *Blood*, Vol. 30, No. 5 (Nov. 1967), pp. 669-673.

6 Dr. Henry Nadler, "The Role of Amniocentesis in Intrauterine Detection of Genetic Disorders," *New England Journal of Medicine,* Vol. 282, Part I, Jan.-Mar. 1970, pp. 596-599.

7 Ibid.

8 National Foundation/March of Dimes Original Articles Series, Vol. VIII, No. 4, July 1972, pp. 5-6.

9 A. J. Dyck, "Ethical Issues in Community and Research Medicine," *Linacre Quarterly,* Nov. 1976, p. 222.

10 *Advances in Human Genetics and Their Impact on Society,* National Foundation/March of Dimes Original Article Series, Vol. VIII, No. 6, p. 29.

11 Arno Motulsky, "Brave New World?" *Birth Defects,* Proceedings of the Fourth International Conference, Vienna, Austria, Sept. 2-8, 1973, sponsored by the National Foundation/March of Dimes.

12 Aubrey Milunsky, *The Prenatal Diagnosis of Hereditary Disorders* (Springfield, IL: Charles C. Thomas, 1973), pp. 166-167.

13 Germaine Greer, op. cit., p. 336.

14 Ibid.

15 Desmond Zwar, *New Frontiers in Medical Research* (New York: Stein & Day, 1983).

16 Ibid., p. 137.

17 Ibid., pp. 137-138.

18 Ibid., p. 138

19 Ibid., p. 139.

20 Ibid.

21 Ibid., p. 138.

22 Ibid., p. 141.

23 Nat Hentoff, "The Awful Privacy of Baby Doe," *Atlantic Monthly,* Jan. 1985, pp. 54-62.
24 Ibid.
25 Interview with the author.
26 *Who's Poisoning America* (San Francisco: Sierra Books, 1981).
27 1983-84 National Foundation/March of Dimes grant list.
28 Aubrey Milunsky, *Genetics & the Law II* (New York: Plenum Press, 1976).
29 Ibid., pp. 61-62.
30 Ibid. pp. 66-67.
31 Ibid., p. 67.
32 Margery Shaw, "The Potential Plaintiff," *Genetics & the Law II,* p. 227.
33 Ibid., pp. 228-229.
34 John Fletcher, *Ethics & Trends in Applied Human Genetics,'' Birth Defects,* National Foundation/March of Dimes Original Articles Series, Vol. 19, No. 5, 1983, p. 145.
35 Ibid.
36 Ibid., p. 146.
37 Robert C. Baumiller, "Clergy Involvement," *Hospital Practice,* April 1983.
38 Ibid.
39 Robert C. Baumiller, "Legal and Ethical Considerations," *Birth Defects,* National Foundation/March of Dimes Original Articles Series, Vol. 19, No. 5, 1983, p. 160.
40 Ibid.
41 Ibid.
42 Carolyn Denning et al., "Psychological and Social Aspects of Cystic Fibrosis," *Cystic Fibrosis: Projections Into the Future,* ed. John Mangos & Richard Talamo (New York: Symposia Specialists, 1976).
43 Ibid.
44 Ibid.
45 Ibid.
46 Ibid.
47 Ibid.
48 Ibid.
49 *Screening and Counselling for Genetic Conditions,* p. 93.
50 Ibid., p. 97.
51 Interview with the author.
52 *Attitudes Toward Prenatal Diagnosis of Cystic Fibrosis Among Parents of*

Affected Children, published with the support of the March of Dimes Birth Defects Foundation.

53 Ibid.

54 Interview with the author.

55 Richard Restak, "The Danger of Knowing Too Much," *Psychology Today,* Sept. 1975, p. 22.

56 Ibid.

57 Ibid.

58 Ibid.

59 Dr. Charles R. Shaw, "The Psychiatrist in the Genetics Clinic," *Genetic Screening and Counselling A Multidisciplinary Perspective,* ed. Steven R. Applewhite (Springfield, IL: Charles C. Thomas, 1981, p. 117.

60 Nancy S. Wexler, "Will the Circle Be Unbroken? Sterilizing the Genetically Impaired," *Genetics & the Law II,* pp. 314-315.

61 *Man Alone,* ed. Eric & Mary Josephson (New York: Dell, 1962).

62 Gunther Anders, op. cit., p. 289.

63 Tom Riggs, "*Roe v. Wade*—The Abortion Decision—An Analysis and Its Implications," *Miami Law Review,* Vol. 10, No. 844, 1973, p. 853.

64 Dr. Leo Alexander, "Medical Science Under Dictatorship," *New England Journal of Medicine,* Vol. 241, No. 2, July 14, 1949, p. 47.

65 Thomas Marzen, "Aborted Babies Born at Hospital With 'Model' Eugenics Program," *National Right to Life News,* May 22, 1982.

66 David Rorvik, *Brave New Baby* (Garden City, NY: Doubleday, 1971), p. 68.

67 Randy Engel, *The Rising Tide of Eugenic Abortion* (privately published), p. 13.

68 Joshouha Lederberg, "The Genetics of Human Nature," *Social Research,* quoted in Randy Engel, op. cit., p. 204.

69 Interview with the author.

70 Interview with the author.

71 "Blue Cross: Fetal Death Good Business," *Catholic League for Religious and Civil Rights Newsletter,* June 1976, Vol. 3, No. 5.

72 G.K. Chesterton, *Eugenics and Other Evils,* from *G.K. Chesterton, Collected Works* (San Francisco: Ignatius Press, 1987).

Other fine books available from Magnificat Press

The Ananias Precedent by Floyd Allen
A novel of Acts 5 in the 20th Century. Does God kill unrepentant sinners?
$3.50

Angels Get No Respect by Cecile Bauer et al.
8 delightful stories about encounters between angels and people. **$3.50**

Blow the Trumpet in Zion by Richard Booker
Israel: its past glory, present crisis and future hope. **$5.95**

Childless But Not Barren by Kristen Johnson Ingram
Counsel and comfort for women waiting for motherhood. **$4.95**

Choices in Matters of Life and Death by Judie Brown
The facts on abortion, birth control and euthanasia. **$3.50**

A Covenant With Life by Clifford Blair
Tired of killing, a secret agent quits—but is hunted by the spy organization because he knows too much. An exciting novel! **$4.75**

The Elijah Task by John and Paula Sandford
The prophet's role in the church. **$5.95**

Healing the Wounded Spirit by John and Paula Sandford
How to overcome hidden hurts. **$8.95**

Light this Day by Toby Rice Drews
Meditations and prayers for families of alcoholics. **$6.95**

Mary: Mother of Christians, Messenger of God by Stephen Dunham
Describes many apparitions of Mary and her words to the world and the church. **$3.50**

Mona/Lu: The Monster Within by Cecile Bauer
Don't hurt your kids! Help for angry parents, from a mother who's been there. **$3.95**

The Other Side of Christ by Father Robert D. Smith
A straightforward presentation of Gospel truth. "A spiritual blockbuster"—*The Boston Pilot*. **$6.95**

The Power of Praise and Worship by Terry Law
This exhortation to praise God is enlivened by Law's stories of his mission work in communist countries. **$6.95**

Praise Releases Faith by Terry Law
An in-depth look at the keys to victorious living. **$6.95**

A Quest for Discipleship by Father Claude Buchanan
A gentle challenge to change and to grow. **$4.95**

Radical Christian Living by Richard Booker
A call to deeper commitment and maturity. **$4.95**

Restoring the Christian Family by John and Paula Sandford
How to resolve marital problems and family conflicts. **$6.95**

Transformation of the Inner Man by John and Paula Sandford
How to achieve inner healing and real change. **$6.95**

Urge to Live by Boleslaw A. Wysocki
Survival and triumph in a WWII Spanish concentration camp. **$12.95**

Worship as Jesus Taught It by Judson Cornwall
How Jesus worshiped, what He taught about worship, what He expects from us. **$6.95**

Wounded Warriors by Loren Sandford
How to deal with stress. **$4.95**

order from:

MAGNIFICAT PRESS
PO Box 365, 315 Main St.
Avon, NJ 07717

NJ residents add 6% tax. Shipping & handling: $1.50 per order.